"A powerful indictment of 1 bulldoze Chicago's most colorful, vibrant, historic but poor peoples' neighborhood and of the resolute and courageous individuals who fought to save their community."

—Dr. Irving Cutler, Chicago State University

"Near West Side Stories are our st [Eastwood's book] delights, informs neighborhood that is the soul of Chic

—Professor Steve Balkin, Roosevelt University
Maxwell Street Historic Preservation Coalition

eals with ordinary
y community."

Roosevelt University
HOOL of Policy Studies

an encapsulated
stories of Harold,
g human interest
a. . . . While explor-
ss that is sweeping
the workings of our
ke precedence over

z, The Industrial Worker

ary 2002)
inter 2002)

Also from Lake Claremont Press

Chicago's Midway Airport:
The First Seventy-Five Years
Christopher Lynch

A Cook's Guide to Chicago
Marilyn Pocius

Great Chicago Fires:
Historic Blazes That Shaped a City
David Cowan

The Chicago River:
A Natural and Unnatural History
Libby Hill

Graveyards of Chicago:
The People, History, Art, and
Lore of Cook County Cemeteries
Matt Hucke and Ursula Bielski

Chicago Haunts *and*
More Chicago Haunts:
Scenes from Myth and Memory
Ursula Bielski

Haunted Michigan: Recent
Encounters with Active Spirits *and*
More Haunted Michigan
Rev. Gerald S. Hunter

Literary Chicago: A Book
Lover's Tour of the Windy City
Greg Holden

"The Movies Are": Carl Sandburg's
Film Reviews and Essays,
1920-1928
Edited by Arnie Bernstein
Introduction by Roger Ebert

Hollywood on Lake Michigan: 100
Years of Chicago and the Movies
Arnie Bernstein

Ticket to Everywhere: The Best of
Detours Travel Column
Dave Hoekstra

Coming Soon

A Native's Guide to
Northwest Indiana
Mark Skertic

Traces of Checagou:
Mammoths, Mounds, Forts, and
the Fur Trade in Northern Illinois
Christina and Nicole Bultinck

A Native's Guide to Chicago
4th Edition
Lake Claremont Press

The Hoofs and Guns of the Storm:
Chicago's Civil War Connections
Arnie Bernstein

Chicago's Midway Airport
audiobook
Christopher Lynch

Muldoon: A True Chicago Ghost Story
Rocco A. Facchini

Finding Your Chicago Ancestors
Grace DuMelle

The Chicago Firefighter's
Best Friend: Windy City Fire
Dogs Past and Present
Trevor and Drew Orsinger

The Politics of Recreation
Charles Shaw

Lake Claremont Press books celebrate what's distinctive about Chicago's history, culture, geography, spirit, and lore. Join us in preserving the past, exploring the present, and ensuring a future sense of place for our corner of the globe.

Near

WEST SIDE STORIES

STRUGGLES FOR COMMUNITY IN CHICAGO'S MAXWELL STREET NEIGHBORHOOD

Carolyn Eastwood

FIRST EDITION

4650 North Rockwell Street • Chicago, Illinois 60625
www.lakeclaremont.com

Near West Side Stories:
Struggles for Community in Chicago's Maxwell Street Neighborhood
by Carolyn Eastwood

Published June 2002 by:

4650 N. Rockwell St.
Chicago, IL 60625
773/583-7800; lcp@lakeclaremont.com
www.lakeclaremont.com

Publisher's Cataloging-in-Publication
(Provided by Quality Books, Inc.)

Eastwood, Carolyn.
    Near West Side stories : struggles for community in
Chicago's Maxwell Street neighborhood / Carolyn
Eastwood. — 1st ed.
    p. cm.
    Includes bibliographical references and index.
    LCCN 2001096725
    ISBN 1-893121-09-7

    1. Ethnic neighborhoods—Conservation and restoration
—Illinois—Chicago. 2. Maxwell Street (Chicago, Ill.)
—History. 3. Near West Side (Chicago, Ill.)—History.
4. Chicago (Ill.)—History.   I. Title.

F548.68.N43E37 2002   977.3'11
                             QBI33-299

Printed in the United States of America by United Graphics,
an employee-owned company based in Mattoon, Illinois.

07 06 05 04 03 02   10 9 8 7 6 5 4 3 2 1

PUBLISHER'S CREDITS

Cover design by Timothy Kocher. Interior Design by Sharon Woodhouse. Editing by Bruce Clorfene. Proofreading by Karen Formanski and Sharon Woodhouse. Index by Karen Formanski. Map by Carolyn Eastwood. The text of *Near West Side Stories* was set in RhymeLight; heads and sub-heads in Maiandra GD.

PHOTO CREDITS

Philip Albert, Chicago Historical Society, Chicago Transit Authority, Irving Cutler, Nate Duncan, Anthony Eastwood, Carolyn Eastwood, Jeff Fletcher, Harold Fox, Lori Grove, Bernice Latoria, Mildred Wittenberg Mallin, Norma Portillo, Florence Scala, Norman Schwartz, Greg Stepanek, University Library at UIC, John Walker, Elias Zayed, and Leo Zayed.

NOTE

Although Lake Claremont Press and the author, editor, and others affiliated with *Near West Side Stories* have exhaustively researched all sources to ensure the accuracy and completeness of the information contained within this book, we assume no responsibility for errors, inaccuracies, omissions, or inconsistencies herein.

CONTENTS

Introduction..3

1. The Jewish Neighborhood.....................................19
2. Harold Fox 33
3. Harold Fox (continued)...61

4. The Italian Neighborhood...................................105
5. Florence Scala...119
6. Florence Scala (continued) 153

7. The Black Neighborhood 201
8. Nate Duncan 215
9. Nate Duncan (continued)....................................231

10. The Mexican Neighborhood...............................265
11. Hilda Portillo..281
12. Hilda Portillo (continued) 297

Epilogue..331

Bibliography...341
Index 345
Acknowledgments..354
About the Author 360

The 600 block of Maxwell Street on a Sunday morning in 1915.

INTRODUCTION

Photo by Carolyn Eastwood.

The intersection of Roosevelt Road and
Halsted Street looking west, with the steeple
of St. Francis of Assisi Chruch in the foreground
and Holy Family Church in the background.

INTRODUCTION

IN A CONVERSATION with a Chicago City Hall official several years ago, I spoke up on behalf of what ordinary people—in this case, street vendors—were saying about an issue. He abruptly dismissed my comment with a growl, "Oh, that's demagoguery!" His implication was that I had expressed an emotional, biased view. This retort was a shock because until that point he had been friendly and informal. Suddenly, the gulf between the viewpoint of power and influence and that of ordinary people was apparent.

Later, at a neighborhood meeting concerning the future of the 120-year-old Maxwell Street Market, I had an opportunity to observe the ordering of a gathering that juxtaposed these two views. City officials and outside experts, formally suited and equipped with elaborate graphics, were lined up at a table in the front of the room. Concerned citizens filled the remainder of the room except for the numerous policemen around the perimeter. Officials spoke first, with no apparent time constraints, whereas ordinary citizens were limited to three to five minutes. What was striking to me was the eloquent expression of passion, home truths, and valid arguments that were expressed repeatedly by the ordinary people in the room, and the realization of how rarely they are really listened to.

The neighborhood where many of those people had lived and worked is a wonderful corner of Chicago centered on Halsted Street and Roosevelt Road (formerly 12th Street). This Halsted-Roosevelt neighborhood, bounded by Harrison Street on the north, 16th Street on the south, Jefferson Street on the east, and Racine Avenue on the west, has been jam-packed with history. (See map of Halsted-Roosevelt area on p. 5.)

Part of the officially-designated Near West Side Community Area, the Halsted-Roosevelt neighborhood has, from its nineteenth century beginnings and on into the twentieth century, been a port of entry for immigrants and migrants, including French, Irish, German, Bohemian, Jewish, Italian, Mexican, African-Americans, and Gypsies. It has been a neighborhood always in flux and never, in its long history, lacking for problems to be solved.

While some parts of the Near West Side Community Area have contained blocks of affluent homeowners, this corner of the area has always had poor-to-modest-income residents, and by 1910 it contained the densest population in Chicago.[1] One way to indicate the pressures on the Halsted-Roosevelt neighborhood is to say that it is within sight of Chicago's downtown business district, the Loop, and has been alternately sought after for its convenience and location and despised for its crowded, and often unsanitary, living conditions.

We may wonder can we define this as a "neighborhood"

Photo by Carolyn Eastwood.

This 1992 view of the Sunday Maxwell Street Market
indicates its proximity to downtown Chicago.

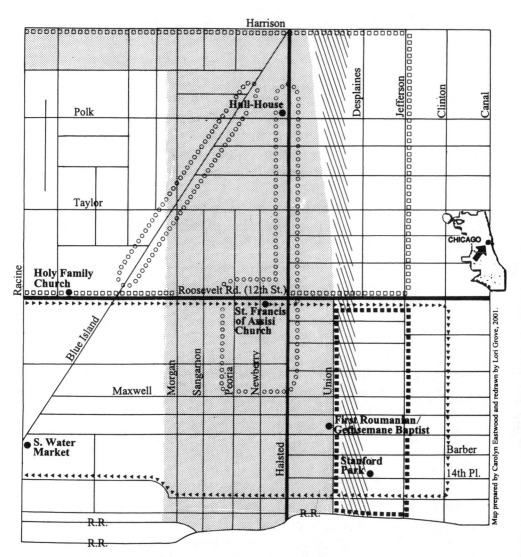

Ethnic Groups of Halsted-Roosevelt Area

Ethnic Groups[1]

Jewish	(1900)	▸▸▸▸▸
Italian	(1925)	◻◻◻◻◻
Black	(1930)	▪▪▪▪▪
Mexican	(1930)	○○○○○

Dan Ryan Expressway

University of Illinois at Chicago

[1]Predominant Group -- all sections have some ethnic mix.

when there are no clear barriers and every portion of the section outlined on the map has been in a state of flux for the last 120 years? Even though the geographic area retained the same configuration and street names for most of its history, the reality of the city always had different meanings for different people.

The oral histories of Harold Fox, Florence Scala, Nate Duncan, and Hilda Portillo contained in this book are a way of listening to what four ordinary people of different ethnic backgrounds have to say about the meaning of this neighborhood during their growing-up years, and later as they were drawn into the struggles of their neighborhood as adults. Each one was part of an ethnic group with a loosely-circumscribed area of residence and had predominant relationships with family, church, commerce, and customs of their own group.

Yet the neighborhood boundaries were permeable, and each ethnic grouping had a tapestry of members of other ethnic groups within its area. Throughout the Halsted-Roosevelt neighborhood there was more of an ethnic mix at any one time than most people realize, even in an area as generally recognizable as Taylor Street ("Little Italy"). Not only that, but the image was more kaleidoscope-like than a tapestry because families were constantly moving in and out of the neighborhood and to buildings on other streets and to other blocks within the neighborhood.

We may ask if this neighborhood is unique or like hundreds of others in its fights to maintain its housing, businesses, and institutions. Political analyst Paul Green asserts, "Power and influence will always beat out culture." Can we, therefore, see this neighborhood as a metaphor for the struggle to survive of every community in the face of the greater power of a city hall, a university, or an archdiocese?[2]

While the threats to this Halsted-Roosevelt neighborhood were specific, many of the issues and actions that challenged residents, shop owners, buyers, and parishioners in the past half century could be subsumed under the heading "urban renewal" and have been repeated endlessly in poor neighborhoods throughout the city and in countless cities throughout the United States. Viewing the changes in this neighborhood from this greater perspective clarifies the players' positions and their respective power quotients.

The process and history of urban renewal in the Halsted-Roosevelt neighborhood and elsewhere in the United States highlights an often-overlooked question: Whose neighborhood is it anyway? As the history of the Halsted-Roosevelt neighborhood and the recollections of Harold Fox and the other oral histories show, a neighborhood is created day in and day out by the people who live there. In that way and in that sense, those people own the neighborhood. They define its tone, and they determine what life is like on its sidewalks and in its stores and in its backyards. They give it its character.

But another form of ownership is the stewardship that public officials have. In theory, these officials make decisions on the basis of what is best for the community. This may be interpreted to mean what is good for the immediate neighborhood, or perhaps, for the entire city. In practice, those decisions may be based on private gain (including that of family and friends), or on favoring or protecting more powerful segments of society.

Much of what happened to the Halsted-Roosevelt neighborhood transpired because its residents were poor and relatively powerless. More upscale neighborhoods, middle-class or affluent, would have had more clout to fight and defeat efforts by the city to put an expressway and a university where their homes and businesses stood. Instead, they were placed where the residents were less organized (in a middle-class way) and lacked both clout and ready financial resources.

If you are a resident losing your home or a business owner deprived of your livelihood, you see things very differently than the developer who hopes to benefit from gentrification of your area or a city hall official who expects to reap kudos for "cleaning up" a neighborhood.

For some, "urban renewal" is a form of urban destruction because displaced residents have no affordable place to go when their homes are demolished, nor can they pay the rents of replacement housing if it does eventually appear. In the 1950s an Englishman came to Chicago for the first time, looked around, and wondered what had happened to make parts of

Chicago look so much like bombed-out London after World War II. Urban renewal had happened and left wide open tracts of land.

Throughout its long history this Halsted-Roosevelt neighborhood had experienced the normal forces of change. There was constant movement among ethnic groups, immigrants, and migrants—moving in, establishing their community, and then moving on to other parts of the city or suburbs. Many others stayed on, either as business owners or as residents. Housing deterioration could be expected and was ongoing. Yet there were also internal attempts to rehabilitate the housing such as the efforts by a post-World War II group in Little Italy whose plans for improvement met with full City Hall approval. Urban renewal, however, took several drastic forms in this particular neighborhood, and the cumulative effect was catastrophic in altering the community's nature.

The first major change came about in the 1950s with urban renewal projects of the Chicago Land Clearance Commission that left open spaces where homes and businesses had been. The general intention was to "renew" with light industry and commercial development, but in many cases that did not happen. Although undoubtedly substandard, the former buildings had represented life and livelihood in the neighborhood rather than the sense of abandonment implied by the empty stretches of land that remained for decades. Only destruction, not renewal, had transpired.

Although it was badly needed to move traffic in the metropolitan area, the construction of the expressway system meant the demolition of more homes and institutions, arguably, more frequently in the poorer, more powerless, sections of the city. In this particular Halsted-Roosevelt neighborhood the second major change occurred when the Dan Ryan Expressway was built, and its north/south pathway necessitated the elimination of all buildings from the western edge of Jefferson Street to the eastern edge of Union Avenue. In the process, the Maxwell Street Market, which had previously lined Maxwell Street all the way east to Jefferson Street, was truncated.

The third major shock to the neighborhood came about in

the early 1960s when the Harrison-Halsted area was chosen as the Chicago site of the University of Illinois campus, and most of the Italian neighborhood was demolished to make way for it. Although few would deny the need for making higher education convenient and affordable for citizens of Chicago, it is the use of power and the manner of choice in the decision-making process regarding this site that make this particular event so memorable.

Although the eastern stretch of the Maxwell Street Market had been eliminated with the building of the Dan Ryan Expressway, a fourth major blow to the Halsted-Roosevelt community came with the final eviction of the Sunday market as it had existed along Maxwell Street and westward past Halsted Street into surrounding streets for 120 years. The Maxwell Street Market was widely known and patronized by shoppers from many parts of Chicago, as well as from other states and countries. For hundreds of vendors and shoppers it was a crucial part of their coping with financial necessities. The City Hall-University coalition was, again, impervious to any solu-

Photo by Carolyn Eastwood.

Co-existence has worked for hundreds of years for the market
and the prestigious Cambridge University in Cambridge,
England, but was not considered for the one-day-a-week
Maxwell Street Market and the University of Illinois at Chicago.

tion other than displacement.

The final example of trauma in the neighborhood is note-worthy, not for its major effect on the entire community, but for its illustration of institutional disregard by the Archdiocese of Chicago for the people most affected by its decisions. This involved the closing and proposed demolition, without warn-ing, of the historic St. Francis of Assisi Church at the corner of Roosevelt and Newberry. For some time the Archdiocese of Chicago had been experiencing serious financial problems, and it was the difficult task of the leaders to make hard decisions concerning parish closings in order to help resolve the crisis. St. Francis was a flourishing, solvent parish that sustained five crowded Spanish language masses each Sun-day and drew Latino worshippers from all over the Chicago area. So the question was, "Why St. Francis?" The church leaders refused to discuss the matter with parishioners. Until members took unprecedented, dramatic action, no meaningful conversations took place between the authorities of the Arch-diocese and the congregation of the church.

In these five instances of a neighborhood which has been profoundly affected by the power of City Hall, the University of Illinois, and the Archdiocese of Chicago, the significant factor is not so much the power—these institutions come by that legitimately—but the matter of how the power is used. Finan-cial resources, time, and places to meet are significant assets of these three institutions, but the crucial factor in the power equation is the ability of these organizations to withhold infor-mation. This ability conserves power within the ranks of those who share information and diminishes the capability of the opposition to make plans for the future. The importance of this factor became clear during the tenure of Mayor Harold Wash-ington, because suddenly access to previously withheld records was possible through a freedom of information law—Mayor Washington's first executive order. As a citizen, your "right to know" became an acceptable premise. Since the days of Harold Washington, city government has gone back to the old system of obscuring public information, and many commu-nity groups have stopped filing for freedom of information because they cannot afford the legal fees for appeals.

Roslyn Brown, a school and parks activist, summed up the

problem, "If there was information, you could know what to fuss about . . . if you don't see it you can't fuss what you don't know."[3] The sociologist Max Weber wrote, "Every bureaucracy seeks to increase the superiority of the professionally informed by keeping their knowledge and intentions secret   . . . it hides its knowledge and action from criticism."[4] Both Brown and Weber say essentially the same thing.

One of the great losses to public information in Chicago occurred in 1993 when Mayor Richard M. Daley wrote the Municipal Reference Library out of his budget. This institution had been a key resource on Chicago's city government used by 20,000 visitors a year; now there is no central place to gain this information and much, such as a clipping file of community and ethnic newspapers, is lost altogether.[5]

Institutions such as City Hall, the Archdiocese, and the University of Illinois all manage public information through experts who have been hired for this task and are adept at "we haven't made a decision on that" answers. Anyone pursuing information by talking to lesser officials may find that cooperative informants have suddenly been left out of the information loop or have been transferred to another administrative post. Then, when the plan has already been set in motion, ordinary people are presented with a *fait accompli* when it is too late to inform public opinion or mount opposition.

Another bureaucratic technique for handling opposition is to belittle the opponent. During the final years of the Maxwell Street Market affair, Alderman Ted Mazola led the City Hall fight to close the market, and he was fond of saying that he could understand that vendors would not want the market to move because, "Change is scary." This condescension implies that the vendors are not-very-bright children rather than adults concerned with their livelihood.[6]

Even though City Hall, the Archdiocese, and the University have had a preponderance of assets and have persevered over the long term in order to achieve their goals, ordinary people of the Halsted-Roosevelt neighborhood also have possessed resources. First of all, they have had a sense of place. The people who have lived in the neighborhood, traded in the market, worshipped in the local churches, or shopped in the local stores have had mental, social, and physical associations with that place, and even though they might be critical of their surroundings, it was *their* place.

Although no living person goes back to the beginning of the neighborhood, all people who have lived there since it was first settled have contributed to a complex mix of associations. For example, the market grew out of a need of newly-arriving immigrants to secure the necessities of daily living at a manageable price and of the need for peddlers to gain the means for survival. It endured because it filled a need.

Despite the major losses for ordinary people in the Halsted-Roosevelt neighborhood, they did have some partial victories. For these people, the neighborhood is an important part of the fabric of their day-to-day living. Because they really cared about it and it was tied to home, belief, and financial necessity, they could interest others in the rightness of their cause, and they were not entirely alone in fighting for what mattered to them. Outsiders began to write letters to newspapers, and editorial writers and talk show hosts took an interest in the cause. When interest is intense and sustained, the neighborhood cause may gain enough strength to win concessions, if not outright victory.

Several examples illustrate these partial victories over a period of time. When Florence Scala led the fight against the elder Mayor Daley's plan for the demolition of most of Little Italy to make way for the construction of the University of Illinois at Chicago, her group lost and much of the neighborhood disappeared. But because of that struggle and the publicity that accompanied it, urban renewal has never been the same again. Even though this occurred more than 40 years ago, Florence Scala's name is still well-known in Chicago circles while the names of the lieutenants working for the mayor and the university have long since passed into oblivion.

Another partial victory occurred in the struggle to save the Maxwell Street Market in the face of the aim of City Hall and the University to eliminate it completely. This issue also raised a storm of long-term publicity and demonstration. Finally the market was removed from the Halsted-Maxwell area, but because of the outcry and widely-perceived need, instead of disappearing altogether, it was reincarnated in a gentrified version on Canal Street and is thriving there. A sidelight on the struggle to save the market was that a vigorous effort by an interested group was made to acquire landmark status for the Maxwell Street Market district. It was an innovative plan that won *unanimous* approval by the state landmark commission, only to be rejected by the state landmark officer. The grounds for his rejection of the plan were less than persuasive.

Finally, the fight to save St. Francis of Assisi Church resulted in forcing the church authorities to take a second look at ethnic group issues and to reevaluate the true facts in the case. Although church officials consistently ignored the protestations of parishioners and the information presented by them, finally, just before demolition, one official really listened to them and said, "We *have* to take another look at this."

No one would claim that there is equality in the power equation or that protagonists for the neighborhood won complete victories in any of these struggles, but they have not lost altogether either because they did influence the outcome. A look at the stories of four ordinary extraordinary neighborhood individuals illuminates that process. All four have spent their lives in the Halsted-Roosevelt neighborhood or have major associations with it, and the issues of power and access to information, urban renewal, and neighborhood vulnerability are played out in real life terms throughout their oral life histories.

Harold Fox, born in 1910, remembers in detail everyday particulars of the Jewish ghetto, from what they ate to rules of the games they played, from selling socks on Maxwell Street near his father's store to celebrity associations through his suit-designing business and activities as a band leader.

Florence Scala has rich memories of her childhood in the Italian sector of the neighborhood and of times she spent at Hull-House settlement house. Her keen sense of right and wrong clarifies the reasons why she risked so much to save her neighborhood and why these issues will not go away today.

Nate Duncan's story spans the transition from the Jewish neighborhood to black community as he relates growing up in Black Bottom, thriving on local park district sports, and working in a matzo factory and in a Jewish deli that he eventually purchased. His story demonstrates how an ordinary person can be genial and peaceful and foster friendly exchange, yet at the same time remain steadfast about issues.

Hilda Portillo relates how she came from Mexico to Chicago as a teenager and St. Francis of Assisi became her community and her "home." The moral support she received there throughout her personal traumas over the years provided her with the faith and will to fight to save St. Francis. Her story also makes clear the more subtle aspects of prejudice as it is directed against Latino immigrants to Chicago.

These oral histories are based on interviews conducted over a period of more than two years. Most of these interviews were informal, open-ended, and conversational, usually conducted while seated at a kitchen or dining room table. All were tape-recorded and later transcribed, and since all four of these informants had been interviewed at different times by media representatives and others, the tape recorder did not seem to inhibit their conversations in any way. Although I usually had some questions in mind before each interview, our talks were never bound by those questions and were often quite free-ranging.

The only exception to this procedure was in collecting information from Harold Fox. Since he lived in Sarasota, Florida, and he had originally contacted me by mail, some of his narrative is gleaned from the lengthy, expressive letters that he wrote over a period of five years. He also had a habit of tape recording "letters" when he was tired of writing, so I have a collection of those. He had previously made a series of tapes for his family and I had access to two or three of those. We also had numerous phone conversations to answer questions and fill in gaps, and finally, I went to Florida and we had two full days of interviews at the kitchen table.

My intent in presenting the oral histories was to make certain that the narratives were entirely the words of the subjects and not my own words or my opinions. Therefore, I saw my role not as editor of the final product but as someone who might rearrange the order occasionally for the sake of chronology and coherence. My contention is that editing would lose the true nature of what extraordinary "ordinary" people think and feel and say when they are being themselves. What they are—their quality of character and how they have acted out their lives—is a major point of the book. Individual introductory chapters to each of the four oral histories will present some background of the particular ethnic group in question and its association with this Halsted-Roosevelt "community of communities" of the Near West Side of Chicago.[7]

NOTES TO INTRODUCTION

1. Chicago Fact Book Consortium, *Local Community Fact Book Chicago Metropolitan Area* (Chicago: Chicago Review Press, 1984), 75-79. The first Fact Book about Chicago communities areas was published in 1938 under the direction of Ernest Burgess. The community area concept has helped to provide consistent demographic information about designated census tracts.

2. Quotation is from a "Chicago Tonight" public television interview with John Callaway. In a 1997 telephone conversation Paul Green said, "That's something I've been arguing for years."

3. Neal Pollack, "Public image limited: Mayor Daley's ministry of information versus your right to know," *Reader*, 5 May 1995, sec. 1, p. 1.

4. Hans Gerth and C. Wright Mills, *From Max Weber: Essays in Sociology* (New York: Oxford University Press, 1946), 233.

5. Neal Pollack, "The late, great Municipal Reference Library," sidebar in "Public image limited," *Reader*, 5 May 1995, sec. 1, 22.

6. Alderman Mazola was generous with an hour-long interview when I talked with him in 1994 but there was no information forthcoming concerning the future of land south of Roosevelt Road. All his answers were of the, "We haven't discussed that yet," or, "We haven't made any decisions about that" variety.

7. I thank Patrick Reardon, *Chicago Tribune* staff writer, for this felicitous phrase when he wrote (personal communication) that the Jewish Community, Little Italy, Black Bottom, and the St. Francis parish are pieces of the Halsted-Roosevelt community, but not the whole. He wrote, "The whole—in one of those beautifully urban realities—is the community of these communities."

I don't consider a man as a Negro, Jew, or Italian, or a member of his particular race. I consider him as a member of the human race striving for existence in a mixed up world.

—HAROLD FOX, 1947

Courtesy of Harold Fox.

Hal Fox measures Rabbi Morris Gutstein,
rabbi at Shaare Tikvah Schul, for a kosher suit.

1. THE JEWISH NEIGHBORHOOD
2. HAROLD FOX
3. HAROLD FOX (CONTINUED)

This storefront tobacco factory in the Maxwell Street area, c. 1905, like many on the Near West Side, provided piecework for regular workers, and after school employment for enterprising youngsters like Hal Fox.

1

THE JEWISH NEIGHBORHOOD

INTRODUCTION

IN SPITE OF cultural traditions that extended hundreds of years into the past, the Jews in the Halsted-Roosevelt ghetto on the Near West Side of Chicago seem to have been in fast forward motion. The story told by Harold Fox provides details of daily life of an ethnic group in transition. He was born in 1910 at a time when the Jewish population of the Maxwell Street area was beginning to move out of the area to other parts of Chicago and to the suburbs. Many moved a couple of miles west to Lawndale. There they had ties with new homes and institutions, yet still retained many links to family, friends, and businesses of the old neighborhood. It was also a period of movement and change in the music and tailoring worlds, and it held the seeds of big changes in the areas of civil rights. Harold Fox participated to the hilt in all of these worlds of this Near West Side neighborhood.

In 1910 the area around Halsted and Maxwell Streets fulfilled a meaning of "ghetto" that, according to Wirth, had become more or less standardized throughout Europe. It was an area predominantly, if not exclusively, inhabited by Jews.[1] By 1910, in this area where the Russian-Jewish immigrants were concentrated, the population was 90 percent Jewish.

Although the first Jew, a peddler named J. Gottlieb, arrived in Chicago as early as 1838, he is believed to have moved west soon after his arrival. By the Great Fire of 1871 many

German Jews had moved to Chicago and had established homes and businesses in and around the Loop. The fire destroyed most of these buildings and five of the seven synagogues in the area, and five hundred Jewish families were left homeless.[2]

A second devastating fire occurred in 1874. This fire swept away homes on the Near South Side where many poor Eastern European Jews lived. A secondary effect of the Fire of 1874 was that many businesses that had been burned out of the Loop moved into the Maxwell Street area that was just outside the paths of the fires, and a burst of considerable activity amid prosperity ensued in this neighborhood. The few Jewish families who had previously crossed the river into the Maxwell Street area were now joined by others who had lost their homes east of the river.

Typical of immigrants flocking to the area was Bernard Horwich who arrived from Lithuania as a "greenhorn" and asked for directions to a Jewish neighborhood.[3] A bystander pointed west and said, "If you go across the bridge, you will find a great many of them." Horwich inquired as to where the better class of Jews resided and was told that on Canal Street he would find all kinds of Jews, but mostly poor ones.

The Eastern European immigrants were used to living close together in small, homogeneous communities in their former countries where a set of Jewish values prevailed and there was a real sense of belonging. In the smaller communities, they lived in a central section near the marketplace, whereas non-Jews lived in the outskirts; in the cities they were concentrated in particular neighborhoods. Therefore, when they arrived at the Halsted-Roosevelt area on Chicago's Near West Side, the neighborhood may not have been the fulfillment of their dreams, but it had a familiar "feel" about it.

When the first Jewish settlers moved to the Near West Side it was occupied by a large number of Bohemian immigrants. Many of the Jews came from Bohemian sectors of the Old World, so often they could communicate in a familiar language. They shared some traditions with the Bohemians, and the two groups were used to trading with each other. Eventually the non-Jewish Bohemian immigrants moved south of the 15th Street railway tracks to what came to be called Pilsen, while the Jewish immigrants stayed in the area north of the tracks. The Irish and German immigrants who had also been living in the area gradually moved out until this part of the Near West Side was predominantly Jewish.

In the ghetto, bounded by 12th Street (later to be named Roosevelt Road), Halsted Street, 15th Street, and Stewart Avenue, nine-tenths of the population of about 16,000 people were Jews. Here newly-arriving immigrants would find familiar sights: kosher shops, peddlers' carts, synagogues, bearded men, women wearing shawls, and every kind of trade from tailors' shops to matzo bakeries. The immigrants were used to hardships, and the physical conditions of the ghetto gave them no respite. The neighborhood became more and more crowded as newcomers moved in and no new buildings were built. It was said that if all of Chicago were as densely populated as the Maxwell Street ghetto, the city would have 32 million people instead of 2 million.

In 1910, Jane Addams, the founder of the Hull-House settlement house, said that the houses, mostly wooden, had been originally built for one family but were now occupied by several families. Along with overcrowding, there were narrow streets, overflowing garbage boxes, outdoor toilets, and no running water.[4]

At first, the major business center of the Jewish settlement was Jefferson Street, a paved street with an electric trolley, stores, pushcarts, and peddlers. As early as 1893 the World's Fair guidebooks for Chicago described the Jewish market on Jefferson Street as one of the interesting sights of the city.[5] As peddlers grew more numerous and Jefferson Street more crowded, the activity spilled over onto Maxwell Street until, in 1912, the city council formally certified Maxwell Street as an official open-air market. Eventually the focal point of the ghetto became the intersection of Maxwell and Halsted Streets.

Roosevelt Road was the chief arterial street of the neighborhood and was slated for widening as part of Daniel Burnham's Plan of Chicago of 1909. The widening was begun in 1916 and this improved road served as a link between the old

Photo by Charles R. Clark, Chicago Historical Society, 00273.

Jefferson Street, c. 1906, was a main north-south
thoroughfare with vendors lining the sides of the street.

Halsted-Maxwell ghetto and the newer Lawndale Jewish district.

Making a Living

On the Near West Side of Chicago there was a common pattern
of advancement among the Eastern European Jewish settlers.
An immigrant might have peddled from a pushcart throughout
the neighborhood in the 1880s, then progressed to vending
from a stand along Maxwell Street, initiated a commercial
enterprise in his own shop on Halsted Street, graduated to a
wholesale business on 12th Street, and by 1910, moved family
and business west to Lawndale. When these immigrants arrived on the Near West Side they found a teeming population
living in need of goods. There were ready-made customers

Robinson's Department Store, 657 Maxwell Street, was still in business in this 1956 view.

whose likes and dislikes were familiar and who could be served daily on the streets or in the back alleys for the most convenient kind of shopping. Peddlers brought everything from trinkets to clothes to food, including bread, milk, fish, fruits, and vegetables.

Sunday brought buyers from all over the city to Maxwell Street, and as Meyer Laser described it, "For blocks and blocks, it was thick with people, shoulder to shoulder . . . Maxwell Street itself was a poor man's paradise . . . the 'State Street of the ghetto,' it was known as."[6]

After the construction of the Dan Ryan Expressway the market continued on Maxwell Street from Union to Morgan and filled in the empty blocks that had been demolished by urban renewal from Maxwell Street south to 15th Street. With this development, instead of being linear, the market took on the form of an old city market square. The Maxwell Street Market continued to attract as many as 20,000 visitors each Sunday and helped furnish a living for approximately 1,000 vendors, until 1994 when City Hall shut it down in order to turn the land over to the University of Illinois.

There were dozens of small shops in the Maxwell Street area and a few large ones. Robinson's Department Store, on Maxwell Street between Union Avenue and Jefferson Street, was founded by Joseph Robinson who came from Russia when he was five years old. In 1920 he purchased the department store from the former owner and enlarged it until it filled a block. His son, Sheldon, recalled, "We had forty employees and customers from all over—advertised in all the newspapers—and sold expensive lamps and all kinds of high class merchandise—even mah jongg sets."[7]

Courtesy of Philip Albert.

Several Maxwell Street businesses, such as the Maxwell Fur Co. (left) and Joe Fligelman Watches (below), seen here in 1956, were still active when their buildings were demolished in the late 1950s for construction of the Dan Ryan Expressway.

Ben Lyon, another long-term businessman on Maxwell Street was born in the area in 1908.[8] His parents came from Eastern Europe in the early 1900s and bought a deli on Jefferson Street; eventually Ben took over that business. The food was kosher, conforming to Jewish dietary laws, and it was a popular place with customers from all over Chicago. Later he rented the ground floor of a building west of Halsted Street on Maxwell Street. One of his employees was Nate Duncan, whose oral history appears later. Finally, when Ben Lyon wanted to retire in 1973, he sold the business to Nate, a black man. Ben reflected on the sale, "He was an honest boy—I knew he'd do well—it was good for me and good for him."

Not all Jewish immigrants on the Near West Side were in the food business or retail trade; some turned to various industries for their livelihood. An inspection of detailed, turn-of-the-century maps, such as Robinson's and Sanborn's, makes it clear that there were innumerable little factories

scattered throughout the neighborhood.

On Jefferson Street near Maxwell Street, was a matzo company owned by the Wittenberg family. Mildred Wittenberg Mallin explained that her grandfather started with a bakery

Photo by Carolyn Eastwood.

Nate Duncan purchased the delicatessen at 807 W. Maxwell from Ben Lyon, his former employer, in 1973. The building was built in 1896 and had served as a deli from the 1920s or 1930s.

where he made bread and cakes.[9] Then in 1921 her father converted to making matzos on the second and third floors of the building and her grandfather continued the bakery on the lower floor. Their living quarters were in back of the bakery. Mildred described how conveyer belts took the matzos to the third floor and sometimes some dough caught in the mechanism and would start smoking. Everyone on Maxwell Street would see smoke coming from the back of the building and would shout, "Oh, the Wittenbergs are having a fire again!" At that time the Wittenbergs had the only matzo factory in Chicago and "shipped thousands of pounds of matzos to Jews all over." Later, in his oral history, Nate Duncan relates how he also worked in this factory as a teenager.

A relatively small number of Jews worked for the tobacco industry, which had numerous shops in the area, and substantial numbers of the immigrants turned to various manifestations of the clothing industry. Harold Fox had associations with both of these industries. In the following chapter he recounts his experiences as a child worker in a small, neighborhood sweatshop of the tobacco business. He also describes his lifetime connection with the tailoring and designing trade from his grandfather's and father's trimmings and woolens shops to the Fox Brothers tailoring business he shared with his brother.

Courtesy of Mildred Wittenberg Mallin and Irving Cutler.

The Wittenberg Matzoh Company, 1326 S. Jefferson, c. 1919.
The company had customers worldwide, but was known
in the neighborhood for periodically catching on fire.

HELPING EACH OTHER

CONSISTENT WITH LIFE in their former village communities, the
Jewish immigrants on the Near West Side continued close ties
with family and friends. Family gathering were frequent and
sometimes these took the form of "cousins' clubs"—semi-
formalized groups of relatives who organized mutual savings

and self-help associations, as well as socialized.

Also ubiquitous in this neighborhood were small religious congregations that formed, often as quickly as they could gather the required 10 men (a minyan) for group worship. These little groups had no elaborate synagogues, and they often met in private rooms or store-fronts. Harold Fox describes his relatives and other businessmen who formed a congregation in the Maxwell Street area so they could worship near their work during the day although they no longer lived on the Near West Side and belonged to other congregations.

Two buildings at the corner of Union Avenue and 14th Street illustrate the ethnic transitions that took place here. In 1886, the wooden building on the corner was the German Evangelical United Church and next to it was the German school. By 1914, both of these buildings were Jewish synagogues.[10] On the corner was Congregation Paole Zedeck Anshe Sfard and the building next to it was the First Roumanian Congregation. In 1935 the Roumanian Congregation building

Photo by Dr. Jack H. Sloan, courtesy of Norman Schwartz.

Two of the many synagogues of the Maxwell Street area were still standing on Union Avenue when this photograph was taken in 1943. Congregation Paole Zedeck Anshe Sfard is on the left; the Roumanian Congregation building, later Gethsemane Missionary Baptist Church, is on the right.

was purchased by a black congregation that gave the wooden building a brick veneer and named it the Gethsemane Missionary Baptist Church.

Another important source of mutual support in the lives of Eastern European Jews as they faced the insecurities and hardships of life in the new world was the *landsmanschaften*. These were societies formed of people who had emigrated from the same area of the Old World. They provided friendship and everything from matchmaking to burial plots.[11]

There were also numerous, more formal, groups within the Jewish community directed to meeting needs of poor and unskilled immigrants who faced harsh conditions. For example, on the Near West Side was the Woman's Loan Association that loaned hundreds of thousands of dollars in short-term, low-level loans. Minnie Low, the founder, said that throughout the entire district there were comparatively few of the peddlers, vendors, and keepers of small stands and shops, who had not been given a start in life or helped over rugged places by loans from local organizations.[12]

When the Eastern European Jews first filled the Near West Side there was really only one social center—Hull-House, founded in 1889. By 1893 the idea of settlement houses was beginning to catch on and the Maxwell Street Settlement was opened. In 1908 the Chicago Hebrew Institute had purchased a convent on Taylor Street and this also became an intellectual and social center for young people and adults of the neighborhood. Many donations to charities came from private individuals, but business people were pressured to give funds or goods, and often there was a political angle involved.

Mildred Wittenberg Mallin of the matzo business relates that during Passover many poor people of the neighborhood could not afford matzos. Then a big truck would come to their factory and workers would fill it with matzos. As Mildred said, "That was the alderman's political end of it. He made a show of giving away what he got free from us. And it was really something! We used to give away whole truckloads, and then everybody would thank Alderman [Moe] Rosenberg because they got free matzos."

An intense love of learning prompted a number of Jewish

institutions. One of the first projects of the Hebrew Literary Society was opening a library on Canal and Polk Streets. For school children in the heart of this neighborhood there were the religiously oriented schools—the Talmud Torah, Moses Montefiore Hebrew Free School, and the Jewish Training School—but most Jewish children also attended one of the three public grade schools—Foster, Smythe, and Washburne. In 1914 the enrollment in those public schools was 80-90 percent Jewish.

In other ways the world was opening up for the new Eastern Jewish immigrants. Yiddish daily newspapers finally were successful after several false starts. The local Yiddish theater and vaudeville were favorite forms of entertainment; they enlightened and yet were, at the same time, comfortably familiar.

In the public domain there was Stanford Park, founded in 1910 at 14th Place and Union Avenue. This park seems to have provided satisfaction out of all proportion to its size. It was to furnish a recreational outlet for young people and green relief from the crowded conditions around Maxwell Street for all ethnic groups in the area.

TRANSITION

BY THE 1930s most of the Jewish residents had moved from the Maxwell Street area to other parts of the city, although some older Jews remained for a time and a number of Jewish businessmen retained their stores in what was left of the Halsted and Maxwell business center. A surprising number of individuals who had familial ties to Maxwell Street went on to become prominent in various aspects of American life. They included Barney Balaban (President, Paramount Pictures), Walter Paley (CBS founder), Arthur Goldberg (Supreme Court Justice), Admiral Hyman Rickover (father of the atomic submarine), and Saul Alinsky (community organizer).

In addition to the tailoring business, the other world of Harold Fox was music, and his two worlds overlapped in many ways in the 1940s. First of all, Fox Brothers designed and tailored uniforms for nationally-renowned big bands and for many of the musicians on an individual basis, which brought them to Fox Brothers on Roosevelt Road. Secondly, Harold Fox led the Jimmy Dale band—a band that played at Hull-House on Sundays and practiced in Stanford Park—and also served as back-up band for better-known performers such as Nat "King" Cole and Stan Kenton.

In 1947 Joe Segal, Chicago's jazz impresario, was studying and presenting shows at Roosevelt University when he wrote an article for the student newspaper, the *Roosevelt Torch*. It was headlined, "Stan Kenton was fine—but Jimmy Dale stole the show." Segal praised the musicianship, but also made note of the mix:

> Jimmy (Harold Fox) fronts the band with unbounded glee and energy, and is to be complimented for his determined policy of resisting all offers for better jobs when those jobs meant playing with a strictly white band. As it stands today, Jimmy Dale's band is undoubtedly the greatest mixed organization in the country. Orchids to him, and may we hear more of him.[13]

Fifty years later, Joe Segal reflected on the nature of Harold Fox and his band, "He was innovative—there was not much in the way of mixed bands before. Some had a couple of guys as a feature, for example, Benny Goodman's band. But Hal really had a mixed band—maybe even more blacks than whites. Sometimes the music was a little rough because he used a lot of subs, but he had some good guys."[14] Among these were some who made names for themselves in the music world, such as Lee Konitz and Junior Mance. Harold Fox, with his exceptional combination of vitality, showmanship, caring, and broad-minded interest in people of all backgrounds, provides a glimpse of an ideal transition attitude when a neighborhood changes.

NOTES TO CHAPTER 1

1. Louis Wirth, *The Ghetto* (Chicago: University of Chicago Press, 1928), 3.

2. Irving Cutler, *The Jews of Chicago* (Chicago: University of Illinois Press, 1996), 29.

3. Bernard Horwich, *My First Eighty Years* (Chicago: Argus Books, 1939), 118-19.

4. Jane Addams, *Twenty Years at Hull-House* (New York: Macmillan, 1910), 97-100.

5. Edith Abbott, *The Tenements of Chicago* (New York: Arno Press, 1970—originally University of Chicago Press, 1936), 88.

6. Ira Berkow, *Maxwell Street* (New York: Doubleday, 1977), 57-64.

7. Telephone interview with Sheldon Robinson, 1997.

8. Telephone interview with Ben Lyon, 1997.

9. Interview with Mildred Wittenberg Mallin, Chicago, 1996.

10. Norman Schwartz, "Photographs of Wood Synagogue Picture History," *Chicago Jewish History* 16, no. 4 (Chicago: Chicago Jewish Historical Society, 1993).

11. Sidney Sorkin, *Bridges to an American City: A Guide to Chicago's Landsmanschaften, 1870-1990* (New York: Peter Lang Publishing, 1993), 3.

12. Shelly Tenenbaum, "Immigrants and Capital: Jewish Loan Societies in the United States, 1889-1945," *American Jewish History* LXXVI, no. 1 (September 1986): 70.

13. Joe Segal, "Stan Kenton was fine, but—Jimmy Dale stole the show," *Roosevelt Torch* (1947).

14. Telephone interview with Joe Segal, 1997.

Courtesy of the Chicago Historical Society, ICHi-31927; located by Lori Grove.

The grandfather of Hal Fox owned this tailor supplies
and trimmings store at 606 Maxwell Street, c. 1915.

2

HAROLD FOX

THE RELATIVES

I WAS NAMED Conrad Fox after my grandfather when I was born on July 9, 1910. Eventually my family started calling me Harold because Conrad was a sissy name in our neighborhood, and I wasn't a very good fighter.

When we came home from the hospital we lived in a little flat on Ashland Avenue, which was one step beyond Maxwell Street. First the immigrants came to Maxwell Street, and then there was the upward movement of the Jewish people who made progress by moving into neighborhoods that were all Gentile neighborhoods. One Jew would manage to sneak in and pretty soon he would have quite a few of the Jewish people moving in. But at that time my father and two uncles and my grandfather all still had shops on Maxwell Street.

The real name of my grandpa, my pa's dad, was Kalman, but they called him Conrad. Grandpa Fox left Russia because of the pogroms—the Cossacks would come in the villages and beat them all up and destroy their houses. When Grandpa got to Ellis Island he said his name was Fuchs, but the customs man couldn't understand him, and he kept asking Grandpa to repeat his name. Finally he said, "I tell you what, your name is Fox." So he wrote that down. Grandpa Fox came to this country about 1880, and he established his business on Maxwell Street, almost at the corner of Jefferson. Actually, he came to New York first, but since there was a Jewish colony

Photo by Carolyn Eastwood.

Hal Fox and his family moved west to this home in Chicago's
Lawndale neighborhood while his father, uncles, and
grandfather still had shops on Maxwell Street.

from his *shtetl* here in Chicago he came to the Maxwell Street
area. The Jewish families would always help each other and
they would take in boarders so it made it easier for newcomers
to get started.

The oldest in the family would always come first and as
soon as he had a job or got into business and made a little
money he would send for the oldest son so that one could help
out too. So Grandpa sent for his oldest son, Ben, and then next
came Ike, then Healy, and then my pa, Leo, came from Russia
when he was five years old. My pa had two sisters too, Dora
and Eva, so it was a big family to bring all the way from Russia.

Grandpa Fox was probably the most respected gentleman
around, and he was really a beautiful person with a long beard
and very pious. Everyone in the neighborhood respected him.
While Grandpa Fox was well liked, he was very shrewd. Whenever anyone in the neighborhood needed advice they would
come to him. He seemed to be pretty wise and had all the right
answers. I remember seeing my Grandpa when we'd visit in
the relatives' homes and also when I went to visit my relatives'

shops on Maxwell Street. Another memory I have is of being in my bed and my pa woke me up and said Grandpa passed away. We waited a long time in the cold for a streetcar to take us to his house.

My grandpa's store was a kind of walk-up; you had to go up a few stairs to enter the store, and he would have bolts of linings and special notions and Wiss scissors, all kinds of cottons (O.N.T. thread), and tailor's trimmings, and buttons and hooks, and tailor's chalks—anything that tailors needed. He also had some woolens too. It was supposed to be wholesale, and mostly the tailors went there to get their supplies, but he sold retail too.

All four sons of my grandfather went into business of one kind or another. First was Ike—Ike was a handsome, tall man, bright red hair and a big strong posture. All the Fox brothers were big boned and had a good physique. Later they got a little big around the belly because they were all good eaters. Uncle Ike worked on a matzo truck; he delivered matzos for a company called Wittenberg Matzo Company. They used to manufacture their matzos on Maxwell Street. That seemed to be the place where most of the Jewish people went and most of the other ethnic people went too.

He'd deliver these matzos and that way he'd make a lot of connections with some of the grocers, and sometimes they would trade matzos for canned foods. And his particular fancy was canned fish of all kinds; kippered sardines, salmon, tomato herrings—so when we'd go to his home, he'd immediately take us to the basement to see all the cases of imported salmon and sardines. He was so proud of his food because food was really important to everybody in those days.

The second son, Ben, had a fabulous store. He started with toys. He got to know the Marshall Field's person and he would be their main connection on getting rid of their toys each season when they were ready to put in a new line. And he would sell them in his shop. Around Christmas time Marshall Field's would job a lot of Christmas ornaments to him, and he'd put the ornaments outside on a stand. One Christmas I sold these ornaments for him because he was always busy inside. I think the weather was about 20 degrees below zero. There I was hawking these ornaments—two for a nickel. I didn't know too much about them, but I was a pretty good salesman.

At first Ben's store was on Maxwell Street near Jefferson, and he began to handle some of the finest Dresden chinaware and marble statuaries. He would go on buying trips to Europe—to Germany for china and Italy for statuary. He was proud of all the genuine things he had there. He'd click on those cups and hear that ring that would prove that the article was genuine and that it was a very fine article. He had statues and things like that that would go for $50,000 today. Customers used to pull up in chauffeur-driven cars. It was hard for those big cars to get in on Maxwell Street and the vendors would yell at them for taking up all the room.

Eventually as he got more popular and his business grew, he bought the nickel movie show on Halsted Street just south of Maxwell and made a big long store out of it. That show was from the real old days when we'd always go for a nickel and get what you'd call a "late check" and get to stay for the second show. Uncle Ben and his family continued to live in the old building on Maxwell though and it was still just Uncle Ben and my Aunt Mahtel running the shop. She still wore her Jewish wig and never wore any makeup or anything.

The third son, Healy, was my favorite uncle. He was always nice to me and made sure I'd always have a few pennies in my pocket and things like that. He wanted to be a social climber—he was the first to move into neighborhoods where there weren't any Jewish people, and he bought the first building of his own. He lived on the second floor and when you'd get up to his apartment you'd see beautiful furniture, especially for those days—marble-topped tables, and a lot of statuary—just gorgeous. But the furniture wasn't to enjoy or sit on, most of the time it was covered with plastic or tapestries. Also, Uncle Healy was the first one in the family to have an automobile, a Buick. In those days if you could just go for a ride in a car it was considered great. When we knew he was going for a ride my brother and I would be sitting and hoping on the curbstone.

My dad and Uncle Healy had their woolen store at 648 Maxwell Street, a half a block away from my grandpa's store.

Even as a little guy I would go to see my father in his shop. For three cents I would go on the 16th Street streetcar all the way from Lawndale, where we lived then, to Maxwell Street, about three miles. The streetcars had a motorman in front and a conductor in back, and I used to like to watch the conductor punch out the transfers. It was just kind of entrancing so I would stand on the back platform and watch him.

My grandpa's store was concentrated on trimmings and my dad's store was sort of one step up the ladder to the finest materials from the finest mills. At that time serge was the big thing. My father's was more or less a higher-class business. His shop was a very clean store, and the name on the window was Fox Brothers Woolen Company and Tailor's Trimmings, and to this day we're Fox Brothers, but we're tailors.

Grandpa furnished their first woolens and then my dad and uncle started doing business directly with the woolen mills, and they bought by the bolt. The bolt usually had 60

Chicago Transit Authority.

Streetcars along Roosevelt Road were convenient and frequent, as seen in this 1944 view looking westward from the intersection of Roosevelt Road and Halsted Street. The "Red Rocket" streetcar stops in front of the well-known Gold's Restaurant.

yards, and in those days, I would say $1.50 a yard was high for the best woolens. Later on, when they were doing pretty good in the woolen business, they called themselves Fox Brothers Woolens and they moved from Maxwell Street to Roosevelt Road, or 12th Street, as it was called then. That was around 1915.

At that time they weren't getting people coming in off the street; mostly the trade was people who wanted to buy their own goods and take it to their tailor and have it made up. Or the tailors themselves would come in because my dad put out a sample line that he called Master Fabrics. He would go to a certain company and they would cut up a yard of goods into these squares and put them on a card, one sample per card. They had a big box and the cards would fit in there. They would have, maybe, a hundred different patterns. Later I used the sample line in New York. That's how I helped him sell material.

They didn't need Maxwell Street anymore because now they had the sample line, the tailors would come to them, and when my brother and I took over we would let the tailors know, just call in and tell us what you need, and we would jump in the car and deliver it that afternoon.

One reason moving to Roosevelt Road was a step up the ladder was because there weren't such things as pullers and there weren't carts outside the stores, nothing like that. People could just walk in the door or they used the tailors' sample line. When my dad and uncle started they didn't even have a yardstick. To measure a yard you'd measure from your nose to your outstretched arm and hand. Eventually they got yard-sticks that they nailed to the counter. My uncle couldn't add and he used an abacus. They didn't have registers either; the money all went in the pockets, and then in a box. Most of the family didn't go to school very much.

In spite of the fact that he didn't have any education, Pa kept his own books and he had a very beautiful way of writing. He would use a wide pen and then press heavily while he was writing to make some of the lines wider. He became head of his Masonic group and to this day we have a picture of him in his uniform and there was another Oddfellows group that he belonged to. The uniform looked almost like a soldier's uniform. People would say what war was your dad in? He told us to tell the kids that he was in the Salvation Army. I was kidded a lot for that because I thought he was in the real army.

Pa was a very religious person and he would do prayers every morning. Every Saturday he would go to the temple. But my dad and I never got along. He was very strict and felt, "Young man, get down to business and don't be running around." And I was kind of a "chaser" so I'd get home late, from the time I was young, and he'd be waiting with that big old broomstick and he'd beat me up with it till it would break. I guess it was through that that I never had much love for my dad. He never seemed to sit down and talk to me. But I didn't realize that he was busy earning a living. I think he was a little on the selfish side. At dinner he had a strict rule—you don't talk at dinner—you eat. After dinner he'd leave. Finally we found out that my dad had been going down and getting a coke, but he never thought of taking any of the family.

One of my father's sisters was Eva, and she married Charlie Geertz. He had a successful cigar company called Cyrus the Great run by Ehrlich and Geertz, and he was the Geertz part of it. Barney Ross, who was later the world lightweight and welterweight boxing champion, was orphaned when he was about 14 years old, and he went to the Marks Nathan Home, which was a Jewish charity. My Aunt Eva and Uncle Charlie were on the board of the Marks Nathan Home, and they took Barney into their home and raised him. Years later there was a program called "This is Your Life" and one of the programs was about Barney Ross, and my uncle and aunt were part of the program.

My mother was Sarah Pearson. Her father, Grandpa Pearson, was in some kind of business and he and his wife, Rachel, were traveling in Great Britain when they had their family so the children were all of different origins. Jennie, my aunt, was born in Scotland; a couple of them were born in London; but when they got to America, my mother, Sarah, was born. My mother went to Foster School on Union near Maxwell. A lot of Jewish kids went there.

My Grandma Pearson's name was Rachel, and I remember

some of the food she served. I guess you remember some of your family by the different things you have to eat when you visited them. She also wore a *sheitel* (wig worn by Orthodox married women), like my Grandma Fox. My mother really didn't know the European recipes, but she and Auntie Ella, the wife of my dad's brother, were good friends. They were used to eating that way, so through Auntie Ella my mother learned to make all the things like cholent and gefilte fish and all the Jewish pastries and pickles and green tomatoes. Our basement was full of canned things.

My mother was always close to her sister, Jennie, but when I married a Christian girl, Jennie wouldn't talk to my mother for 10 years. She said I disgraced the family, but before that she was my best aunt. Another sister, Tillie, married a man named Max Goldman. He had a tailor business on the South Side. He worked very, very hard, but he was always saying that he could never make enough money. One day he was so depressed about business that he just walked to the end of Belmont Harbor to Lake Michigan and jumped in and drowned.

In those days we didn't have much entertainment, but we'd go to visit the relatives. I have a picture of a family gathering in Uncle Ben's apartment above the store, and there must have been about 50 relatives at this party—family and in-laws. People sometimes called these gatherings "cousin's clubs" and ours we called the Fox club.

None of Uncle Ben's five daughters married and they always blamed it on the fact that they lived above the store on Maxwell Street. They'd be ashamed to invite anybody other than relatives to their home. One daughter was Hindi and another was Richie. Richie loved to dance and we'd roll up the rug and dance like mad. I can remember playing the violin and Hindi would play the piano.

The relatives mostly talked English because we younger ones didn't understand Yiddish, but some of these Jewish people talked Yiddish to each other because then they didn't have to think of the English words. They were just learning English. Most of my relatives had Jewish names and with some of them I never did know their English names. When I

Courtesy of Harold Fox.

A Fox family gathering, c. 1918, in Hal's Uncle Ben's apartment above
the store at 620 Maxwell Street. Hal is seated center front.

was little, one reason hardly any of us talked Yiddish was
because you'd be in trouble with the kids and everybody else
because they'd say you're a greenhorn—"You're a greenhorn!
Speak English! You're a greenhorn!"

The Glickman Theater was a Jewish theater, and I used to
go and sit right out in the front row. I used to love to go and see
Yiddish plays, even though I didn't understand too much of
Yiddish. I was schooled, but unfortunately we didn't learn to
speak Yiddish, and I learned to read Hebrew, but I didn't know
what I was reading. I can say the prayers in Hebrew, but I
don't know what I'm saying. Even though I didn't know much
of what they were saying at the plays, I enjoyed the music.

I always had a weak spot for Yiddish things and Jewish
things—I really love the Jewish religion. While I go to a Con-

servative synagogue, I still like the Orthodox way of doing things. Now they have Bingo in the synagogue so while we're having *kaddish* and saying our mourner's prayers, we'll hear, "number 7, number 10," and I think that's really terrible and sacrilegious.

But back to Uncle Ben's family. Besides the daughters he had a son, Sam. Sam was the oldest and he had a pop factory called the Perfection Pop Company. He made a famous drink called the "Oh Henry"—it was a combination of Coca Cola and cherry, like a Dr. Pepper. This was a pretty popular business because most of the Jewish people wouldn't run to the store and buy a bottle of pop or a can of soda—they would have their pop delivered regularly because they drank it instead of coffee and milk and all these other things. They never drank wine except for Friday night for religious occasions. Pop was a favorite drink, and I still like to have strawberry pop. Another favorite drink was chocolate phosphate, and they called it Jewish beer.

So that was a pretty good business that Sam Fox had. While his main drink was Oh Henry, the Oh Henry candy bars came out that were made by Curtiss Candy Company. Curtiss put up a bunch of signs and all they said was Oh Henry, and that gave Sam's pop a lot of business. They tried to get him to change the name of his pop and he wouldn't do it, so eventually they paid him off. Anyway, during Prohibition Sam still had the pop factory, which was two blocks from Maxwell Street, and that was a short way from Little Italy. So the Capone people got acquainted with Sam and they needed some place to keep their bootleg booze, so they rented space in Sam Fox's pop factory. That was when all these gangsters would come in and sit in the office and talk and make deals. I met some real tough characters there.

In those days we used to go to the corner grocery for a glass of strawberry soda for 3 cents, but if you only had 2 cents, you could get it plain, and that's where the term "two cents plain" comes from. I'd ask for strawberry soda and ask for it sweet. I'd drink about half and say, oh, you made this too sweet, could you just add a little more seltzer, and he'd add some seltzer water. So by the time you finished you'd had about three glasses of soda. I wasn't the only kid who used this racket—we all used it. The grocer who had the soda fountain, I think he knew the racket, but these were only kids and he'd go along with it.

Tea was a very important item, especially for the older Jews, and they would sit down and have a glass of tea at night or at noonday at lunch and sometimes just sit there and put it in the saucer and blow on it. They'd have this thing where they would put the lump of sugar in their mouth and sip the tea so it would get some of the sweetness without putting the lump in the tea.

THE NEIGHBORHOOD

IN THE MAXWELL Street area the actual stores would be back from the sidewalk and the owners could lock the door and go home at night. Then a lot of the stores had little tables in front of their stores, and they would have merchandise displayed— dresses hanging and all kinds of things. They also had the people who were called "pullers" outside the stores for the customers who didn't want to go in the store because they figured they'd get hooked if they went in there. These customers knew there were really high pressure guys inside the stores. So these pullers would try to talk and pull customers into the store. They'd say, "Come on mister, you need a suit, I've got a good bargain for you—I'll give you a good price. Come in right now—please come in." Once you came in they'd work on you pretty good.

My Uncle Louie would say, when the customers would come in, "I'm going to give you a good deal, mister, give you a good deal because you're my first customer. You've got to start me off for the day so you'll be lucky—you'll get a good price." Then usually they'd dicker and dicker, and if the customer was still not satisfied with the last price, he'd say, "I'll think it over and I'll be back." Then my uncle would always say, "Mister, my grandfather went away, and he never came back. Let's do business today. I'll give you another fifty cents off on the yard."

At the outside of the walk by the curb there were always

pushcarts. Sometimes the owner of the store would own the carts on the curb; sometimes they were owned or rented by the vendors. Some stores were a little farther back so they had a little more room. But my father's store was right up to the sidewalk so all he had was the sidewalk and in front of his store were two different pushcarts. Who owned them, I don't know.

Once I sold shoes from one of the pushcarts when I was around seven or eight years old. Believe it or not, they were always mismates, two left shoes, two right shoes, but there were people who would still buy them. While the shoes didn't match, they would still have a couple of pairs of shoes out of it. Also I sold socks from his cart, twelve pair for a dollar, and when the customer got home he'd find the toes would have holes.

When they closed at night the store owners would pull all the stuff in except the pushcart—the pushcart guy would have to take care of his own. The peddlers were kind of rivals of the people who had the stores; even the mom and pop owned stores didn't like the vendors because they resented it that the vendors didn't have to pay building rent.

But the pushcart peddlers did pay a fee. Every day the Maxwell Street Market Master would go round and collect a certain amount of money from everybody who had pushcarts. If you didn't pay you would be put out. There was a fellow by the name of Red Glickman who was Market Master and he was connected with the politicians downtown. Through him, his brother, Maxie Glickman, got this choice spot. He would have mostly fruit—boxes and boxes of fruit. Red was a tough guy and everybody who wanted any breaks at City Hall had to go through him.

On the corner of Union and Maxwell was the snake oil medicine man. He was a big husky man and he had a big snake like a cobra. He would make talks and he had a little bit of a spiel, and people liked to listen to him. He did tricks with the snake and would wind it around his neck and all that. An International Newsreel came and took pictures, and I was in it because I always went to that corner to hawk socks because there were so many people there. That was the place to find customers.

There were lots of streets with houses and there were other peddlers that would go up and down the streets and alleys. It was just amazing these peddlers came to visit my mother and bring all their wares. Panties, foodstuffs, notions of every kind, and loads and loads of cutlery and everything. The peddler would have a pack on his back and he would unfurl it on a table or on the floor.

Then my mother would ask for certain items and he'd know where these items were—hundreds and hundreds of items in this pack. And when he was finished he would just pack them all up very neatly so he could always go to a particular item. If he wanted a thimble he knew exactly where it was. It was just a miracle. In those days you could knock on doors and someone would answer.

The icemen came through the alleys with horses and wagons and they would be chopping up their ice in the wagon and shouting, "Ice." The kids would jump up on the wagon and pick up pieces of ice, especially in the hot weather and suck on them. You'd have to sneak in back and when the iceman would find out about it he would go back there and chase all the kids.

There were also installment dealers; these were peddlers also. They had certain places along Roosevelt Road and Maxwell Street district. These were merchandise places owned by Jewish merchants such as dress stores and men's clothing stores, and these installment peddlers would get customers that they would deal with all the time. They would have a little book and they would go to their steady customers weekly or monthly and whatever the customers would need they would pick out.

The customer could pick the dresses she wanted and then the peddler would record it in the little book. She might pay the regular price of $100 for an item, and he would pay the merchant $40. So the installment dealer made quite a profit, but of course a lot of the time some of his customers would move on him and he had a lot of losses. But every week he would go and collect so much money from these people, and whatever they wanted they would keep adding more stuff.

One thing my mother did every single week. She'd get up at 5:00 in the morning and take the taxi to Maxwell Street to the market. She knew if she got there early she could get the best antiques. You never paid the right price on Maxwell Street and of course, if you were working there, you never gave the right price.

There were all different kinds of stores on Maxwell Street. There was a shoe store and I remember his name was Temp-kin, and when I was little and needed shoes my father would take me over there. I was always looking for style and my father was looking for a pair of shoes that would wear to death.

Another place I'd go on my own when I was quite young was to a tailor's shop on Roosevelt Road. I always had a flair for clothes and it probably started when I was about five years old. My father would have leftover goods from the bolts and he'd give me a little piece of material and he'd say, "O.K., take it over to the tailor's and have them make knickers for you." These were short pants, or knee pants, gathered just below the knees.

I'd go over there, and the tailor would say, "O.K., come back a week from Tuesday, I'll have them ready then." I'd say, what do you mean, you'll have them for me? You didn't ask me how I wanted them made. He said, "I'm the tailor, I'll make them for you. What does a kid know anyway?" I'd say, I know you're the tailor, but I know how I want them.

Then I'd start showing just how I wanted mine made, and I'd say, I want the buttons to show on the fly, and I want them contrasting. At the bottom of the pants, at the knees, I said I didn't want the elastic that they usually have. I said, I want you to have three inches of flap, and I want the buttons to match the ones on the fly. He made them the way I wanted them, but he said he'd never heard of such a thing.

The shop next to my father's was kind of a junk shop—a rags and iron place. Rag pickers would come and the junkman would buy rags and tin cans and other stuff they had picked up. He was sort of a middle man. The thing I remember best about him was what he ate. The religious Jews would make a dish (cholent) on Friday night so they wouldn't have to light the fire on the Sabbath. They'd start cooking at sundown and the dish would cook until the next day at twelve when they would come home from the synagogue. I got a kick out of it because the fellow who owned this rags place would eat this cholent cold every day at lunch.

Down Maxwell Street towards Halsted was Hymie's—the original hot corned beef place. He was right at the alley which was about three stores east of Halsted. My father would give me about ten cents to go to Hymie's and I was going to make the most of it, I had a big appetite, so instead of getting a sandwich I'd buy half of a springbread (like an Italian bread) and a nickel's worth of corned beef and free mustard, so I'd have like three sandwiches, and they always gave me a slice of pickle.

Jim Stefanovic had his own kind of a drink that he sold from a pushcart for two cents. It was a drink that tasted like a combination of lemonade and tea. That was the most unusual taste to me, and had a real good taste. Everything had a good taste in those days because we were hungry and we didn't have any money. When we paid two cents we made it last.

There were the Wilners who had the fish market and there was an old man outside who ground horseradish and then mixed it with some sort of potion of beet juice and a little sugar so you just didn't get the strong horse radish. It was a strange kind of a combination, and it was really good.

The Wilners were cousins of "Fishky"—Leapin' Lena Levinsky—who managed her brother, Kingfish Levinsky. He was the great heavyweight fighter and pride of the Jews. She also had truckloads of iced boxes of fresh fish delivered to her and her daughter there on the curb at Halsted and Maxwell. They had a big old-fashioned scale and sold the fish and cleaned them right off the truck. They were two very strong women and threw the boxes of heavy iced fish around like nothing you ever could imagine.

Just west of Halsted was Lyon's Deli—later it was Nate's Deli. I knew there was a Nate who worked there, but in those days Lyons owned it. It wasn't so much corned beef then; we went there for good lox and bagels. I never went there to sit down and eat; I'd get my lox and take them home. For corned beef we went across the street to Levitt's. Levitt's was the place where Stefanovic had his place outside. Stefanovic had the hot dogs and the pork chops going, and Levitt's was the corned beef part. I used to enjoy walking to Maxwell Street, but after my brother and I had Fox Brothers I was so busy that I didn't have much time to walk around.

The farthest I would get would be the place that handled all the Vienna stuff and they would take care of all the poor people. They made their sausage in back there, and in front you could buy salami, corned beef, whatever. But then if the poor guys would come in the people who ran the store would put bits of salami and corned beef on a plate on top of the counter and these guys could have it free.

Right outside of Lyon's Deli was where Sol the shoe shine man built a stand. He was a helluva shoe shine man, and all of the black people were very neat and fussy about their shoes. They kept them shined so you could always see your face in your shoes.

When my dad and uncle moved to Roosevelt Road, the big department store, 12th Street Store, was on our corner—four doors west of Fox Brothers. Across from that was the United Cigar Store that used to give you coupons. Three doors away from there was the famous Gold's Restaurant with a banquet hall upstairs where you could get married and have the wedding party. Everybody would go to Gold's if you wanted a real good meal. Gold's was kittycorner from St. Francis of Assisi Church. We were right next to the Roosevelt Cafeteria and two doors from the Central Bank. The university took over all of that.

There were four brothers who had a rag business and they got together with the merchants, including my father and uncle, and the jobbers, all Jewish people. Most of these business people no longer lived in the area—they had moved to other parts of Chicago. They couldn't stay away from their businesses for long periods of time, so if they wanted to go to a synagogue it was a problem. So they got together and pitched in and bought a little building on Union and made their own synagogue. Then during the week when there was occasion for a service they would close up their businesses and attend the service.

Fox Brothers was close to the Italian section and I got to know some of the people and visit their homes. When the Italian immigrants came to Chicago they would come to the neighborhood, but often the young people, as soon as they got a little money, didn't want to live in the ghetto because it was kind of beat up and they'd want to move out. Their folks didn't want to move because they had friends there, and they had all their shops there—the meat markets, the bakeries, and they knew exactly how to buy. So when the boys would make a lot of money they'd want to take their folks out of the ghetto, but the folks refused to go.

Sometimes these buildings would look beat up outside, but if you'd go inside, you'd see a millionaire's apartment because their sons would make sure they had the best in furniture. They'd have plush carpeting and you'd think you were entering a Gold Coast apartment.

I enjoyed blacks—that wasn't the way my family raised me, it was just the way I was—but later I brought my mother into it. My brother didn't care one way or the other. In the days when I went to see my dad in the store as a kid, there were no blacks coming into the store.

Later when my brother and I took over the store, a black family that I was very close with was called Graves. They were customers at Fox Brothers. There was Clarence, the oldest, and Benny, and Clarence wanted to play the trumpet. I said if Clarence would get a trumpet, I would give him lessons free. So I would manage to leave Fox Brothers on my lunch time and go to Sangamon Street where they lived and give him trumpet lessons.

Then one day one of the brothers was spotted by the FBI or someone else who falsely accused him of being a communist. So because of that the whole family got up and moved to California. Once when I went to California I looked them up and I found out that the youngest son, Clint, became an architect and worked for Frank Lloyd Wright, and he designed a building in Las Vegas. Benny became a lawyer and Clarence manufactured carts for supermarkets. So that was really a loss to the neighborhood.

There was one feared cop at the Maxwell Street police

station and his name was Smitty—he was like a 300-pound bruiser and didn't like black kids and when they got in trouble he would beat hell out of them. Most of the blacks knew me at Fox Brothers, and they would send someone in like their father or their brother to beg me to get in touch with Smitty to lay off. By contrast there was another cop who pounded the pavement who had a good reputation with everyone, with the blacks and the Chicanos. I remember he was very proud of his son at Northwestern University who became a great concert pianist.

I've heard the words "kikes" and "Jews" used in derogatory ways many times in my life, but we tried to forget about it and get on with our everyday life. They'd say, "We don't want that kind here—let's keep them out of our clubs." But we're really all human beings. There are good Jewish people and bad Jewish people. One time I was in front of my store and a little black kid about five years old came up to me, "Please, can you tell me where's Jewtown?" Blacks have always called the Maxwell Street area Jewtown, but they don't mean anything bad by it—it's just a name because that was where all the Jews used to live and work.

Growing up—Work and Play

I WAS FROM the age of three always out and about. I've talked to my sister, Beatrice, who was eight years younger and she tells me there was a lot of fighting going on in our home and I was always smart enough to get out as soon as it started. She said she and my brother Aaron took the brunt of it.

It seems as if I always had a desire to work and be on my own and be independent as far as finance was concerned. When I was very young my mother had an old lamp and it had hundreds of beads. It was no longer usable and was down in the basement. I took all the beads and went out in front of house and set up a little table and sold about fifteen beads for a penny to children in the neighborhood to use for marbles. That was a bargain because real marbles cost a penny for only two or three.

A little later I graduated to selling papers. I used to put a stand out in front of the Central Park Theater, and rather than just hawking the papers I would sing a song to attract people to my stand. When my mother would go downtown to Marshall Fields I'd tell her to bring me some cough gum (like Chiclets) that sold for about three for a nickel. I would take them and put them out in a little dish and this way I could sell something to people on the way in to the theater and then they bought papers on the way out. I would sell these pieces of gum like three or four for a penny and I'd wind up doubling my money and I'd give my mother the money I had earned and she'd buy me some more.

Right after that I got a job with the corner grocery and I used to take care of the stock. We would take fruit, such as oranges, and make them like a pyramid, and I had the job of piling them up. Sometimes I would wait on the people. Everybody would come in with a list and the owner would take the list and there would be a tab—a little book where they would write down what they got. Then at the end of the week when the husbands got paid the customers would come in and pay their bills. I would help in compiling these things. I also had the job of picking out all the bad vegetables and fruit and throwing them away.

We used to put sawdust on the floor and people would come in and walk on the sawdust and the sawdust would absorb the dust so it wouldn't go on the vegetables. The other job I had was delivering. I went all the way home with the people or they would phone for their groceries. I had a little wagon outside, everything was on foot, and I would deliver these things.

At one time there was a cigar factory about eight or ten blocks from my home. I had been playing peg 'n' stick and I beat everybody on my street so I'd go to the next street and look for somebody to beat there. Then I came across a store-front cigar manufacturer, and since I was always looking for ways to make money I walked in and asked him if he needed any help. The guy kind of looked at me and laughed. I said, well, I just thought I would ask. He said, "Well, maybe there is something you could do. Come and try this."

He had a whole lot of paper bands. These were the bands

you find on a cigar with the name of it about a quarter of the way down the cigar. You took a whole bunch of bands in your mouth—there used to be 50—you'd wet a band with your mouth at the glue end and then you'd wrap it around the cigar and glue it. You'd take the box of cigars that had been packed by a packer—he'd take the best looking cigars and he would put them in a pile—so in a box of 50 there'd be 13 on bottom, then 12, then 13, then 12, and the 12 on top were always the prettiest ones.

I'd come in after school and I'd go to work in the cigar factory and ask, well, you got any work for me. They'd say, "Yeh, we've got five boxes." And the work would consist of taking the cigars out, putting the bands on and putting them back in the box in the same way. They were in pretty tight. For at least five years I worked after school every day banding these cigars. There were other cigar factories that opened up, usually in basements. They'd put in a little window and the people would be working inside. I'd have, maybe, five different factories, these sweat shops, and I'd go from one to the other. If I did five boxes I'd get fifteen cents.

As I got a little older and wiser I held out for five cents a box. I got so I could do 15 boxes an hour. I was pretty fast at it. I worked for the boss, so to speak, and when I left I always asked him if everything was all right. The boss to me was the kingpin. Today it doesn't mean anything. I was very friendly with the bosses and as far as I was concerned, they treated me like their own sons.

In two or three of the factories I made a little progress and got a little better position. One of the positions was to become a cigar stripper; it's really a tobacco stripper. You take a bunch, say fifty, strips of tobacco, and there's sort of a wooden horse in front of you and it has sort of a rounded top. You take one of the cigar leaves on this rounded top and you pull the center of it—there's sort of a string that holds the leaf together and that's too tough for wrapping (the tobacco leaves that show). You'd pile up one over the other till they pile up about one hundred high.

The next job up on the cigar factory totem pole was to pack and you'd go around to all the men making the cigars and pick up the cigars. Then you'd bring them over to a table and you'd sort out all these cigars and sort out the prettiest and put them on the top. There was also another job that came very much later. An enterprising maker decided he wanted a silver wrapping. We took sheets of silver and we would wrap the cigar in silver foil. That would pay almost three times as much as banding and in that case they eliminated the packer who could spot the good cigars and he was probably the highest paid man in the business.

When I would get hold of this money I always enjoyed buying things for people and uppermost in my mind was my mother and I would bring her chocolate ice cream. Before I would go to the ice cream parlor I'd stop at a deli for a bologna sandwich. I always like the ends and he'd save the end for me.

Another way to make money in those days was by collecting things off the street so we would go around taking seltzer bottles that were lying around in backyards or by the alleys. Even in those days they paid 20 cents a seltzer bottle, so you could see that was a heck of a lot of money back then.

Also we would save silver foil; we would go around trying to find the silver cigarette wrappers and turn them into silver balls. Then we would take them to the junkyard and they would pay us for the silver. Also we would go around in back alleys and places where they'd been tearing down houses or shacks and we'd pick up iron and we'd manage to get it down to the junkyard and he'd give us a few cents for the iron. That was another way of making a little money.

When I was in high school I had a sort of peddler job. I worked on the trains that ran weekend excursions. They started on Friday and they would go to Fox Lake and come back on Sunday. The Harvey Company handled all the food and the "candy butchers" as we were called. Before we left on Friday we'd go to the Harvey Company in the train station and we would pick up baskets of candy and cookies and fruit and soda pop. Then we'd go through the cars hawking our wares.

The Harvey Company would charge us ridiculous prices but we had to buy all our stuff from them. Everything was almost double what you could buy it wholesale. Like a nickel candy bar was ten cents whereas you could buy it for five cents in a store; by the time I hawked it I had to charge twenty cents—and that was a little tough.

I had a friend in Norwood Park and I would take a minimum at the Harvey Company and my friend would meet me at the station in Norwood Park and bring a lot of cases of soda pop and put it in the freight car. I would buy it from him for three cents instead of the ten cents that I had to pay Harvey. I also bought boxes of Hershey bars from him. But when I got caught that was the end of it.

When I got to Fox Lake I played with this little dance band. But while I was on the train I had a small Victrola and I was a pretty good Charleston dancer—they had Charleston contests and I would often win those—so as I was hawking my wares I'd announce, "Come to the baggage car at 4:00 for a show. You're all invited." So they'd come and I'd put on a show and then pass the hat. So I made a little more money that way.

In high school I got a job working in a public garage. People would leave their cars for so much a month and while the cars were there we had to wash them. When an owner came to the garage he would honk his horn and you would have to drive him home and then bring his car back to the garage. One of the customers was named Maxie Eisen and he was president of the fishmongers union. He'd have four hoods with him with machine guns and I'd kind of have to crawl over them and drive them home in Maxie's big old Cunningham.

In those days different kinds of cars had different shifts; the Dodge had one kind, the Haines had another kind, and the Cunningham had another. There were about five different kinds altogether. When I got the job the man asked if I knew all the cars and I said yes, but I really only knew how to drive my dad's Haines and I didn't know was how to work all the different shifts. The first day on the job I had to drive a Buick home. I didn't know that shift and I put it into reverse instead of forward and almost went into the lobby with that car. That was a pretty scary moment.

Another job I had in high school was delivering fish to hotels on the North Side. I carried the fish in a basket on the handlebars of my bike, and you had to pack them just right in order for them to balance. To get the bike going you would push off by running along beside it and throw your leg over the bike. But the first time I did it I hadn't done a good job of balancing the fish and the wheel turned sharply and I went over my head onto the ground. Even though I hurt myself I wouldn't let the boss know. And it never happened again; jobs weren't that easy to get.

I guess I've always had what my black friends call "street learning" but school was something else. My teachers were always disciplining me and I was constantly into mischief from day one. An embarrassing incident happened when I was in grade school and I got into a fight over a marble game (I always had to have more marbles than anyone else). My teacher, Miss O'Leary, took a large safety pin and attached it to her skirt and the other end to my shirt sleeve. I had to walk all day attached to her. However, on Passover my ma would fix a big platter of Passover foods and I would take it to Miss O'Leary—probably to make up for all the trouble.

I met my first girlfriend in grade school. I rode her on back of my three-wheel bicycle and bought her penny candy with the money I saved out of my job earnings. There was a candy store across the street from the school and they always had a great big jar of large kosher dill pickles. I would also buy those, three for three cents, and there would be one for her, one for her best friend, and one for me.

I am a high school graduate, but they really graduated me to get rid of me because I had a straight "D" academic record. My picture wasn't in the annual because they didn't expect me to graduate, but I guess the deans got together and decided it was better to give me a diploma and get me out of there.

I was popular with the gals, but not because I was good looking. On the contrary, I was a scroungy, skinny, ugly dude, but I was number one with the gals as I was a first-class jitterbug dancer. All the gals wanted to be my partner, and in exchange, they did my homework papers for me, so my grades on tests were never passing grades since I had never done any of the work.

I was always a ringleader to get parties going and I always had a little band so we would play for the parties. I also played in the high school symphony. As I had no violin teaching to speak of, I didn't play with the first violins, but I was leader of the second violins, and I did play in the pit for operettas such as *Bohemian Girl* and *The Mikado*.

One day while I was in high school I was sitting on the curb and heard the band which was rehearsing on the 3rd floor. They sounded real good, and as the school provided the instruments and lessons, I hustled up and waited until practice was over and confronted the band master, Mr. Condy. I asked for a school trumpet to join the band. He looked at me and remarked that due to my fat lips I could never play a trumpet as the mouthpiece was too small for my embouchure.

So I arrived home that day with a great big tuba. Since our house was small, Pa and Ma kicked me out with the tuba which I returned to the school, and I never did get to play in the band. This was a tragedy as Mr. Condy's theory was nuts! Dig the best jazz trumpeters in the business, today and forever, are black, and they all have fat lips. I missed an opportunity to get some legitimate learning.

I was also a member of the R.O.T.C., which was a sort of army training camp for students. I attended summer R.O.T.C. camp and there I was punished for talking after taps. The punishment was to walk within a square roped area with packsack and rifle on my shoulder, continually, non-stop, for a number of hours. Thereafter, everyone called me Bull Pen Fox.

By the end of high school I was a pretty good violinist so I was assigned to play a violin solo at my graduation. But come time for my spot on the program, no Harold could be found. I got nervous and ran out and stayed away the entire time. So I missed the march to receive my diploma. My ma was in the hospital with flu and only my pa attended. He was worried when I disappeared and eventually went home without me. When I finally did get home the broomstick was waiting for me.

When we were young we had all kinds of games that we would play, and I had to be the best in everything. I could hit more home runs, be best at peg 'n' stick. I was the marble champ, and fishing—I had to catch the most fish, the biggest fish. And later blowing my horn I had to be good, but it just so happened I couldn't make that. I was a big fish in a small pond.

But there was a problem; my mother always taught me to be afraid of everything. She had a motto that it was better to be a live coward than a dead hero. And so she'd say, don't do this and don't do that and don't touch this and don't touch that. Don't run too fast; don't fight with anybody. Unfortunately I grew up to be afraid of everything. I had great coordination, but I wasn't very good in a game because if someone came running towards me, I'd just let them go on by. If I'd bump into somebody, I'd just practically give them the ball because that was the way I was brought up. I wanted to be best, but I had this fear.

I was always collecting different things, and one of the things we used to collect was bottle caps. There was an Edelweiss Beer factory on 22nd Street, and 22nd Street was beyond the boundary of the Jewish neighborhood and was in the Polish neighborhood. The Polocks hated the Jews and sometimes we'd go over in their neighborhood and we weren't supposed to. I liked these bottle caps so much and there were always a lot of them behind this beer factory and I'd kind of sneak around and get into the backyard of this factory.

I remember once I had a whole sack of these bottle caps and I was just about ready to go and here came this gang of Polish kids and they said, "Come on, Jew, what have you got there?" I said, oh, I've got these caps. They said, "Drop those caps immediately," and they all started beating on me. And so I never did go back for any caps over there again.

Then I graduated to marbles. I was a great one for playing by myself and I would kind of lock myself into the bathroom and organize a little kind of a marble game in there. When we'd play with friends, first we'd make a ring and each of us would put five marbles in the circle. Then you'd keep shooting until you missed and each time you shot a marble out, it became yours. So I'd always try to have more marbles than anybody else until sometimes I'd have a large, heavy bag of them—some of them beauties.

Another game that we'd play with marbles, we'd go into a schoolyard and we'd go to the back of a building and one fellow would take a marble and he'd hit it up against the building, and it might go back 10 feet. Then you'd hit your marble close enough to his marble that you could "span it"— "span it" was to span it with your hand. If you could pick up his marble with your hand, then it became your marble. Then you would throw yours against the building and he would throw his and try to pick yours up; if he couldn't, it would stay there, and sometimes there would be five or six marbles. I always had the most marbles and I would sell them; marbles, marbles, marbles, that was the big thing for me.

I would take the prettiest marbles and they would be the shooters when we played marbles in a ring. Each shooter I would have a fictitious name for; the big heroes then were the movie stars. Maybe the best shooter I would call Tom Mix, another was Douglas Fairbanks, and another was Hoot Gibson.

We had a special Passover game. You'd start out with about a dozen or so round nuts and we'd make a line on the sidewalk and get about five feet away. There'd be four or five boys in the game, and each boy would have a chance to lag three or four nuts. Then the one who was closest to the line would win all the nuts and you'd put them in your *pushke* (bag). Usually I'd wind up with a lot of nuts and I'd go home and look at them and count them, Brazil nuts and all kinds. Then the next day I'd go out again, and this happened all through Passover. In those days there weren't Chanukah gifts, there was Chanukah *gelt* (money). Your uncle would give you some and your mother, usually people older than you, would give you some money.

My favorite game of all games was Peg 'n' Stick. For this game you take a broomstick and cut off about 14–16 inches and that's the stick. Then you take about six inches of the broomstick and saw that off. Then you cut a point at each end of this stick, or peg. Then, when you put it on the ground and you tap it near the end with the longer stick, it flips up in the air. The object, when the peg flies up in the air, is to hit it as far as you can. I could just kind of tap the thing and away it would go. At the time, we'd wait until the street was being paved and we'd take the broomstick and make a little hole about one inch deep and this would be the goal. You could place the peg any way you wanted, and naturally you'd place it in the direction you'd be hitting.

Now the fellow that you'd be playing against, he'd be out in the field, so to speak, but really he'd be in the street. In those days there'd only be an automobile coming through about once an hour so we'd play kick the can and peg 'n' stick in the street all the time. The other fellow gets out in the field just as far as he thinks you're able to hit the peg. The object is, when you hit the peg it would kind of go up in the air and if he can catch it, you're out. And when you're out he can place the peg right at the spot where he caught it and it's his turn to hit. He waits until you get placed further out in the street to catch it.

If you don't catch it he puts the stick in the hole and he holds the stick and he stands behind it. You're to throw the peg as close to the stick as you can and naturally, you're quite far away so it's pretty hard to get it close enough so you can get him out. How you get him out is you can either hit the stick or you can throw it so it can't span a whole stick, which is 16".

You measure the distance and if you have like 10 sticks, then that's 10 points. You can play for 100 points or 50 points—whatever you make up at the beginning. Naturally the further you can hit this peg, if he doesn't catch it, the better chance you have of getting points. So this is the way with peg 'n' stick. We'd play for a couple of pennies a game and if you'd win you'd win the money.

THE END ?

HAROLD FOX ENGAGED IN ONE OF OUR FAVORITE POSES..... KNOCKING OUT THOSE FRANTIC FASHIONS AT TOP SPEED...

Courtesy of Harold Fox.

Hal Fox, as rendered by suit designer and cartoonist Earl "Quack" Palmer who worked for Fox Brothers for many years.

3

HAROLD FOX

(CONTINUED)

BETWEEN HIGH SCHOOL GRADUATION AND MY CAREERS

RIGHT AFTER HIGH school, about 1928, I worked for Harriss Pies loading the trucks. They'd put the pies in one side in the oven and they would go on a conveyor belt till they were baked. Then you'd slip them onto the truck right from the platform. We'd fill the orders. At that time there were saloons, and they served free lunch if you'd buy beer. So I could buy beer for five cents and then have a free lunch, and that was what I'd do. The other workers would take Polish sausages and put them on those ovens and heat them, but there were cockroaches all over the place and I couldn't imagine eating there by those trucks. They didn't really have inspections in those days.

From there I got a job at a smaller pie place off of 47th Street, and then I'd come early in the morning, around 6:00. A black guy on the corner had a newspaper stand, and one day when I came by he said he'd noticed I came by every morning, and he asked if I could do him a favor. I said, my name is Fox, and I'll help however I can. He said, "A lot of times it's cold out here and as soon as I leave to take a pee, someone comes and steals my money, so this morning could you just stand by and see if you can catch him." And I caught the thief! And we got the police and put him in jail.

And then this vendor said to me, "I appreciate what you did, but I don't only sell newspapers, I take bets." So he said,

"I'll give you a tip. I know it's going to win the Derby. Your name is Fox and the horse's name is Gallant Fox." I never bet, but that time I gave him a buck, and I won about $60 back on Gallant Fox.

Another job I had was at Goldblatt's Department Store. We were working on commission and I was always a high pressured salesman. I was working in the dinnerware department, and I would find a likely customer for a set of dishes and then I'd take her back and there'd be a great big platter that cost as much as the whole set and I'd say, this is slightly damaged, but if you'll buy this set I'll throw in the platter. Most times when I went to get my check it didn't amount to much because I high pressured these folks when they couldn't afford it probably, and they'd get home and their husband would chew them out, and then they'd bring the set back. So by the time Goldblatt's would take off all my refunds, I wouldn't have much of a salary.

I also took an overtime job there at Goldblatt's reading all the registers. We had to go to all the different departments and read the register and I'd put down the reading for the day. The scary part of it was that there was a night watchman and he had four large Doberman dogs that could tear you apart. He kept them pretty well chained, but I was on pins and needles all the time though.

When the 1933 Century of Progress fair was in Chicago I had a job playing my violin with a trio at a place called The Oasis. We would get the overflow from the Sally Rand show in the Oriental Village down the street. Part way through the season the owner of the club decided to move the tables back so the customers would have room to dance, and he wanted a dance band for that. So my violin was out, and I was given two weeks notice. I had a friend who played trumpet and when I told him what was happening to me he said he'd teach me to play trumpet so I could stay on the job—in two weeks! Anyway, we made it. I wasn't very good, but some of it I faked, and I was good on really high notes, so I kept the job all summer.

I always loved to dance and danced my way through high school. This was when the Charleston dance contests were popular and I won contest after contest, but when we were jitterbugging my favorite partner was Vivian. We would give dancing exhibitions with a lot of fast and furious dances; she was so athletic that I would throw her up and she would land in a split. Vivian was a wildcat, a real fighter. Later she was a partner of Johnnie Weissmuller, and she was one of the best diving champions of the time.

In those days the Balaban and Katz theaters, in addition to the movies, had stage shows and they had some of the greatest bands. On Friday nights, after the last show they would set up in the lobby and ordinary people could dance. One of the agents saw us dancing and hired Vivian and I to give exhibitions. One thing I'm proud of is that we gave exhibitions at the Regal Theater. That was in the black area of Chicago and in those days both blacks and whites went to the Regal Theater.

We got married when I was 18 and Vivian was 17, and I stayed with her for two years. We went to Detroit and danced for a living. We got in fights and she was so tough. One time I pushed her out in the hall and put a dresser against the door but she was chopping at the door with a knife so I called the police and asked them to put me in jail to protect me from her.

The relatives never approved of the marriage, and finally they came and got us and that ended that thing. So our marriage was annulled even though we had a daughter, Letty. Later I married Helen and went to New York with her. She is the mother of my other three children—my twin daughters, Audrey and Sandy, and my son, Leo.

I'm thankful that I've never been to war because I don't think I could ever really kill anybody, and I never learned to shoot a gun. In those days they had the draft, and I was just lucky at my draft examination. When the examiner learned that I had four children, he remarked that the government was crazy if they sent me over. He said that it would cost the government more money, there were many single men who could do the job just as well, and I'd be worried about my family. I didn't argue with him because, really, I didn't want to go. If they had sent me there would have been no protest, I assure you, and I would have gone into the army. The examiner sent me to the psychiatrist and I had no trouble proving that I was a little off in the upper story—I always kind of acted that way anyway. The examiner called up the psychiatrist and tipped him off and lo and behold, I ended up with 4F status, so that's one of the reasons I've never been in the army.

When I married Helen my folks kind of disowned me because I married out of the faith, so I got an idea to go to New York. When I had finished playing at the fair in Chicago I was offered a job in New York, so I was counting on that. After paying the bus fare for myself and my wife and baby I had about $7.50 left when I landed in New York. And the job fell through—what a jam! We found a room for $4 and I had to get a job. I had passed a restaurant that had a sign in the window "busboy." I was afraid to go in since I'd never been a busboy, but I got to thinking about it in the middle of the night and thought, I could do that. So I ran down to the restaurant but the job was already taken. So after that I started looking for busboy jobs at different restaurants.

Finally I went to Grant's Bar and Grill in the Times Square area. They said they could use a night busboy and I could hardly wait to go back that night. They had me fill out an application and when they asked the nationality I put down "Jewish." He said, "I'm sorry, but we have all Chicanos that are busboys, and I don't think they'll take kindly to you being a busboy." Then after thinking a little he said, "I tell you what, I know you need the money so I'll start you out as a counter-man."

I didn't know anything about that job, but he said, "We're so busy that in one hour you'll know the job or quit." I figured I had as much experience being a counterman as a busboy; so I became a counterman and learned quickly. Later I learned to work the hot dog station and the soda fountain and the station where they carved meats—all the different stations—and they made me relief man.

The restaurant was about two blocks from where the Navy fleet came in, and sometimes there'd be 40 or 50 sailors lined up at the counter. Also, this grill was right across the street from Minsky's Burlesque and lots of entertainers would come in and I got to know them. Sometimes one of them would ask me to let him know if I heard of a job. Or somebody would come in and say, "Hey, I need a sax player for Saturday night.

Have you heard of anyone?" I'd tell him to leave his number and if anyone came in I'd give them the number. That way I helped some of the players get jobs and some of the entertainers find players. I didn't make any money at it, but I did make lots of contacts.

I had playing jobs myself at night. The manager liked me and sometimes he would let me take off Saturday night. That didn't make me very popular with the other workers because that was the biggest night of the week. I was always hustling for jobs and making all these contacts and one of the men who came in the grill ran a radio station at Times Square. I'd always fix his lunch and one day he asked me if my band was good enough to play on the air. So once a week we had sort of a jam session on the air with different prominent musicians coming in to play.

Years later my former boss at the bar and grill summed me up. I wondered what had happened to him and tried to track him down. Finally I found him in Miami and when I called him I just said I was a former employee from New York. Anyway, he asked me to come over and when I went he said, "Why didn't you say you were Fox?" I said, well, you wouldn't remember me; you've probably had 100,000 employees since then. He said, "Yeh, but I'd always remember you—you know why? You were always a character." So you see, it pays to be a character. I've always been a non-conformist and people remember me more easily.

We lived about eight blocks from the restaurant. The rent was four dollars for a small room, one bed, dresser, table, and all the cockroaches and bedbugs you could want. So, after about two weeks at the restaurant I became friendly with a fellow employee. He knew I was renting, and one day he approached me and said he had a large living room in his apartment in the tenement district. If I would agree to be his tenant for six dollars a week he would buy furniture for this empty room, including a pullout bed and a sleeping couch—all new furniture. Wow! It sounded great, and so we left our room and he took us by subway with all our belongings to his mansion sight unseen.

Never again! We were in a room facing the alley in a

six-floor walk-up tenement, and we were on the fourth floor. The tenants would yell, "midnight garbage," and down came their garbage past our front window. The toilet was a one-seater out in the hall, used by eight tenants, and there was always a waiting line. The bathtub was under the kitchen sink, and come Saturday night you would warn the rest of the household and sit out in the open and take your bath. But all the time you kept whistling so anyone coming home would know to stay in the hall until you were through.

About that time my father was having financial problems with his business. Since my father and uncle had their Master Fabrics sample line of woolens, I suggested that he could send me a box of his samples and I would hustle up some business at work since there were about 100 employees in the restaurant.

I always had a flair for designing so I'd show the kids at work the samples and then on our lunch hour we'd go over to a tailor's shop on Broadway where I'd tell them exactly how to make up the suit. That's when I really started working out some of the ideas for the zoot suit design because I began to design wide shoulders and a roomy fit. The tailor was usually skeptical and would say that it wouldn't fit right. But I told him we were paying for it and that's the way we wanted it. The customers were always pleased with their new suits and finally the tailors had a little more confidence in my designs.

Another job I did while I was in New York was some modeling for *Liberty* magazine. They wanted a model who could play trumpet for an illustration for a story they had going. In one picture I was a trumpet player and in another I was pictured dancing with the girl who was the girlfriend of the trumpet player. So from then on I did modeling jobs from time to time. That was the way it was then—lots of jobs crammed into each week. Sometimes I was so tired that when I'd take the subway I would tell the motorman to wake me up at a certain stop. Most of the sleep I had was on the subway because I'd work a full day and then did all the playing and other jobs for four or five hours at night.

FOX BROTHERS

I MENTIONED THAT business wasn't going so well for my uncle and father. Actually their woolen business had been going very well. By that time the Fox Brothers had established a reputation and they were making a lot of money in woolens— but everyone was in those days. Their big thing was, they invested their money in real estate. That was their downfall.

They went out and bought a building for $80,000 and sold it immediately for $120,000. They bought a building for $100,000 and got $200,000 for it—and they thought, what are we doing in the woolen business? They were so happy that the next thing they bought one for $400,000 and mortgaged everything they owned—their business, their homes, and their cars, and they bought the building. Just then a little depression set in and their building income started dwindling. The rents that were something like $75 went down to $20 a month. And expenses were high, coal was high, and they just couldn't keep up.

So they would borrow and borrow and borrow to keep the building going in hopes that someday they could catch up and hang onto their building. But it was kind of a sad thing; while they borrowed thousands from banks to keep their business going, they just borrowed $300 from a neighbor one time. Everybody else gave them a little more time because they knew they'd lost all their money that they had invested in Fox Brothers, but this so-called friend pressed charges and they lost their building and I don't think they ever got over it.

My dad took it hard, but not as hard as Uncle Healy, and soon after that Uncle Healy was dead. This thing of the building really got him. My dad was pretty honorable and he went to Uncle Healy's family and said he would keep the store going and send them a weekly check. Well, like most families when it comes to money—they were always thinking he was cheating them. So finally they got together with a lawyer and my father bought the business and paid them. When I took over, the business started paying off and then the family came to me and said they got a bad deal.

This was in about 1938 when my ma sent for me and said, "Your dad is very ill and isn't expected to survive." He was in the hospital and in a lot of pain. Then he got a little better and he decided he wanted some of Grandma's soup and he wanted to go home. And he got to meet Sandra and Audrey and he accepted Helen, their mother. And he was home about three days before he had to go back to the hospital. When he died he was a charity case at Mt. Sinai Hospital, and he died with $1 in his pocket. Years later when Fox Brothers was doing great my ma wrote a big check and donated it to Mt. Sinai Hospital, so the kindness at the time of his death was repaid.

For years I kept that $1 wrapped in brown paper in my wallet, and then I lost it when I was playing a dance with Billie Holiday at the Pershing Ballroom. I sent word through the black grapevine offering a reward. Soon after that I got a call from an elderly lady. She wanted a description of my wallet as her children "found" many wallets that week. I described it to her and she brought it to Fox Brothers and claimed the reward. I looked for Pa's dollar, and sure enough, it was there. However, a couple of years later my sister wanted to see Pa's last dollar, and when I took it from my wallet and unwrapped the brown paper the dollar was gone. Wow! And all those years I thought it was my good luck charm!

When my dad was so deeply in debt a man named Schwartz came to him and they made an agreement that Schwartz would send him woolens and my dad would send him a regular amount of money. But he started sending dad the pieces that no one else wanted and little by little things got worse and worse my dad couldn't make the $250 a week payments. My dad wouldn't take any salary—and my brother Aaron would sometimes get $25 a week, but still he couldn't make it. Schwartz got all the gravy and he did pretty well.

When my dad passed away my brother, Aaron, and I took over the business, and we had all these creditors that we owed money to. One of them was Schwartz and then there were some New York dealers. We called them all in. We said, "This is the situation. I'm the oldest son and my brother and I are taking over and we want a clean bill. We can't be paying off $120,000 and at the same time keep selling material." At that time we weren't in the suit business yet, so it was tough. I said, "we've got $8,000, and we'll cut it up proportionally." So the New York dealers agreed. But not Schwartz. He said, "No, I want you to continue buying from me." So I said, "we'll keep the $8,000 and I'm not going to be buying from you and I'm not going to be paying off that debt."

So he thought it over, and he said, "O.K. then, I'll settle providing you buy all your goods from me in the future." I said, no way, I'm not promising that. Then he put a name on me—he said, "O.K., I knew your father, we were friends, and we did business with a handshake, and then along comes Harold Fox, a real New York sharpie. You don't know how to buy—you'll go out of business before you know it." I said, well, I'll take my chances and I will buy some from you. When I need materials I'll come down and see what you have. But he never liked me after that.

When my dad died my ma seemed to get old overnight. She wouldn't do anything but cooking and housework, and she was always dressed in old house dresses. She just didn't care about her appearance anymore. We hated to see her getting like that because she always used to be immaculate, so I got the idea of telling her that we were short of help at the store and needed her to fill in. She said she didn't know anything about tailoring but we told her there was plenty she could do, and after a while we persuaded her to come down to the store. What a change! She would come to work neat and clean with her hair groomed and her nails done. She was like a new person.

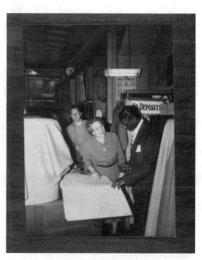

Courtesy of Harold Fox.

Hal Fox, his mother Sarah Fox, and Nat "King" Cole at Fox Brothers tailoring shop.

On the other hand, my big fight at Fox Brothers after I got my mother into the store and the thing that always would bug me—she would speak in Yiddish sometimes when she didn't want any of the black kids or any of the non-Jewish customers

to understand what she was saying. She wasn't saying anything bad, but if you're talking Yiddish they know you're
talking about them, otherwise why don't you talk in English.
I'd get madder than hell, and I'd say, Ma, if you don't talk
English I'm not going to answer you. But she'd still use that
stuff. Even about the Arab tailors; they would bring a lot of
food and sometimes the grease spots would get on the suits,
and that used to bug her and she'd say in Yiddish, "Tell them
to eat back on the table and not at the machine." They were
words I didn't know anyway, but I got the idea.

At the beginning we were still just selling yard goods over
the counter, but what I really liked was the satisfaction of
creating suits. Just cutting off pieces didn't do anything for
me because I was full of ideas and wanted to do designing.
The real break came when we started making band uniforms,
and the first band I made uniforms for was Bill "Bojangles"
Robinson's band. He was the tap dancer that later danced
with Shirley Temple.

What happened was, Irv Brabec was manager of the band
(later he became president of MCI), and he happened to go to
a ready-made tailoring place that was two doors away from us.
This was in the middle of the week and he said he needed 18
uniforms for Friday night when the band was opening at the
Oriental Theater. In those days band members always dressed
in uniforms. The ready-made shop didn't have the 18 suits so
he came to us and asked if we could do it.

I said, O.K., we can do it, but then I was in trouble with our
tailors. When I talked to our people in the shop and put the
proposition to them they said, "If we want to get into this
business, we'll work our tails off and do it. We may have to
work all night, or whatever it takes, but it'll be a break for all of
us." So they agreed, and they did it—and the uniforms were
beautiful.

This was the start of our uniform business for all different
bands, and by the 1950s we were the largest band uniform
company in the world, making uniforms for every top band;
Duke Ellington, Count Basie, Stan Kenton, Gene Krupa,
Tommy Dorsey, Woody Herman, and Billy Eckstine were just a
few. And through the bands we began doing work for enter-

Courtesy of Harold Fox.

Left: An advertisement noting the band leaders who had selected Fox Brothers
Tailors to make their band uniforms. Right: Hal Fox with champion Olympic
runner Jesse Owens and ventriloquist Skeets Minton in Fox Brothers Tailors.
Some of the signed pictures on the "wall of fame" can be seen behind them.

tainers from all over the world. In the '40s we had more than
600 signed pictures and letters on the wall of fame at the store.
Some of those pictures are still there on the wall at Fox
Brothers.

I had my own styles for the band uniforms. I figured up
until then the musicians would wear these close-fitting
clothes, and when they'd get up to play, they were in trouble
because when they'd raise their arms to play the jackets were
too tight across the shoulders. So I said, O.K., we're going to
make loose clothes, but I was in trouble with the tailors. They
said, "How can we make bags to fit." I said, O.K., I want them
not to fit good. So that's how they started the Fox Box.

When I was just getting started in the band business there
was a Mr. Rosenthal who was a customer. He and his wife
came in to have some clothes made and he had a whole set of
neckties with him. Very colorful—the loudest ties in the world.
He said, "If you want to come with me, I go to all the shows
backstage and I sell all the musicians and the band leaders
these ties, and I can introduce you." For example, he'd go in
and Louie Armstrong would buy 20 or 30. So that's how I got
entree to some of these bands; I'd go backstage and talk to

them.

When I'd go to measure the band members for uniforms I'd wear a really attractive new suit with all the accessories just right. Then the band members would start asking me to bring along samples so they could pick out material for personal suits. They'd say, "Since you have our measurements, how about bringing some samples and we'll pick out what we want and you can make them up while we're on the road." So I was shipping suits all over the world.

Courtesy of Harold Fox.

Buddy Childers and Maynard Ferguson of the Stan Kenton band clowning around at Fox Brothers after a fitting.

I'd measure a band for uniforms on Friday when they first came in to town and try to get them done by the following Thursday. Then they would get their pay and they could pay for their suits. But if they didn't get paid, sometimes I'd end up giving them money. Nobody would give musicians credit, and anybody that needed credit I would give it to them. They were all my friends, and if they came in the store, it wasn't just, "Sell me a suit." We'd get into conversation and hug each other.

There were two methods of paying for uniforms. There was the method Lionel Hampton used; Lionel would pay personally for all the uniforms and when the men wore them on the stage they would have to remove them before they went out on the street, and hang them up nice and neatly. They didn't own their own coats. But most of the other outfits would make the fellows in the band pay for their uniforms. There was even a system in the union where when you hired a union band they had to play in a tuxedo. But if they played in a uniform that was anything other than a tuxedo, you had to pay $2 or $3 extra for that uniform band. So these musicians would have to pay for their own uniforms. If the musicians paid for their uniforms they had the privilege of wearing them on the street. They were mostly suits, cut real sharp like a black or blue or gray suit, and they could wear it outside.

Now Earl Hines was a famous band director and well respected by all of the musicians. He had a beautiful style on the piano, he was a good jazz player, and he had good jazz players in his orchestra. I made all his uniforms.

Then he decided to buy a nightclub. It was called the El Grotto, and it was below the Pershing Ballroom, and the Pershing Ballroom was one of the leading ballrooms of Chicago. So Earl Hines had bought this nightclub and put a lot of money into it, so naturally he was a little short of money. One day he came in and wanted to know if I wouldn't make a set of uniforms so the band could open up real neat, you know, in this beautiful club. And he would be sure to pay me. At that time we were having a little trouble collecting debts, etc., and the folks at the store were against making those uniforms. When I first approached them they said, "No way, everybody owes us and we're not going to make this set of uniforms for Earl Hines."

The black musicians union at that time was called The Protective Union; now they're affiliated, and the black and white union are all one, but in those days they were separate. The musicians would never make enough money and they'd always be short of funds, so they had a very efficient black union official who would always come to these dances and he would want to see all the union cards to make sure that the musicians were all paid up. And he would always find three or four that were not paid up—and the rule of the union was, you couldn't work if you weren't paid up.

When I had my own band I got to know the union delegate. He'd always come to me and say, "I know you're doing a lot for our people, and I'm not going to pull them off the job because I know that you need them—if you'll guarantee that when the job is over you'll hold out the union money, I'll come by and get it from you." So I got to know this particular union delegate, Bill Dover. Things have a way of working around. It seems like if you do a good deed, they come back with something else, so I was always a friend of his and I'd give him gifts and I'd give him a discount on his own personal account at Fox Bros. So through our friendship he'd let these kids play.

So they brought William Gray, the president of the union, and Bill Dover, the delegate, to see me. The president said, "Earl Hines is starting this club and he's going to be hiring a lot of black musicians and doing a lot of good for the community, and I will guarantee for the Earl Hines uniforms. If he doesn't pay you, I'll make sure that the union pays you because they have to put so much money in after every job and they have quite a treasury." So I brought this to the meeting of Fox Brothers and they said, "Well, we can't go wrong with the president of the union, so if he says he'll guarantee them, we'll make the uniforms." So we did make them.

To make a long story short, Earl Hines never paid us. His place went broke and naturally we couldn't press him till he got on his feet again. He lost money at the El Grotto and it seems like the club didn't go over. When I went to the union president and reminded him that he said he'd make it good he answered, "Well, I was just talking at the time, but I really can't because the board said I'm not allowed to. I had a lot of confidence in these boys, but the fact is, you can take a loss." So it was kind of a bad thing for us.

Most people think we only made uniforms and zoot suits, but we made suits for businessmen and all sorts of people—politicians, rabbis, sports figures, underworld figures, priests—people from all different walks of life. We were also one of the few places that handled kosher clothes. All these people didn't want zoot suits, but they wanted something different, so they would come to Fox Brothers.

First we were the home of the New York Harlem Fronts. That was a drape suit, sort of like the zoot suit; the zoot suit was more exaggerated. The way that name came about was because the kids would come in and they always had their own names for things and they'd say, "Hey, I need a new front for the dance Saturday night." Then it became the Drape Model King because the jacket hung from the shoulders in a kind of drape. Then we had the We Create, Others Imitate.

So every customer that would come in I would design something for each one of them. Our specialty was to be original, so there was always a difference between one suit

Courtesy of Harold Fox.

An adveristement for
Fox Brothers noting the
"specially selected styling."

and the next. They'd decide the color, the material, whether they wanted patch pockets, where the buttons were to be placed—every customer dressed individually.

So this made for a lot of excitement because everyone was looking at everyone else's suit and asking where they got it. When they said, "Fox Brothers," then we'd get some more new customers. Also, people in the neighborhood, all the different ethnic types like blacks and Jews and Chicanos, knew they could get credit at Fox Brothers if they were short of money. They knew I liked having them come to the shop. It was lots of fun having a bunch of them in the store laughing and shouting and telling jokes.

After we had been running the shop for a few years the black people began to realize that the Foxes were on their side. We became sort of a favorite among the black people. Very often we'd have some kids in that would want something right away rather than waiting for the designing and tailoring and we would sell them something that was just hanging there because it had never been picked up by a particular customer. I'd say, just wait one minute because I'm going to take the label off and they'd say, "Oh, no, no, no, don't take the Fox Brothers label off—we want the Fox Brothers label." I'd say, well, I'll put another label in with your name on it, but it will still have the Fox Brothers label.

A picture taken in front of Fox Brothers shows some kids in zoot suits and the little guy with his pants all doubled up, he was one of the Hampton brothers. There were three of them; they were six, four, and five years old. They had their little old shoe shine boxes, and they would go out shining shoes on the street every day. So one day they stopped on the way home and gave me a $1 bill towards paying off their suits. I thought about this and decided to call their parents.

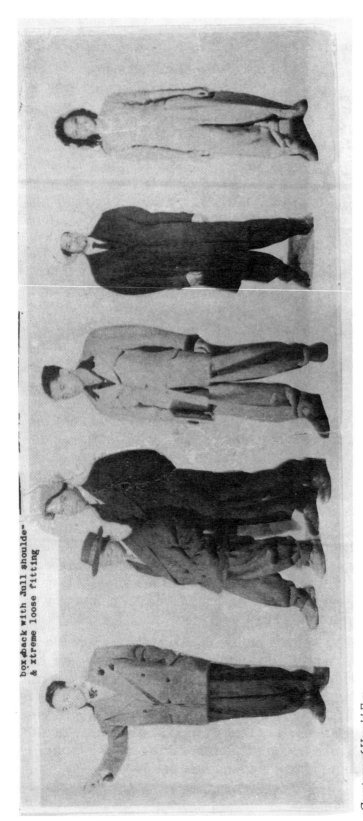

box back with full shoulder
& xtreme loose fitting

Courtesy of Harold Fox.

Modeling zoot suits for Fox Brothers Tailors. The smallest is the youngest (5 years old) of the Hampton Brothers, siblings who all saved their money from shining shoes to buy their own zoot suits.

Some Jewish zoot-suiters showing off their new suits in front of Fox Brothers. Whitey Borman is on the far left and Bernard Rosenthal is on the far right.

I asked them to come down, and said I wanted to talk to them. Since we charged $18 for all suits, I felt guilty sometimes that these little kids would pay the same for their suits as a 300-pound man would for his. Also, I really didn't think the kids should be saving all this money that they worked so hard for for buying suits, because before they know it, they'll be outgrowing them. I said it would be a better system if they would get one and he would pass it on to the smaller one. When they came to the shop their folks said, "No, they work very hard shining shoes, they make their own money, and the thing they love is Fox Brothers clothes and Fox Brothers' label. So we appreciate your telling us about this and trying to help them as much as you can, but that's their enjoyment so it's O.K. with us."

Pretty soon the black publications would come around and write stories about us. One was written in the magazine called *Flash*—it was a national magazine for black people. The date was December, 1950, and there are pictures showing those of us who ran the store: Ma Fox, Victor, my sister's husband, Aaron, my brother, and me. The title is "This Fox is crazy: his vines don't cling, they drape." Another piece of publicity for the zoot suit was the song by Ray Gilbert and Bob O'Brien that became popular when Kay Kayser's band featured it—"A Zoot Suit (For My Sunday Gal)." The lyrics went, "I want a zoot suit with a reat pleat, with a drape shape, and a stuff cuff to look sharp enough to meet my Sunday gal."

There's always a lot of competition in the clothing business, and at one time I was a little suspicious of a customer named Smokey Joe who came to Fox Brothers because about every week he'd come in and want me to make him another suit. I'd make him some wild clothes. At the time he was working with his father selling suits in a store on Maxwell Street. A customer would come into their shop and say, "Man, I want one like yours." So Smokey Joe would say, "You can have this," and he'd take it off and sell it to the customer. I got a little mad because then one time he had a write up in the paper saying that he invented the zoot suit. I was good friend until then, and I didn't care that he opened Smokey Joe's, but I did get mad about that because I was the guy who invented all the zoot suits.

There was another tailor called Leo Fox Tailors, not related to our family. When I was just getting started he was the big man in Chicago and all the big guys were going to him. I designed this coat with the cape on the back and Quack (who worked in our shop) drew a picture of it. Then one time Leo Fox came to see it and started making it, and he and another guy from down the street went to New York to the sweatshops. He had hundreds of them made with cheap cloth and cheap labor and started selling them. Smokey Joe got that idea too and did the same thing with suits.

When I was getting $35 for a suit he was able to sell them as ready-mades for $8 or $9. My trade always wanted something made up special for them, but he would take a style of mine and have it made up in New York and put it in the window and people would buy it. But those were the people that were satisfied with the ready-made, and people that came to us wanted originals designed individually.

When the zoot suit was kind of over I came out with a new thing that I called the "icicle look." This was the exact opposite of the zoot suit. Instead of real wide shoulders I made very narrow shoulders, no long coat, but very short coat, and narrow skimpy pants. Years later, about 1960 or so, I had a letter from a London Carnaby Street shop wanting me to make them a thousand or so zoot suits. They got the idea from a zoot suit article written in 1942 and thought they could still buy them for $18 apiece in 1960.

We had a rule at Fox Brothers—first come, first served—so it didn't matter how important a person was or whether he had a Cadillac or not, there was a bench along the wall where everybody would sit and be served in turn. Sometimes they'd overflow onto the curb outside. Some of the fat cats might get irritated if I'd serve some little black kid first, but it didn't matter to me—it was still first come, first served.

Back in those days the kids really had their own language, and when they wanted to say they were real happy with something they would say, "It's the end to end all ends." There was a Dan Burley with the *Amsterdam News* in Harlem. He came to Fox Brothers and sat there four or five hours a day for about three months listening to the kids when they would come in and spiel all this jive. Then he wrote a little book with poems and a dictionary of jive called *Handbook of Jive*.

Now when we first designed the zoot style, we needed a name for it and I started thinking about the jive talk. A lot of things rhyme with suit, so I just kept going down the line through the alphabet till the end when I got to Z and I said, well, this is the end to end all ends—so we had "zoot suit." That name ended up in the *Webster's 9th Collegiate Dictionary* as "Coined by Harold C. Fox: a flashy suit of extreme cut typically consisting of a thigh-length jacket with wide padded shoulders and peg pants with narrow cuffs."

We didn't just design suits, but we sold all kinds of accessories, like the bebop caps and the bebop glasses. The kids always wanted the latest, and when we'd design a new accessory we put an ad in the magazine *Downbeat* about all these different novelties. I had the confidence of all these kids, and all I had to do was say, I've got a new novelty out—a new tie, or a bebop cap, or whatever I was pushing at this particular time, like little string bow ties and the Chubby Jackson bow ties.

I'd say, if you want to be the first in your crowd to wear these things, send *x* number of dollars, mailing charges prepaid—like maybe I got $1 for these bow ties and $1.50 for a bebop hat and so they would send the money in. Not only that, most of the kids would like these things so they would show them to their friends, and the mailing list was getting bigger and bigger all the time. And besides that it wouldn't be unusual for me to get four to five hundred letters a week from these kids who had been satisfied with the novelty I had sent them. They'd keep writing and saying, "Hey, have you got anything new? I've been wearing it, but have you got anything new on the scene?" So we'd get a lot of mail from all parts of the country and all parts of Europe.

You couldn't purchase these novelties anywhere else because they were made up by us, for us. There was a young black man, about 16 years old, by the name of Nick Nicholson who came to Fox Brothers. This fellow would buy about 10 ties and then he would peddle them on the South Side just like the Jewish peddlers in the old days. Then he'd come back for another 10. Later in life he became the president of the Prudential Life Insurance Company of Los Angeles. We've been friends ever since, and he has retired to New Orleans.

When King Levinsky quit fighting he used to come to Fox Brothers and he sold ties. While we sold ties too, we never dared say anything to him—he was half there and half not. He'd hang around and sit down and sell everybody a tie that would walk in to have a suit made. Leapin' Lena, his sister and manager, and her daughter were big husky women, and they never could get any readymade clothes so I made clothes for them.

We were also making suits through the mail. I had a little folder that explained to people how to take the measurements, and got these kids again who were happy with the ties and the hats and they'd say, "Hey, I'll trust you to make up a wild suit for me." And they'd just send the money in and tell me to pick something and make them a suit. And there were hundreds of those—so through having these novelties, although we never made a lot of money on them, we got a lot of suit customers that way.

One day I was measuring a little Chicano kid; he wanted a zoot suit and he asked if I had any accessories to go with it. Just then I had to go to the men's room; in those days they had a water tank above with a long chain and you'd pull that to flush the toilet. I went to pull the chain and it came off. I figured well, I've got to get that fixed so I went to the front of the store with it to get someone to fix it.

On the way I passed the room where I was measuring this kid. He said, "What's that?" I said, well, it's just a chain. He said, "Maybe we can use that." I said, maybe we can. There was a wooden handle on the chain so I took the wooden handle and I put that in his pocket and I draped the chain down and all the way up to the belt loop and tied it to that. So then the kids got the idea of walking around swinging the chain in a circle. Another thing that the zootsuiters did was to pose in different positions like a kind of crouching position with their fingers pointing outward.

Each time I would make a new style or a new fad I would name it after someone who was popular in the jazz line—like the Chubby Jackson bow tie, the Stan Kenton hat, the Dizzy Gillespie bop tie. Dizzy was the bop king and I designed the tie to kind of droop in front, and I would sell that to all these kids I had on my mailing list and I would use his name on it. He was very popular and a lot of people were using his name. At first it wasn't too important because he never had a decent lawyer to represent him.

Finally he got one real sharp lawyer and the lawyer said, "Now we're going to take all these people because they used your name without the authorization." As a matter of fact, for years we tried to get Dave Garroway, the talk show host, to allow us to use his name in advertising because he came to Fox Brothers frequently. But when we called his manager he always wanted a big amount of money which we didn't want to pay because we never did that kind of advertising. So all the tailor business we got in the city was by grapevine and one person would tell the other, and I think that's the best kind of advertising.

Anyway, Diz got this sharp lawyer and we got a letter from him that he was going to sue us because we used his name. I

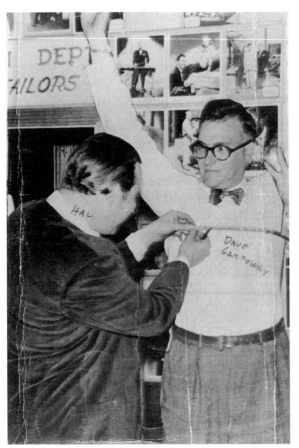

Courtesy of Harold Fox and Elias Zayed.

Television and radio host Dave Garroway called Hal Fox "The Mad One," but entered into the crazy atmosphere himself during his frequent fittings.

don't think Diz had anything to do with it because he was a beautiful cat. Anyway, I called Diz and said, what's up— we're good buddies? I always gave you a good price on your clothes and I gave you a rush job on your clothes when you needed it.

So Diz says, "We really need a set of uniforms bad and we don't have any money. If you want to, we can drop the charges, there won't be any problem, we're suing about everybody, but I'd appreciate it if we could get a set of coats—just the coats —we'll furnish our own pants—we'll pay you back for it by giving you a lot more orders."

I went back to the folks and said, well, Diz's lawyer won't settle unless we make them a set of coats, and to me it looks like there isn't any way out. They said, well, that's probably the best way out because he was suing for something like $20,000. We ended up making him a set of coats and he always appreciated it. And as a matter of fact, he played here (in Sarasota) and I went backstage and he told everybody about the free set of coats that I made.

We had a great staff at Fox Brothers and we never could have turned out all the volume if we hadn't worked well together. We had a graduate draftsman, Bill Fuchs, who would make a pattern for each and every customer from the ideas that I gave him. I would write all the specifications on a blank and then discuss each and every suit with him. A shop of Bohemian women did piecework sewing, and some work went to Billy the Tailor.

We had a man in the alterations department by the name of Nadler who had had a dry cleaning shop that wasn't doing so well so he came to work for us. After a customer's suit was completed and fitted it might then go to alterations if I wasn't satisfied with the fit. I always had an argument with Nadler because I wanted everything to be perfect and he would say, "You're only getting $18 a suit, how can we put that much work into it?" But I didn't want anything to leave the shop that wasn't right.

Morris Milton began doing errands around Fox Brothers when he was 16, but he became a great designer. After about a year of training we were really thinking alike; when a customer would want to know what would look good, we would almost always come up with the same answers. Besides that, Morris learned to sew (which I never could do) so he could even do alterations if necessary. In our own taste in clothes we were completely opposite; I had some pretty wild suits with bright colors, ties to match, conspicuous. Morris was a conservative dresser, everything beautifully coordinated and impeccable. He loves his work and has now been at Fox Brothers for about 50 years.

Two other people who have long histories with Fox Brothers are Leo Zahed who has been tailoring at the store for more than 30 years and Fran Kenney. She has been secretary for about the same amount of time and she knows so much she pretty well runs the place.

Another special person who worked for Fox Brothers for many years was Earl "Quack" Palmer. He had drawn cartoons for the black newspaper, the *Pittsburgh Courier*, and when he worked for us as a designer he was always drawing cartoons all day. He worked fast and maybe while a customer was picking out a style or choosing fabric he would draw a cartoon of them and take it over to them. He did hundreds of cartoons—not only customers but those of us around the shop. Quack knew a lot about music too and for a few years he went into the record distributing business. He was also one of the first nightclub record-spinning deejays.

My brother Aaron and I ran the business together, but he was diabetic and died when he was only 37 years old. He was so good hearted and always gave a lot to charity. After he died my sister's husband, Victor, took over as business manager.

A lot of the Chicago tailors just couldn't understand me or my ideas, but I stuck with the ideas anyway. I don't know what they called me, but it was the T.V. talk show host, Dave Garroway, that started calling me "The Mad One." When some of his friends would come to the shop they'd ask for "The Mad One." That stuck with me for a long time.

One of our customers was Sarah Vaughan, a famous jazz singer, and she came to Fox Brothers often. The first thing I'd do when I knew she was coming was to go around the corner to the Vienna Sausage Company on Halsted Street, and I would pick up a salami. And when she autographed one of her photographs for me she wrote, "To the Fox Brothers Tailors— Great clothes—great salami." So she loved those salamis!

We had started making matching belts for suit customers if they wanted them—a lot of the men liked them. So then we began making matching ties and caps, and we made our first matching cap and Casablanca coat combination for the singer, Mel Tormé. He was a regular customer of ours. Another was Liberace; I made suits for him during his early years when he was in Chicago, and one time he invited the Fox family to be his guests at his performance at the Palmer House. It was a complete surprise when he announced that his tailor was in the audience and that he was dedicating a number to us. It was "12th Street Rags"—a takeoff on our address at 712 12th Street.

Now Sammy Davis, Jr. was also one of our customers. At that time he worked with his uncle, and when he worked at the Regal I used to go backstage and see him. He'd been there several times before—that was before he really got famous. When he booked himself into the theater I'd see him on the first day and make him some clothes and then deliver them on the closing day. Well, this continued for a number of years and he'd always pay me, but this one last time he owed me $20. So I had him on the books for years and years and he was in the movies and had become famous.

Then in the '70s I went to Hollywood for a visit and I was in the studio with Pete Rugolo. We were listening to some of the tapings for some of his shows and he had to do a taping of Theodore Bikel. When they do their vocal tapings they do them in a separate studio.

We went to the studio and there was Theodore Bikel and Sammy Davis, Jr. Pete went over to him and said, "Hey, I've got an old friend of yours." So he brought me over, and Sammy said, "Are you kidding, how can I ever forget him—I think I still owe him something." I said, yes, Sammy, you do owe me something, but no way are you ever going to pay me! I get too much fun out of telling people that Sammy Davis owes me money and that's worth more than the little bit of money you owed me. He really got a kick out of that and said, "Well, I don't mind, I'm happy."

Stefanovic of Jim's Hot Dogs on Halsted and Maxwell was a local customer of mine. I always had a large variety of woolens and Stefanovic would pick the very best woolens and he would send them to his relatives in the old country. This was after World War II and these relatives were extremely poor so I asked why he'd send the finest woolens since they couldn't afford tailors. He said they wouldn't have them made into clothes as you'd expect. They'd take the cloth and sell it to people with a lot of money. Then they'd live on the money.

There was a gambling place above our store. A woman had picketed it because her husband was spending his entire paycheck there, so in order to wait till things quieted down a little, the people who ran the gambling place asked if they could use the back of my store and it would look like their place was out of business. So we were pretty well acquainted that way.

In one of the offices was a fellow who used to like to bake cookies even though he was a Mafia member. He got a friend of his to help, and they started baking cookies and stocked them in one of these rooms, and his name was Bob Stella. The cookies were Stella d'Oro that you can buy in all the supermarkets today. He became very famous and very wealthy, but he was still a Mafia member. Then he moved from Chicago to Las Vegas where he got a job managing the Stardust Hotel in Vegas and then to the Diamond Horseshoe. When I'd go to Las Vegas he'd get me right into the shows and everything was free.

A lot of the Mafia guys that came to have suits made would use nicknames so you never found out their real names, but you kind of suspected that they were in the Mafia. Occasionally you would see write-ups about them in the newspaper. Sometimes we'd never even see the person we were making the suit for—someone would bring in the measurements and an errand boy would come in and get the suit when it was ready. Two of them I knew were juice runners for the Mafia, and both were found dead in car trunks for holding back money.

Occasionally I'd get a call at like 2:00 in the morning. They'd been gambling, playing cards, and they'd win a lot, and they'd call and say, "Fox, come down to your store. I've just made five grand and I want to give it to you and order some clothes. I want to get rid of it in a hurry." So I'd go to the store and wake up the burglar alarm people and they would have to come down to open up the store.

JIMMY DALE AND "THE BAND THAT ROCKS"

WHILE ALL THIS work in the store was going on, I had a second life. In fact, many people thought I was a twin; they thought I was the band leader and my twin brother was the tailor. This is the way it got started. Before World War II I was playing trumpet with a band (all white) called the Jimmy Dale Band. Then the leader was drafted and the members chose me as their leader. We're talking 1941 when I made most of the suits for the bands—Count Basie, Louis Armstrong, Benny Goodman, Vaughan Monroe, even Lawrence Welk. I'd been a musician first, so when they'd come in they'd say, "Hey, man, we need a set of uniforms and we'll give you some of our charts (music arrangements) in exchange." It costs a lot of money to purchase band uniforms so we'd work up a deal with them. We did the same deal with some of the great writers and arrangers.

That meant I had the best music of some of the greatest bands in the country. So then I got a bunch of musicians together, a pretty swinging band because of these great

Hal Fox as "Jimmy Dale" on stage at the Apollo Theater with saxophonist Gene Ammons.

Courtesy of Harold Fox.

charts, see, the musicians were anxious to play in my band. These kids were anxious to play the best music, so I got lots of calls. Many of them were customers and most of them fine musicians so we ended up with a lot of talent—Lee Konitz, Junior Mance, Gail Brockman, Gene Ammons, Cy Touff, Sonny Stitt—some of the great jazz musicians.

There were only two instances when there was a problem over the arrangements. The leaders themselves were giving me the arrangements, but there was one occasion when they came from a player. The baritone player in Count Basie's band was a big guy, big seven-footer, and he never could get any clothes. I had to make his clothes and he'd sneak out all of Count Basie's arrangements and give them to me. Also Count Basie's manager and band boy would give me stuff. But eventually after I retired, Count Basie came to Sarasota to play and I went backstage. He was very sick at the time. I caught some fish to take to the hall for him. First I went to a pizza place and got their biggest box and then fried all the fish.

At intermission time I went back to see Count Basie. He couldn't even walk and he was riding around on an electric cart. I said, Count, I brought you something. He said, "I really appreciate it—you know, I'm very sick—I can't eat pizza." I said, Count, you can eat this pizza. Just open it and see if you like it. So he opened the box, and he was so happy and ate most of the fish. He always called me "Jim Daley" so he said, "Jim Daley, maybe you thought you were getting away with something with that music, but I didn't mind; I knew that Charlie was stealing my music and giving it to you, but I was happy; I was doing good and I didn't mind."

The other instance concerning arrangements was with Lionel Hampton and his big hit was "Red Top." But it wasn't his hit, it was my hit. What had happened was he had a musician in his band who wrote the song "Red Top." I went to talk to Lionel Hampton backstage and asked, "Hamp, have you got any music?" He was a good guy like that. He said, "Well, here's a few tunes that we don't like so you can have them." One was "Red Top" and he gave it to me.

I couldn't record in my own name because the booking agent would not record me unless I signed a contract to work all this out. With working with Fox Brothers I couldn't commit to an agent because I couldn't be free just any night. So they never signed me and they wouldn't record me either. So I told Gene Ammons, who played sax in the Jimmy Dale band, you can get a little group together and go to one of these out-of-the-way recording studios and make this record. So he made "Red Top" and sold a couple of million copies.

So now Gladys, she always managed Lionel, she found out about it and said, "That's our song." I said, well, he gave it to me. She said, "No he didn't." So we went to Hamp the next day and he said, "Yeh, I gave it to you." She said, "It doesn't make any difference, I want a cut of it." I said, well, it's Gene Ammons, it isn't me anymore, he doesn't have anything, but if you want to sue anyone, sue him. But she never got very far.

Those were the only two that ever gave me any problems. I didn't have my own arranger, I just had other peoples' stuff because it was the big bands. I didn't have that kind of money. I can't even arrange a note. I can't even play my arrangements. I play by ear. I had the best musicians, but I couldn't play the music. I didn't have the chops and I couldn't read music that much. Jazz is hard to play when you play those big arrangements, and there's all kinds of rhythms that I couldn't read. Once I had the music, I had a gift that when the band started to play, I could tell if they were playing it wrong or not. I could tell how it was supposed to go, and I was gifted enough to get good tempos.

My band was "Jimmy Dale, the band that rocks." Little Richard was the guy who started rock and roll, but even before his time, I called my band "the band that rocks" so you might say that rock and roll came a lot sooner. I always had so much energy and in Chicago they said "Jimmy Dale was the natural high cat" because I didn't need pot; I didn't need anything. I didn't use booze, but they said I was still higher than anybody in the band. That's why I got a lot of good stuff out of the musicians. I'd start out by marching back and forth on the stage, and the band would be waiting till I got the right rhythm going and then I'd say, "O.K., one, two, three, four," and the band would start.

Around about 1945 I started changing some of the person-

Hal Fox as "Jimmy Dale" conducted his "band that rocks" with great energy— including this leap into the air.

nel in the band because I wanted to include black musicians. This was the first mixed band in the country. Some people say, "Well, Lionel Hampton played with Benny Goodman and that was before you," and I'd say, yes, but that was just a token. There were always the token blacks occasionally in white bands such as Benny Goodman's or Artie Shaw's band—but our band was really integrated with about 12 blacks and six whites.

The first black member of the band that we hired was a vocalist with a wonderful voice, Leon Kechum. We were beginning to be known around the city so then we had a call to play at Melody Mill which was in Oak Park. Everything was going along fine until intermission when one of the staff came up to me and said the manager wanted to talk to me. What he wanted was to say to me, "You know we don't allow any niggers in our ballroom and so I would appreciate it if you would have your vocalist leave."

I told him I was hired by Oak Park, not by him, and then he said he'd blackball me and the band, and that he didn't want niggers singing in that ballroom. So at that point I said, no way is he leaving; if he leaves, we all leave. Finally he had to back down because he couldn't get another band on such short notice, and I made sure Leon sang a few extra songs that night.

We had a helluva job on the road finding places to eat because a lot of places wouldn't take the so-called "niggers." They'd say, "Let them eat in the kitchen." Musicians don't know any color line and if we couldn't all eat in a place, then none of us would eat. So what we'd do was we'd pull up in front of some place like a White Castle and I'd take orders from all 30 or so in the bus. Then I'd collect a $1 from each person; that would buy 20 hamburgers apiece. That's 600 hamburgers!

One place we played was the Club Riviera in St. Louis. It was unusual for a black and white band to play there, and besides that, it didn't go over well with the Ku Klux Klan for the audience to be mixed. So they picketed the place and we always had to leave the club through the alley.

My very first Jimmy Dale gig was in Stanford Park, at 14th and Union, for Fox Brothers customers. We gave out free admission cards in the store and that brought listeners to the park and more customers to our store. The fellow who was in charge was Brooks; he was the head of Stanford Park. He would let us use the auditorium for free, and when he needed uniforms he would come to Fox Brothers. Later on, our 18-piece band, black and white, played in Bowen Hall in Hull-House for dances every Sunday afternoon. Those were admission dances and we kind of broke even because we had to pay for the hall.

We wanted to publicize our Jimmy Dale Band so when we had our dances you have three or four hundred kids who were Fox Brothers' customers in there jam-packed having a good time and the band was good. So now if we'd go to play at the Pershing Ballroom on 63rd Street, we'd have a lot of these kids would come by to see us because they knew the Jimmy Dale band. Another piece of publicity was that I appeared pretty often as Jimmy Dale as a cartoon in the Mary Worth funnies in the daily newspaper.

I had a lot of Mexican trade at Fox Brothers, and there was a Mexican fella named Zuniga that had a grocery store across from the St. Francis Church, and he used to come and get his clothes from us. So then he was getting married and they came over and made arrangements for the Jimmy Dale band to

Courtesy of Harold Fox.

Playbill for the Jimmy Dale Band at the Club Riviera in St. Louis.
Musicians are, beginning with Hal Fox, "Jimmy Dale," at the top, clock-
wise: Pat Bolby, Sam Player, Hog Mason, Jonathon Eng, and Lee Konitz.

play for his wedding. This was the first time that this band of mine played for a Mexican affair, and we had to play some rhumbas and some Spanish music. We knew this one fellow, Sparky, who played bass and was also a capable drummer, and I got him into the band for just such occasions. We had a rehearsal at Stanford Park just before we played for the wedding, and Sparky sat in on drums and he taught all the fellows the Latin beat. The band was pretty capable; they could play the swing stuff which everybody liked, and they could also play the Latin with a little help.

So at the Zuniga wedding we played this Latin music and even though this was the first time we ever played it, we were very well-received at this wedding. The reception was in the banquet room at Gold's across from St. Francis on Roosevelt and we played at that Zuniga wedding till late in the morning.

But one thing resulted from it—the fellow who married them was Father Pat, a well-known priest because he worked with all the poor and he was affiliated with St. Francis. Later he went higher in the Catholic Church and was transferred and now I think he's in California. So he heard our band at the wedding and it gave him an idea for raising some funds.

So they had a big hall at the church and one day he came in and wanted to see me, and I said, what can I do for you Father Pat? He said, "Well we're in very bad need of funds. There are a lot of poor people here and we have to feed them, and we're way behind in our endeavors to help these people." I said, I'll be glad to help in any way I can, Father Pat. He said, "Well, in exchange for it, all the priests need black suits and a lot of them like them made to order, and I'll make sure I steer them in here."

I said, that isn't necessary; you don't have to bribe me or anything like that, I'll be glad to do it. He said, "It's a good cause, and what I want you to do is donate your orchestra and I know that all the kids heard you at the Zuniga wedding, I know they'll all be there and we should pack the place and make a lot of money."

So I agreed to play, and then about a week later he said, "Well, it would be kind of nice if we had some entertainment, too. Do you think you could get us somebody with a big name so we could splash this thing all over the newspapers?" So I said, well, I'm going downtown to the Oriental Theater to measure the Louis Prima band, and I'll see what I can do. They were playing there at the time, and they had a couple of stars with them and one was Jane Withers, the movie star, and the others were Buddy Lester and Jerry Lester. They had an act sort of like Martin and Lewis.

So I had Louis Prima introduce me to these stars. I told them that I was playing for this charity affair and they would very much like to have someone make an appearance; it's a good cause. Buddy Lester said, "We were brought up in the ghetto district ourselves so you've got us, but we'll have to talk to Jane Withers because maybe she don't understand those things." In a few days they got Jane Withers, too. So when we advertised them and Jane Withers also, we really got a crowd and they made a lot of money for the church from that.

When Father Pat came to the store to thank me he said he was going to give me a card belonging to the St. Jude Society. Pretty near all the policemen in Chicago belonged to the St. Jude Society. I said thanks very much, but how is this card valuable? He said, "All the cops belong to the St. Jude, so if a cop pulls you over for speeding take that card out and show it to him and you'll have a free ride."

So I kept the card in my wallet, and I was doing a little speeding around Grand and Western and a cop pulled me over and said I was going 10 miles over the limit. I said, I'm sorry and all that, and he said, "Let's see your license." I kept the card right alongside my license and he said, "Oh, I see you're a member of the St. Jude. I'm a member too." I said, yeh, they said if sometime I'm in trouble I should just show this card and you'd give me a pass. He said, "Well, I will give you a pass; this and $5 will get you a pass." So he still got his cut.

For Christmastime the kids in the neighborhood always had to have a new suit. They might be wearing workclothes on their regular jobs, but for the holidays they wanted to look really sharp, so Fox Brothers tailors and seamstresses worked 24 hours a day getting out the orders. In about 1944, International Harvester called me and they said, "The black kids have recommended your band to play at the employees' dance at the Union Park Temple for Christmas Eve." I had made suits for all these kids, four to five hundred of them, and they also knew the band from the gigs in the neighborhood.

The night of the dance they had a buffet table with about 10 chefs; everything you could think of. Nine o'clock came and nobody showed. Our band was on the stand and the International Harvester president was there. "When are these kids going to show up?" they were asking. Well, to make a long story short, nobody showed up.

Four days later when the kids came around we said, "Hey, what happened, they had all these eats. The band had to take all the eats home." One of them answered, "Well, we found out that they ran two dances, one for the whites at a ballroom on Crawford, and ours, and we weren't going to stand for that. We work together, and we can dance together." So they boycotted the dance.

Back in those days ballrooms would book two bands on one night and they had a popular feature called Battle of the Bands. Each would try to outperform the other. So one night we had a Battle of the Bands with Stan Kenton at the Pershing Ballroom on 64th and Cottage. Stan Kenton was the star and I was the fill-in band, but Pete Rugolo did the arranging and he was my good friend. So Pete Rugolo sent me Stan Kenton's arrangement of "Sorrento." These guys gave me the arrangements, but I always changed them. Vito Musso, who was a jazz tenor man, played in Stan Kenton's band, So then Stan Kenton plays his arrangement of "Sorrento," and Vito Musso, who was well known as a jazzman, played the solo part.

Stan Kenton was a precision man; when he played any place, he played everything exactly the way it was on his recording. When you record, usually there's a chorus and then you let the soloist play. Well, the soloist just plays one chorus on the record—32 bars. He did improvising, but only 32 bars. So that night Vito Musso plays the 32 bars. That was Stan Kenton's version of it.

And now it comes my turn and I'm playing the arrangement of "Sorrento" and when we get to the tenor sax part, I put Gene Ammons up there, and instead of 32 bars, I let him play for half an hour. And the blacks are so enthusiastic and go crazy the more you play. So I won that night because I knew the audience and I let Gene Ammons go—as you play you build up more. They would cluster around the stage shouting, "Go! Go!" But it didn't really cause any trouble; Stan Kenton and I were always good friends. When he autographed a picture for me he wrote, "I wish all my friends were like you."

When the band played the Regal at South Parkway (now King Drive) and 47th, a lot of the people didn't know us yet. I had a different kind of beginning for our performance because I had the rhythm section on the stage, and then at a given time I'd give the signal and the saxophones would walk down one aisle and the trumpets blowing like the saints—blowing their way up the sides to the stage.

After the first show I used some of Stan Kenton's stuff, and Junior Mance had kind of a classical opening. I had him play a lot of classical stuff—real heavy. So we played two of Stan Kenton's; one was "Concerto to End All Concertos" and the other was "Sorrento." After the first show the manager called me and said, "I know you're white, but you're black too and you know music, but you don't know the Regal audience. I think you should change your show. Count Basie-style things, that's what they like."

Courtesy of Harold Fox.

Band leader Stan Kenton and Hal Fox were friends in spite of a friendly rivalry at Battle of the Bands at the Pershing Ballroom.

I said, why don't you give it a chance? These are people like anybody else; I'm sure the way we do it, they'll like it. After the last show he called me in and he admitted I was right because I played all that stuffy stuff, but I played it swinging. They were people that had never heard that kind of stuff before, but they enjoyed it.

We had some great experiences at the Regal Theater. When Billie Holiday performed there we used to be the house band and sometimes I would act as the M.C. One evening she played a trick on me. I went backstage to check and make sure she was ready to be introduced, she said she was, and I went out and made the introduction. But she didn't come out, so there I was feeling stupid. So I went backstage and checked on

Courtesy of Harold Fox.

The Jimmy Dale Band was the house band at the Regal Theater while Nat "King" Cole headlined. Nat and his wife Maria were also regular customers at Fox Brothers.

her again, and when I came out there the whole audience was really getting impatient, but still no Billie Holiday. Finally I went back and told her she could introduce herself—and she did—just as if that was part of the act, and then she put on a fantastic show.

In those days Nat "King" Cole was a great jazz pianist and his trio was featured at the Regal. The stage curtain would go down after the movie and our band would lead out and announce Nat. Then they'd pull the piano out and he'd do something. Then the curtain would go up and my band would be there and my band and Nat "King" Cole would both do something together. He liked that; he'd say, "Bring out Gene Ammons and let him blow."

So what happened was, he decided to marry Maria so they went to the city hall to get married and they did it between shows. So now they're downtown and I don't know this and I'm out leading our band. We did some pieces and then I announced the great Nat "King" Cole. Then I heard a whisper from the stage manager—"Keep it going, he isn't back yet but he should be here any minute." Well, I began making some announcements and then I started running out of announcements.

So the stage manager had a nephew backstage and he just came in from school and had his books there. So I took one of his books, a geography book, and opened it to the map of the world. I said, Nat just spent eight weeks in Copenhagen where he played to big crowds, then he was 10 weeks in Paris where they mobbed him, and Pittsburgh, and Johannesburg, and on and on, telling a story about Nat in each city. Finally I could announce, here he is, Nat "King" Cole! Nat was one of the greatest; both he and Maria were customers at Fox Brothers and he was a really pleasant person to be around.

Probably the high point of my musical career was when the band played at New York's Apollo Theater and Savoy Ballroom to packed houses. When we played the Apollo Count Basie was in New York playing the Capitol Theater, and his show started later than ours. Wow! There he was in the box seat almost on stage and I was a bit nervous coming out for our first performance. It was a petrifying moment, but I was cool and announced, "We are honored to have the great Count Basie with us today. Stand up and take a bow." And when he sat down I said, "Guess he's here to dig a great swingin' band. Not as good as his, but worthy of his giving a listen to. So we are indeed honored."

When you play at either the Apollo or the Savoy you really have to be on your toes because you know there are a lot of the top jazz musicians in New York and they may be stopping by to hear you. Dizzy Gillespie and Thelonious Monk were there on that first night, too. Also, the audiences were pretty sophisticated because they're listening to the best bands and they expect a lot.

We got good reviews for those engagements and were booked into the Howard Theater in Washington, D.C., but I had to leave the band in New York because Fox Brothers was getting busier all the time and they needed me back at the store. Gene Ammons took over the band after that. I never had any regrets; it was a great jazz band and we played some of the top spots.

The whole music scene was changing about that time. I mentioned earlier about Earl Hines's club that went broke. Most of these clubs were starting to fold. People weren't attending them; they were staying home to watch television or else going to little clubs where they could just sit and drink and listen to music. After the zoot era there came a "cool" era where everybody was considered hip if he was cool. A black fellow didn't want to be considered a jitterbug—he just wanted to be a cool fellow and have that icicle look.

Even these kids, I'd see them in front of the band, and that's one of the things that made me quit the band—they'd come to hear the band, and they'd love to hear it, and we'd always be playing opposite the big names like Billie Holiday, so they'd come to these attractions, but very few of them in this particular era, after the zoot era, would dance. And I'd hear young girls, when someone would come up to them and say, "Hey, you want to dance?" And the girls would say, "You're out of your mind, that's just for jitterbugs. I just came to dig the music."

So this would bug me because these little kids that were 14 and 15 years old, it's all right to be cool, you see, and to grow up, but not to grow up before your time. When they're 14, that's the time they should be jitterbugging, be out there bouncing and dancing, but instead, they wanted to impress each other.

All they wanted to do was go to a nightclub, and they had a place on 47th Street near the Regal Theater where this fellow installed a juke box. It was one of the first juke boxes, and it replaced live bands. He used to get most of the business on the South Side and the dance halls all went out of business. He would just play slow, romantic music and they would just kind of stand and cling to each other, no jitterbugging or anything like that.

GONE FISHING

IN 1950 MARIE and I were married. At that time the twins were 16 and Leo was 8 years old. Then in 1954, I retired to Florida. To me an easier life was more important than being rich. I could have been a millionaire by staying at Fox Brothers, and everyone thought I was crazy to leave so early, but I have never regretted the move and have been enjoying Florida living ever since. I am happy and have everything I want—maybe no Cadillac, but I do have a Buick.

Part of the deal when I retired was that I would come back to Chicago every summer and fill in the different positions at

Courtesy of Harold Fox.

Above: Hal and Marie Fox in Florida in 1995.

Below: Hal Fox's memorabilia room has four walls and
a ceiling jam-packed with photos, momentos, and artwork.

Fox Brothers when people went on vacation. The only thing I couldn't do was sewing, but I did everything else and was in the shop every year from June to September for about 15 years.

My daughters all live in California. Letty married Howard "Hotsie" Katz who played trumpet in my Jimmy Dale band, and their children all have careers in movies and television. One of the twins, Audry, is married to Richard and they are head of the Navigators, which is a religious organization. Sandy, the other twin, is married to Tony, and she was in show biz and has had a school of acting and a fashion design business. My son, Leo, is married to Nancy and lives in Orlando. He's a stockbroker with Paine Webber. Once I retired I could see more of the children and grandchildren and great grandchildren, and I had more time to write letters and poetry, which I like to do.

I miss the customers and wonderful staff at Fox Brothers. I have a lot of photographs and records and gifts I treasure like the little beat-up horn of Louis Armstrong's and the medallion he gave me. I'm still in contact with a number of my musician friends, but I miss all the wonderful music we used to have in Chicago, and the smell of that great food on Maxwell Street.

My friends send clippings from Chicago about the demise of the Maxwell Street Market. Some people would give anything to have such a place for a landmark, and here we are giving up such an integral part of our history. I'm sure the Fox family is turning over in their graves. But as Ma Fox always said, "You can't fight City Hall."

You could be St. George and you couldn't slay that dragon.

—Florence Scala

The University of Illinois at Chicago, The University Library,
Jane Addams Memorial Collection, JAMC Neg. 285.

Italian immigrants living in the Harrison-
Halsted area around the turn of the century.

4. THE ITALIAN NEIGHBORHOOD
5. FLORENCE SCALA
6. FLORENCE SCALA (CONTINUED)

The University of Illinois at Chicago, The University Library, Department of Special Collections, Italian American Collection, IAC Neg. 10.01.

By 1929 the intersection of Taylor and Halsted Streets was a center of various enterprises, including shops and lodging-houses of all sorts.

4
THE ITALIAN NEIGHBORHOOD

INTRODUCTION

FLORENCE SCALA WAS born and raised on Taylor Street on the Near West Side of Chicago, but no life story begins and ends with a particular person and his or her period. This is especially true of immigrants who leave their familiar environment but bring with them the language and customs and the influence of relatives left behind. Thousands of Italians immigrated to America and settled in the Harrison-Halsted-Roosevelt area of the Near West Side of Chicago, and each had roots in some small town or village in a particular spot in Italy.

Yet when these individuals came to Chicago in the teens and '20s of this century, each had his or her own adjustment to make. For all the generalizations about ethnic groups, each person was an individual with a singular character, with unique hopes, and with individual responses to this new setting. Oral history helps to reveal that combination of individual experience and cultural surroundings that influenced the children of these immigrants.

Meeting fundamental needs such as housing, food, and jobs, and even coping with Chicago's sub-zero winter temperatures, more often than not meant that the immigrant sought and received help and advice from fellow countrymen. In the case of Italians, "fellow countrymen" usually meant relatives and friends who had come to Chicago from the home village, not just any place in the Kingdom of Italy.

As the Italian immigrants in this Halsted-Roosevelt neighborhood were predominantly from rural areas of the southern part of Italy, many had the adjustments that any rural person would face when they encounter city life. By the time these southern Italians began to migrate to this area, northern Italians who had preceded them were well-established and were harshly critical of the southerners' clothes, manners, views, and the work they did, so the southerners also had to cope with this prejudice.

Finally, as in most immigrant societies, a "generation gap" often existed between the immigrant, Italian-speaking, parents and the assimilating second generation. Jane Addams, founder of the neighborhood Hull-House settlement house, referred to this when she wrote:

> The Italian and Bohemian peasants who live in Chicago, still put on their bright holiday clothes on a Sunday and go to visit their cousins. They tramp along with at least a suggestion of having walked over plowed fields and breathed country air. The second generation of city poor too often have no holiday clothes and consider their relations a 'bad lot.'[1]

IMMIGRATION

WHEN HULL-HOUSE OPENED in 1889 Italians were already living along Halsted Street, and in 1892 when the United States Bureau of Labor investigated slums in four major cities, it found large numbers of Italians in this district of Chicago.[2] By 1905 southern Italians were the dominant group in the neighborhood around Harrison, Halsted, Polk, and Morgan, and their enduring community identity was well-established. By 1920 the Near West Side had an Italian immigrant population of 12,995 persons, and the area around Hull-House contained the largest and most densely concentrated population of Italian immigrants in Chicago. In spite of this saturation, there were other ethnic families in the area, and Italians were only one-third of the area's population.[3]

Although concentrated, this was an extremely fluid population, and one study showed that in 1900, fewer than 50 percent remained at the same address when surveyed just two years later.[4] This does not necessarily imply that they moved away from the Near West Side; a change of address might mean a simple move such as that made by Florence Scala's family when they moved two doors east on Taylor Street.

At the turn of the century, Halsted Street was already lined with saloons, restaurants, clothing stores, and all kinds of shops and cheap lodging-houses. The whole district was described as a region of flimsy wooden dwellings and dilapidated sheds, of poorly paved and unpaved streets, and filthy alleys.[5] Blue Island Avenue, originally an old plank road, cut diagonally through the heart of the neighborhood and continued to do so until the coming of the University of Illinois, when it was truncated at Roosevelt Road.

ASSIMILATION

WHETHER THE SOUTHERN Italians remained unskilled laborers in construction work or factories or moved on to become skilled workers or business owners, many began the transition to working life nineteenth-century Chicago under the direction of a *padrone*, who was essentially a recruiting agent. Chicago, as a major manufacturing center, railway hub, and focal point for seasonal-work recruiting, was an important center of this system.

When immigrant workers tried to enter the regular work force without the "patronage" of some kind of a labor agent, they faced assorted problems. One problem was that they were locked out of some unions, and when the unions went on strike the immigrants were hired as scabs or used as threats by employers to undercut wages. A portion of the anti-immigrant sentiment that permeated American society around the turn of the century was directed specifically at Italians because they were portrayed as anarchists and labor agitators.

In Chicago, contrary to the anti-union reputation that stigmatized them, Italians actually helped organize unions or establish locals for various groups; among these were the garment workers, bakers, mosaic workers, sewer and tunnel laborers, pressmen, macaroni workers, cigar makers, hod carriers, building laborers, barbers, and tailors.[6]

This involvement set the stage for one of the most notorious strikes in Chicago history and one which had a direct effect on the Near West Side because so many local people were involved. This was the Chicago Garment Workers' Strike in 1910 against Hart Schaffner and Marx, the country's largest clothing manufacturer. The strike began in the company's shop at 18th and Halsted when a group of female employees, led by a young Sicilian woman, left their jobs because of a wage cut for piecework. Within three weeks most of the firm's employees had joined the strike, and then it spread throughout the city until 50 firms were involved. Most of the 40,000 striking clothing workers were foreign born; this included many who were Italian.

Courtesy of Bernice Latoria.

When Bernice Schuh married Phillip Latoria in 1950, she bought her wedding dress on Maxwell Street. The Latoria family, with its 20 children, was honored at the 1933 Century of Progress World's Fair for being the largest Italian family in Chicago. Phillip was one of those children.

Italians marched in the picket lines and contributed money when they could to support the strike. The settlement house founder, Jane Addams, supported the workers and a money-raising meeting was held at Hull-House by the Italian Socialist Women on behalf of the strikers. Even though the workers lost this strike, they went on to form the garment workers union and to achieve gains in wages and improvements in working conditions.

Not all Italian immigrants found employment with the skilled or unskilled work force—so they became peddlers. For some, it may have been an alternative of last resort, but for many it was the first step on the road to entrepreneurship using skills they had brought with them from the old country. Italian peddlers sold throughout the neighborhood, not only fruits, vegetables, bread, and milk for daily living, but also hot peanuts, waffles, and ice cream for pleasure.

James Caruso, owner of a produce firm at the South Water Market, the central wholesale produce market for Chicago located just outside the Halsted-Roosevelt area, described how his father, an immigrant from Italy, went by horse and wagon every day to sell produce on the South Side of Chicago.[7] Beginning at the age of eight, James Caruso would leave immediately after school, pay three cents on the streetcar, meet his father, and sell produce with his father until eight or nine o'clock in the evening.

Immediately to the south of the Italian enclave, across Roosevelt Road, was the Maxwell Street Market where a number of the vendors and many of the customers were Italian. Antoinette Scala (sister-in-law of Florence Scala) tells her childhood recollections of going shopping on Maxwell Street with her mother:

> My mother did a lot of shopping there. It was all along the streets and my mother made sure I always saw the woman with the sweet potatoes. I remember the sacks around her feet because it seemed like it was always wintertime. She had a metal cart and there was charcoal underneath and that's how she would roast the potatoes. Delicious![8]

By the late 1920s and 1930s many of those who started as peddlers had progressed to the merchant stage. A directory of Italians in Chicago shows that among Italian businessmen there were 65 Produce Commission Merchants, 47 Fruits, and 84 Fruits and Vegetables establishments. There were also 500 Italian retail and wholesale grocers, 23 Edible Nuts firms, and 9 statuary businesses.[9]

One of the most influential institutions in the assimilation process among Italians of the Near West Side was Hull-House, a pioneering settlement house founded in 1889 by Jane Addams and her friend, Ellen Gates Starr, when they rented some rooms in an old mansion at Polk and Halsted Streets. Jane Addams grew up in the simple, rural surroundings of Cedarville, Illinois, but when she came to Chicago she aroused suspicion by moving to this crowded, immigrant neighborhood, by championing the garment workers, and by proposing pacifist solutions to end World War I. When she fought for a law restricting employment for children under 14 and limiting women to an eight-hour workday, the businessmen who relied on cheap immigrant labor were outraged. One businessman was reputed to have said, "Jane Addams ought to be hanged to the nearest lamppost."[10]

Hull-House was a leader in providing tools for the assimilation of immigrants, and eventually, the "house" became a 13-building complex. There were classes in English, cooking, sewing, baby care, citizenship, crafts, theater, and dancing; there were social evenings and ethnic fiestas; and there were lectures and discussion groups. The first public playground in Chicago was started by Hull-House, and a summer camp provided residents with an opportunity to escape the congestion of the city.

The University of Illinois at Chicago, The University Library, Jane Addams Memorial Collection, Wallace Kirkland Papers, JAMC Neg. 490.

Part of the Hull-House complex of buildings on Polk Street in 1924-25.

Although Italians shared the Catholic religion with other immigrants in the neighborhood—the Irish, French, and Germans—for a long time the church seemed to be a force that kept the Italian immigrants separate rather than aiding their assimilation into American society. A parish history notes that apparently during the Lent of 1892 the Italians were not welcomed in the upper church of Holy Family (a predominantly Irish parish) as indicated by the fact that the priest held services for Italian Catholics in the church basement.[11]

In 1875 a school called Holy Guardian Angel had been built in the community, and in 1899 a church was built next to it for the new Italian parish. By 1905 the Archdiocesan weekly, *The New World*, called the Holy Guardian Angel Sunday school "the largest and most progressive in the country." A further indication of transitions in this neighborhood is that in 1912 the Italian parish established the Guardian Angel Social Center in the St. Francis of Assisi (later Mexican) School building just south of Roosevelt on Newberry Avenue.

Holy Guardian Angel Church was a vital institution in the Italian community, so when the church was razed in 1959 because it was in the path of the coming Dan Ryan Expressway, the parish built another church on a site at Cabrini Street and Blue Island Avenue. This was not a blind choice of site; they consulted with the city and were given the go-ahead. Mayor Richard J. Daley even attended the dedication. By 1960 the city was announcing plans for turning over land to the University of Illinois that included the site of Holy Guardian Angel Church. So the church that had scarcely been erected was demolished in 1963 and the parishioners were told to join other parishes.

Another parish, Our Lady of Pompeii, was organized in 1910 to serve the Italian immigrants around Racine Avenue and Taylor Street because Holy Guardian Angel parish was just too crowded. In the 1950s and 1960s, two-thirds of the housing in this parish was razed for the Eisenhower Expressway (running east and west just north of Harrison Street) and the University of Illinois. Yet, with all this disruption, in 1978, 50 percent of the 660 families in the parish were still Italian, and according to the Archdiocesan history, Columbus Day celebrations still began with mass at Our Lady of Pompeii.

Politics offered another path of entry of immigrants into the life of the city, but prior to the 1930s Italians had held only a few public offices in Chicago. In most wards there were not sufficient concentrations of Italians, but this was not the case on the Near West Side (19th Ward). Only in this ward did Italians exceed 80 percent of the total vote.[12] There was, however, a large proportion of Italian women and children who had no vote, and the votes of those Italians who did go to the polls were often split between the Democratic and Republican parties, limiting their influence.

During the whole first quarter of the century, the Irish politician, John Powers, held sway in the 19th Ward—he won his first election in 1889 and retired in 1927. One of the most publicized of Jane Addams's crusades was her fight to oust John Powers from office during three aldermanic campaigns in the 1890s on the basis of his corruption and lack of concern for conditions in the ward, for the schools, streets and alleys, and parks of the ward, but she failed. Powers was so entrenched through his granting of franchises, distribution of jobs, and general glad-handing, that he never failed to win. At one point Powers boasted that he had 2,600 people in his ward on the public payroll, a third of all voters.[13] As Addams noted, the alderman's greatest power was in being "a friendly neighbor." She was never a quitter, but on this fight, Jane Addams gave up.

Chicago has always had a reputation for a thin line separating politics and crime, but very often the blame for this mix seemed to fall largely on Italians. By the turn of the century, city newspapers were consistently blaming Italians and the Mafia, while Italian newspapers were alternately denying everything or blaming the southern Italians.

Although high-level attention was directed to the Mafia, much of the crime in the neighborhood was more in the nature of bullying by local toughs on the one hand and corruption and neglect of their constituents by the local politicians on the other. Both of these aspects are discussed as Florence Scala tells the story of her life on Taylor Street.

A COMMUNITY'S FIGHT FOR SURVIVAL

THE DEMOLITION OF the Harrison-Halsted neighborhood to make way for the University of Illinois at Chicago has a complex history. The story is told in detail from a scholarly, outsider's perspective in George Rosen's *Decision-Making Chicago-Style* (1980), with broader strokes in Sorrentino's *Organizing Against Crime* (1977), and from a personal, thoughtful perspective by Florence Scala in the following chapter.[14] The brief notes that follow provide some guideposts to a confusing series of events.

SEQUENCE OF EVENTS

1947-1948

West Side Community Committee meets to discuss blight in the area; Temporary Organizing Committee forms.

1949

Near West Side Planning Board forms to represent the community and devise a self-help plan for renewal of the Near West Side area; Chicago Land Clearance Commission offers support for their redevelopment plans.

1951

Near West Side Planning Board presents plan to the community.

1953

Committees are set up by the State of Illinois and the University of Illinois to consider a four-year, Chicago-area school to replace its Navy Pier program. The federal director of Slum Clearance and Urban Redevelopment says that the Near West Side might be designated as a pilot demonstration area.

1955-8

Various sites proposed for U. of I. campus are: Northerly Island (Meigs Field), Miller Meadows, Riverside Golf Club, Garfield Park, Riverview Park, and the Rail Terminal site south of the Loop. City Council approves a plan for Harrison-Halsted area for residential and limited commercial use.

1959

Holy Guardian Angel Church and School are built and dedicated.

1960

Mayor Daley proposes Harrison-Halsted site for campus and formally offers this site to the University.

1961-2

Board of Trustees accepts Harrison-Halsted site offer. Harrison-Halsted Community Group organized under leadership of Florence Scala and demonstrations, protests, and court appeals by community group protesting the site choice follow.

1963

U.S. Supreme Court rejects group's final appeal. Harrison-Halsted area razed.

If Mayor Daley's announcement of the Harrison-Halsted site offer in 1960 appears to come out of the blue, imagine what a shock it was to residents after the encouragement they had received for redevelopment of their neighborhood. They learned about the decision through an announcement in the *Chicago Sun-Times.*[15]

After discussing the urgent need for a decision on the site, the article's writer turns to land prices and makes the astonishing comment that " . . . since a considerable portion of the area is streets and alleys," the price would be within the University's range. The most striking aspect of this article is that the residents, the human beings, of the neighborhood are never mentioned except to say that some have already been "relocated." The reporter does not even include the proposed destruction of their homes as a matter of some importance—only streets and alleys are specified.

As it turned out, the campus displaced about 1,900 families, averaging four persons per family, and over 650 single individuals. Approximately 630 businesses were forced out and several institutions, including Hull-House, Holy Guardian

Angel Church and School, the Catholic Youth Organization, and several schools, were demolished.[16]

Another instructive part of this *Sun-Times* article is that it proposed that the campus would extend from Harrison south to 16th Street (the railway tracks), and Halsted would be moved east to occupy space next to the Dan Ryan Expressway. By January, 1961, this proposed boundary was moved north to Roosevelt Road. In the end, however, the University was to acquire exactly what was set forth in the first plan.

A *Chicago Sun-Times* editorial of 1960 commented on another aspect of the site acquisition when it wrote " . . . once again the Board of Trustees of the University of Illinois has reached a major decision in a secret meeting."[17] With the meeting closed to the public, awkward questions did not have to be answered. Jessie Binford, a pioneering worker at Hull-House, expressed the feeling of betrayal that the residents of the neighborhood were feeling when she said, "They feel forgotten as people; ignored as citizens."[18]

Courtesy of Florence Scala.

Jessie Binford, one of the pioneers and enduring workers at Hull-House, who fought to the bitter end to save the settlement house complex from demolition in the 1960s.

The legal protests and appeals went all the way to the U.S. Supreme Court (October term, 1962), where the nature of urban renewal was the central issue. Throughout the entire fight to save their neighborhood, residents protested that they were not being heard. In the final appeal it boiled down to just that—the Supreme Court ruled that the residents did not have legal "standing." Their views were not admissible because the Housing Act was designed for the community as a whole (meaning Chicago), and not for any group smaller than the entire community. Another argument used for rejecting the appeal was that, by that time (1962), much of the area had already been destroyed. No one could argue with that.

Florence Scala's story is not just about this struggle to save her neighborhood, but about all the reasons, from her earliest childhood experiences and throughout her life, why she felt it was worth saving. It is no Pollyanna view—no whitewash of the neighborhood—but honest and perceptive.

NOTES TO CHAPTER 4

1. Jane Addams, *Forty Years at Hull-House* (New York: Macmillan, 1935), 231.

2. United States Department of Labor, *Seventh Special Report, The Slums of Baltimore, Chicago, New York and Philadelphia* (Washington, DC: United States Government Printing Office, 1894).

3. Humbert Nelli, *From Immigrants to Ethnics: The Italian Americans* (New York: Oxford University Press, 1983), 61.

4. Humbert Nelli, *Italians in Chicago 1880-1930: A Study in Ethnic Mobility* (New York: Oxford University Press, 1970), 49.

5. Edith Abbott, *The Tenements of Chicago 1908-1935.* (New York: Arno Press, 1970—originally University of Chicago Press, 1936), 93.

6. Rudolph Vecoli, "Chicago's Italians Prior to World War I: A Study of Their Social and Economic Adjustment" (Ph.D. diss., University of Michigan, 1963), 27; Nelli, *Italians in Chicago,* 78-87.

7. Interview in the South Water Market, 1987.

8. Interview, 1997.

9. Lisi Cipriani, *Italians in Chicago and Selected Directory of the Italians in Chicago* (Chicago, 1928 and 1933-34).

10. June Sawyers, *Chicago Sketches* (Chicago: Wild Onion Books, 1995), 47.

11. Rev. Msgr. Harry Koenig, *A History of the Parishes of the Archdiocese of Chicago* (Chicago: New World Publishers, 1980), 374.

12. Nelli, *From Immigrants to Ethnics*, 90.

13. Gioia Diliberto, *A Useful Woman: The Early Life of Jane Addams* (New York: Scribner, 1999), 230.

14. George Rosen, *Decision-Making Chicago-Style* (Urbana, IL: University of Illinois Press); Anthony Sorrentino, *Organizing Against Crime* (New York: Human Sciences Press, 1977).

15. Malcomb Wise, "Daley to offer new U. of I. site," *Chicago Sun-Times*, 13 September 1960, 3.

16. Rosen, *Decision-Making*, 141.

17. Editorial, "Another secret U. of I. decision," *Chicago Sun-Times*, 23 March 1960.

18. Jessie Binford, "Harrison-Halsted Group Program," *Chicago*, 1962.

Courtesy of Florence Scala.

Florence Scala's parents, married in Abruzzi, Italy, followed
a familiar immigration pattern. Her father, Alessandro
Giovangelo, came to Chicago in 1915 and established
a foothold; her mother, Teresa (shown here), followed.

5

FLORENCE SCALA

FAMILY AND CHILDHOOD

I WAS BORN in 1918, so I'm pretty well up in years now. My parents were married in Italy, and my father came here in 1915, I think it was. My mother followed him a year and a half later. They came from Abruzzi, which is in the central part of Italy. Almost all of the Italians from that province, from the little town that my father came from, settled in Philadelphia, and somehow, one way or another, he decided that he wanted to go to Chicago rather than Philadelphia. He didn't want to be with all those other people. He was very independent at times, and he wanted to be on his own. Some of my mother's family came to America, but they settled in Philadelphia, too.

Back in Abruzzi my father was a tailor. He had apprenticed in Torino di Sangro, which is a small town there, and worked for another tailor. He had served a stint in the army before war broke out. They sent him to Marseilles on maneuvers, and he decided he didn't want to go to war. So after he got out of the army when he had served his time, he decided he wanted to come to the States, and he did. By that time Europe was already in the war. It was always amazing to me how they were able to cross the ocean during the war, and I always wonder about my mother, "How did she do it all by herself?"

My parents lived in a boarding house right down the street from where I live now on Taylor Street. There were Italians there, mostly from Naples and Calabria. The person who owned the three-story building rented out bedroom space and served meals, like a regular boarding house. They were in that business. It wasn't someone my parents knew, but they were Italian.

I was born in the building next door to where I live now, right in the house with a midwife. I knew midwives in the neighborhood later, and I knew the one who helped with me. She was a lady we would think of today as being a woman doctor or a nurse. She had more the qualities of a nurse—she wasn't as standoffish as doctors can be. When I grew up and was old enough to understand that she delivered babies, she was already an elderly lady, pretty well up in years. Her name was Garibaldi, and she delivered many of these babies around here.

I had two brothers, Ernie was two years younger and Mario was four years younger. When my younger brother was born I didn't know my mother was going to have a baby. Ernie and I were pushed into a bedroom where we slept, and my father said, "Get under the bed and stay there." And we stayed

Photo by Carolyn Eastwood.

The intersection of Taylor and Miller Streets with the building where Florence Scala has lived most of her life, the house next door to where she was born, and the second house to the west where her father set up his first tailoring business and the family lived behind the store.

there under the bed during the labor. I don't remember how long it was, but I can still see myself under there and being really fascinated by what was happening and hearing all this talking and then knowing that there was a little baby there. My mother was in the bedroom just opposite us. I was really fascinated; if she was screaming I wasn't aware of that. At that time we lived in back of the store.

When my father came to Chicago from Italy the first thing he did was to get a job in the manufacturing district on Van Buren Street where they made men's suits. He worked for Scotch Woolen Mills who were affiliated with Hart Schaffner and Marx. That was the business and all of these immigrants worked there. He was working there before my mother came because he had to get the money to get her over here. He worked on men's coats and hand-sewed the lapels, and they were paid by the piece. He worked hard and saved all the time; he was very frugal.

That was just when the labor movement was beginning to stir, and it was in that industry where the movement really took hold. But I don't think that his place was organized at that time. He would be the kind of a guy who wouldn't like that stress of being in an industry that was beginning to have turmoil in it so he'd want to pull away from it. He was pretty much that way.

Also, he just didn't like the piecework and the very long hours. He was an independent kind of person, and he was also one who did better on his own—he was pretty much a loner all his life. But he knew if he was going to get my mother over here he really had to earn some money. So he saved up enough money, got her over here, and about a year and a half later I was born. By that time he had bought into the tailor business that was two doors west of where I am now and set up his own business.

My mother was pretty gregarious and friendly and open. She was a defender; she stood up for us and defended the house, and if she felt there was danger she'd be the one to alert us and things like that. She was barely educated and she could write only with difficulty. My father, on the other hand, had gone through school in Italy, and he could write fluently, read fluently, and taught himself to read English. My mother didn't have the time; she was burdened with all the rotten chores that women are always burdened with, plus helping him with the business. She learned English only as we children began to speak it.

I spoke nothing but Italian until I went to school, and that was also true of my brothers. When I went to kindergarten I couldn't speak a word of English, not a word, and that was true of all my other schoolmates. We had this most wonderful teacher, Miss Kelly we called her, but her name was Miss McClellan, and she just knew how to teach. I don't know—there are two teachers that stand firmly in my mind, and that is Miss Kelly, my first grade teacher, and then the fourth grade teacher. After the fourth grade I was already assimilated. Miss Kelly just took us and made us feel at home right away and spoke to us in English, you know.

We were allowed to go to kindergarten at the age of five, and you understand like animals do, with gestures—"Come and sit down," etc. In first grade, that was where we really began to communicate. That first grade teacher certainly had a chore, but she really got us ready. The school I went to was Andrew Jackson, just a few doors away. They were great teachers in those days; they were children of immigrants (Irish) themselves. Their parents had come here many years before.

We went to public school. My father could never really afford Catholic school and didn't want to spend the money for it, and was not that devout a Catholic, so he had no difficulty in the choice. He felt that we should go to the public school. I did all right in school. I was never in the top of my class; my grades were O.K. and I was always in the good middle. I didn't do too well in math, though.

They were all Italian in grammar school. When we were on the playground or in the neighborhood we spoke Italian, but I began to speak English fairly quickly after the first and second grade. In addition to my learning English, and listening to it all day long, there were other children that were ahead of me that were all speaking English. So I've always been uncertain about my feeling about English as a second language in schools today because it didn't take me long to learn. In some areas of the city, pretty much like it was in my time, the kids all speak one language. But in some areas, on the North Side, for instance, you'll have children of Chinese background, and Japanese, Vietnamese, so that they're all coming from different languages so that makes it difficult to teach English as a second language.

The dialects in our neighborhood were so different because we had the people from Bari who spoke in a very different kind of way. For instance, when we say, "Come here," we say, "Veni qua," and they would say "Viena do," so there were little differences. Their inflection was different, too, like the way American southerners speak as opposed to northerners. Sicilian would be like a different language altogether. Everyone spoke their own dialect; only people like my father, who couldn't understand some of these dialects, would insist on speaking Italian and force the other person to speak Italian to him. It was much easier; everybody wrote in Italian, you didn't write a dialect.

But I want to say this, too, other schools in the neighborhood would be apt to have a mixture of Italian and Greek. Around Harrison and Halsted was a school, no longer in existence, and the Greek families and the Italian families went to that school. And if you went a little farther west there were still some Irish families, so there was a mix of Irish and Italian. They didn't hang around too long, but they were in the environment. The Irish were in a community where everybody spoke a language they didn't know, and the Italians were in an English-speaking city, so I think people moved away from one another, not as much for the fact that they didn't want to see the change around them, as for the fact that they wanted to be with other people that were their own kind.

There must have been a feeling, "Oh, my God, look at these Italians moving in here," but I don't think it had overtones of great dislike. I remember as a young girl being in a bar with our group and people who were nearby were talking among themselves and one young girl said, "Oh, we had to move out of there because all of the Italians were moving in." Even so, some of the Irish families remained; there were Irish people living across the street, living down on Blue Island

Avenue, living over on Aberdeen. They were sprinkled around. They loved their houses and they loved the church, Holy Family, and they wanted to stay.

There were some Mexicans in the neighborhood, too. I think in the very beginning the Italians looked down on them. I remember that when things were very tough when we were just coming out of the Depression we had a vacancy in this building and a Mexican family came to rent an apartment. I remember my father and mother saying, "Should we or shouldn't we?" Finally, he said, "It's ridiculous, why not?" So they rented, and that family was the first Mexican family in this area where we are.

Right after that it was obvious that there were more Mexican families moving into this neighborhood, and there was still some, "I'm better than you," kind of feeling about it, but it didn't last very long because before you knew it, the young people changed things. They were going to school together, or they were dating. I would say that after a very few years that feeling of animosity was gone. Some people might have harbored this feeling of "I'm better than you," but it was not anything overt any more. There was the same religion and family structure, and the fact that they both have baptism and communion and confirmation, all of these similarities, and, they're hardworking. The lady that lived here, Flora, was a single mother with three children. She married later, but she worked hard, and she brought up these three kids, and they were wonderful kids.

When I went to church when I was really young I went to Our Lady of Pompeii, and that's where my mother went too. Later I went to a church that was torn down for the University of Illinois called Holy Guardian Angel, and that's because by that time I was going to Hull-House, and I had friends who lived around that church. I'd spend Sundays at Hull-House and so I went there.

My father was, I don't know, maybe he was an agnostic because when my parents would have these discussions and my mother would fuss with him, he'd look at a picture of Jesus and he'd say, "But he's just a man like me." And I'd think, "Wow! He's going to be struck dead if he says things like that."

But he didn't make much of it, it's just that he didn't totally believe, and I think, from what he said later, it was the church in Italy, the church itself, that caused him to feel that way, and he carried over that feeling and resentment about the church itself here. He didn't like the way the church ordered peoples' lives around. They had so many rules—you can't do this and you can't do that, and he just didn't like that.

One of the big events in the neighborhood was when the visiting nurses used to come down the streets. The Visiting Nurses Association came from the Mary Crane Nursery at Hull-House, and all of the women just looked forward to their coming because they examined all of the children and asked our parents what we were eating for breakfast. My mother would tell them, and they'd say, "Oh, no," because when it was cold we'd get eggnogs beaten up with wine. We'd just have bread and milk when we were just babies. Even when we were going to school we had coffee and milk and bread. We used to break up bread like soup and put it in the coffee and eat it, and on a cold day we had eggnog with wine that my father made.

The nurses then taught the mothers and showed them what kind of food children had to eat. They brought samples of it and helped prepare it for them. They came over with their bags, house to house, and when it was time for the children to be inoculated, they made sure that the mothers took the children over to the Mary Crane nurseries. They made sure that the children were examined for tonsillectomies. I remember that the nurse told my mother that she would have to be prepared in a few years because we would have to have our tonsils out. Everybody had to do that, but they waited at least until you were in school before they removed your tonsils.

They came every week, or every other week, and if there was a new baby, they really spent time. When someone like that comes around they have a kind of an authority that's just in their presence, and it's a friendly situation; they're not imposing, they're offering. And so the mothers really welcomed them. Most of the nurses spoke English when they came around, but they made themselves known. It wasn't difficult to know what they were talking about because they were taking stuff out of the bag, and then performing whatev-

Photo by Carolyn Eastwood.

This view westward along Taylor Street shows Florence Scala
in front of the door that opened onto her father's tailoring
shop—space previously housing a tavern.

er. They would show the mother that you have to buy this, and
cook it, and they would demonstrate cooking it up, you know.

When I was pre-school we always lived behind the store.
In that time my father was in partnership and then he bought
his partner out. After that he had to leave that store because
somebody bought that building who wanted to put their own
business in there. This building I'm in now became available
so my father purchased it. He was paying for this building and
getting a second mortgage on it, and a third mortgage on it
with the Depression, and finally he was making his final
payments during the Depression or soon after.

We bought it from a very nice family, and I don't know
what the mortgage situation was, whether the family held the
mortgage, or if it was through a bank. All I know is, when Phil
Ferrone, whose mother and father owned this building, used to
stop by to see my father, it was always on the friendliest of
bases. I guess he must have held the mortgage because I
remember seeing once or twice that my father gave him
money. He probably held the mortgage and never really put

the screws on my father; this is what made it possible.

The Ferrones had purchased the building from Irish people; there was an Irish tavern here, even while the Ferrones owned the building. On the ground floor was a tavern and upstairs was where they lived. The indented area in this downstairs room was the bar, and later when my father had his tailor shop here, that was where he hung suits. This building is more than 100 years old, built about 1863. It does sag some, caused mostly by their rolling big kegs of beer on the Miller Street side. They'd roll them right down to the posts that were downstairs, so part of the building has settled.

When I was pre-school I don't remember playing outside on the sidewalks because my mother wouldn't let us do that. In the back there was a little yard, and we could play in the yard. I could play outside if I stayed on the doorstep of the store, and there were other little children that were outside, but I had to stay on the doorstep—it was a nice expansive one—and there was another shorter step that went right into the store. Our family sat out on the doorstep, too.

There were shops all the way down Taylor Street to Morgan—a cigar store, Carmi's hat shop, and a place where they just made sausages. Right on the corner we had a wonderful place that sold window shades; they were a French family and they made all these cut shades. They were here many years when there were French people in the Notre Dame parish. Next to them was a shoe store where we all bought our shoes. On the corner was a place where you could buy records and Victrolas.

But the best thing was where the Tuscany restaurant is now. We had the best grocery—meat market and grocery. They were quick to understand that they could combine. You know, in the old days you had the meat market, you had the grocer, and also on the corner across the street we had a fish market, all separate. But over there with the combined meat market and grocer—we thought they were something! And way back when, there was always another place where people made cheese, ricotta cheese and mozzarella cheese. It was a wonderful store.

There was a wonderful bakery owned by the Armando

Above: Much of the life of the Italian neighborhood went on in front of houses such as this two-flat on the 1100 block of South Racine.

Below: Neighbors exchanged gossip, shared special events such as a new car, and met each other frequently on errands to all the small shops in the neighborhood.

family, and all he made was bread—no cookies or anything like that. I loved that because there were times when he'd send clothes over to my father's tailor shop to be done up, and he would pick up his things and not pay for them and he'd say, take it out in trade and we'd get our bread.

There's a lamb shop here today that has a history, too. It's been in the neighborhood for years and it was forced to move because of the university—three times. They located where they thought it was going to be O.K., they were on the corner of Taylor and Blue Island, then they had to move over to Blue Island and Polk, and then they had to leave there and come over here. It was an Italian boy who became partners with a Greek. He does very well because they come from all over just to shop here.

HOLIDAYS AND FESTIVALS

HOLIDAYS WERE REALLY nice, even before my brothers were born, but when they came, it was even nicer. My father didn't work on Sunday; that was so nice, so nice for my mother, too, because it seemed to me that she was always working. My father was great on Sundays because he would take us out. My mother would put the food on to cook and she'd put it down real low, and he'd take us either to the lake or to Lincoln Park. When he took us to Grant Park, that wasn't so much of a treat except when the fountains were on. In Lincoln Park there was the conservatory, and the zoo (you had to go several times to take it all in), and the lagoon. We brought food and had our picnics there.

The Taylor Street streetcar was marvelous; it went all the way to Sedgewick and we'd get off at Sedgwick and Clark and walk from there to Lincoln Park, about two or three blocks. There was so much to do there—you could go three or four Sundays in a row and still not take it all in. These excursions were whenever the weather was nice enough to go out, but mostly we didn't go out in wintertime. We'd also go to places like Riverview and the circus which was held in the Colosseum (on Wabash). It's been torn down now.

Festivals were great events for everybody in the neighborhood. We looked forward to them. They were all religious-based, but that was just a front for gambling because they had a lottery. They sold tickets for a game called *tumbolo*, a very popular Italian game where they put all these tickets in a drum and they would turn the drum around and pick out winners.

They also had a big table set aside on the street for men who were playing Italian card games, gambling right outside on the street. One of them would be held on Morgan Street, I remember. It was separate from the church in that it was a society, for example, Societa dei Cuono (Santa Cuono). To celebrate this saint's feast day they would gather the banner and a replica of this figure as a statue and take it to the church—in a parade with a band—where they had a mass in celebration of this saint's feast day.

Then they would parade through the neighborhood carrying this statue and stop and play their music (they were such con artists) at an establishment, two or three times on a block. The women would rush out (and my mother was one of them) and pin dollars on the vestment of this saint and then kneel on the street and say a prayer. My father just didn't like that; oh, he didn't like that! He wasn't mean about it, but he didn't like it, and he ridiculed my mother for doing what she did.

At first when I saw her doing that, I thought, "Oh, my mother is so holy." It must have hurt her knees like hell on that concrete, but later I thought, "Oh, I wish she wouldn't do that," because I realized, she's giving those guys money. I would say, "Don't do that, don't go out there and do that, I'll give them the money." And finally, she just didn't do it anymore.

Most of these societies grew out of the church transplanted from Italy here because they came from some little town. The people that venerated this saint came from a town just outside the city of Naples, and they made a big thing of that feast day in that little town. So when they came here those feast days weren't necessarily celebrated in the same way, but they were noted only because there were enough people who came from there that they wanted to continue the observance of that saint's feast day, and so the church accommodated that. But right after the event was over the church had nothing to do with this group of people.

Those festivals were great because they provided the entertainment that street festivals do today all over the city. The whole neighborhood just waited for that. It was time to have a good time, have good food, and the parades. I used to love to be awakened on a Sunday morning with the band going through the neighborhood announcing that the festival was beginning and that they were going to mass and all that stuff. So they paraded once a day during the five days of the festival. There was a lot of gambling and drinking, and of course, sometimes there were fights—a mixture of different kinds of excitement.

They were in different places. There was one on Morgan Street (people from Naples), and there was one on Sangamon Street (people from Bari). You had to get a license in order to close off the street during those days. They would block out the area where they wanted to have the festival. We had about three different festivals.

My father just didn't understand why he had to close his business on Thanksgiving. That was not a holiday that they were familiar with. Of course, later on they embraced it. But Christmas was really special, and there was not a lot of emphasis on toys; there really wasn't. We got one toy that we all shared; for instance, a bicycle. My mother might give us small presents, little things that you could hardly remember any more. We didn't celebrate the Day of the Befana; I don't remember ever celebrating that. That's the Italian festival when they give toys, etc. We knew about it because they told us the story of La Befana, but it was not a holiday here.

For Christmas itself, that's when my mother would bake the cakes and the cookies and had a special dinner. I used to have to help her with the cooking. My job was to roll out the ravioli dough and make the raviolis. With that dough we made ravioli and pasta as well. We didn't have a macaroni machine; for this we used to have to cut it by hand. There was a man who made actual macaroni right down the block, and he would have these big poles in the store and have the pasta just hanging from the poles and then he would lift them down and we would buy the fresh, dry pasta that he made. It was wonderful. You could buy it by the week, but you didn't have to, you could just go down the street and buy what you needed.

I had a crinkly cutter for the ravioli, but I would have to crimp the edges down with a fork which gave it a nice pattern. At first I'd think, "Oh, I don't want to make this ravioli," but once I got going, I liked it, and what was challenging was to see how many of them I could get out of that dough. My mother mixed and when it was ready I'd knead it a little bit and then start rolling it out. But we all did it; my father would do it sometimes, my mother did it; mostly she would never have time because there were so many other things she was preparing.

On Christmas Eve, that was very special, the Vigil of Christmas. I think the anticipation of the meal was as much as going to Midnight Mass, but the thing was to buy as many different kinds of fish as you could and prepare them all in a different way and have everybody at the table—Christmas Eve before mass. By the time you sat down to eat, there was all the cooking that had to go on, especially in this family where there was only such a small family—you sat down to eat when it was already dark at about 6:00 or 7:00 and by the time you were finished, it was just about time to clear everything off and go to church.

Even today, for myself, I will stay home and cook a variety of fish. It was always just family; we didn't have relatives here in Chicago. The dinner today is partly traditional, but partly it has been added onto. It was a day that you didn't eat meat, Christmas Eve, so you'd eat a lot of fish.

Christmas Day you'd have to get up early and start doing all this other stuff from scratch. The making of the ravioli and the chopped stuff. My mother had soup, and when we had soup with our meal that was special. We had soup as a main dish, but when we had this soup with tiny meatballs and with escarole, that was Christmas dinner. That soup was made with beef stock, and it was the best I've ever had; I can never make soup like that. Instead of celery we used cardoon, huge stalks and they look like celery, a very sweet-tasting vegetable, not sharp like celery can be. That was cut up in little pieces, so all you had was the cardoon, a little rice, and tiny meatballs, which I had to make. We had polenta and a risotto dish once in a while.

We rarely had cookies or cake—only when my mother made cake because it was somebody's birthday or maybe because my father might have a taste for it, but it was rare that we had cookies or cake. When she would make cookies she would make a lot; they were wonderful cookies. Of course, they would get hard as a rock, but that would give us a reason to dunk them. They were delicious even dunked in the wine.

My mother always made a cake (by hand) for birthdays. Later on when we got a little older, we could invite our friends to the birthday party and she would serve this nice cake in the afternoon right after school. There weren't any presents given, just the cake, that was enough. We didn't get presents for birthdays; I don't remember getting any. We'd get little things from time to time, but even the kids that came to the birthday parties didn't bring presents and we didn't bring presents to them.

Sometimes my father would go somewhere to buy supplies or something and on the way back he would buy a bag of Hershey Kisses, but he would put that bag in a closet in the kitchen way up high, and even he would have to get on a chair to get those chocolate kisses. So we didn't know he would have them, and he'd say, "Go in the store and ask the spider what he has for you today." So we would go in the store and sing a little song. "O.K. come in now," he'd say. And on the floor were three or four kisses. And that's the way he'd distribute the kisses; then we'd forget that he had them. It was the best time! I loved spiders; I'd never kill them.

We got Italian ice from peddlers. There was a man who lived on Carpenter Street who did lemonade and pizzas and he would go with this great big thing on his head with pizzas. He'd always have to go home and get some more, so you could see that his range was limited. He'd go down Taylor Street selling the pizzas by the piece, and in the summertime, more often than not, he would sell his ices.

When we came home from school it would be just a

sandwich and sliced tomatoes. At lunchtime I would always be asked, what do you want to eat tonight? For the evening meal we would have one main dish and a salad, and fruit for dessert, and we would only have meat on the weekend. When we were little my father started buying pop from a peddler, so he'd buy a case of mixed flavors and we could only have that at dinnertime. We couldn't just go and open up a bottle of pop when we came home from school or anything like that. He had his wine and we would have wine flavored with the pop.

My father made his own wine—white wine that was very delicious—from muscatel grapes. One of the men of the neighborhood had a cigar store, and as a sideline, in October he'd go to the railroad tracks off of Ashland, where they had the wine grapes. There were trains that parked off on the side special, and everybody in the city who wanted to buy wine grapes went there and bought these grapes. They would have one man in the neighborhood who would be responsible for hauling these grapes, and he would bring them over here to the neighborhood. The whole place smelled of grapes and in the alley you would see all the piles of dark grape skins. Most of the people made red wine.

My father would go there to collect the boxes he wanted. He'd always mix some red with the white grapes and then he would get them and brought them over here. Then would come the business of making the wine and was that a job! He had a regular winemaking press and he and my mother would work on it.

I remember he and my mother working down in the basement, putting the grapes in the press and turning the press. They would press the grapes three times. They had a crusher first and then it would go into this big thing that would press all the juice out. It took them several days to do this job. Then they put it in barrels. He only made about two barrels. He didn't make a lot, and he just let it sit around in the basement until he thought it was ready to be used. It probably took the best part of a year, and he'd go down and taste it. He used to make the best muscatel.

My father didn't drink a lot at all. He might have a glass of wine at dinner time, and that's all, so the wine lasted him a long time. My brothers and I had wine, but my mother used to dilute it with lemon soda.

MY PARENTS' WORK

IT SEEMED TO me that my mother had so much to do. She was a seamstress so she helped my father in the store. She was working all the time doing all the putzy work such as basting, sewing, and blind-stitching that he couldn't get to because there was too much to do. At first he was doing a lot of real tailoring and then later on he just cut that out because he couldn't keep up with the alterations and repairs. He'd have to press the suits and then there was sewing buttons on and fixing tears, and she did a lot of that work. She sat down at the sewing machine and just did that every day.

In addition to that my mother did what housewives do. She had to go shopping, prepare meals, and of course, doing the laundry was not easy in those days. She had these babies, too, and they were by her while she was doing these things. So we were kind of close in that respect because I'd have to take care of my brothers until I got to the age when I wanted to be with my friends, and then I'd give her a lot of trouble. I'd say, "Oh, I don't want to do it—I don't want to do it," and she'd say, "You have to do it, or you're not going to get . . . " and they'd punish me in some way.

Eventually my father switched over to just doing alterations and cleaning because more and more people then were using the cleaners. In the beginning it wasn't such a big thing. If you had your clothes cleaned at the cleaners, wow, you had money, but then it became affordable for most people. That's where a big part of his business was in the cleaning and pressing and then in alterations and repairs. One of my jobs was to pull down the men's cuffs and brush out the lint that would gather in the cuff. This was when I was young enough to be told to do that—later on I rebelled. And later on he didn't give a darn, he just sent them to the cleaners with the lint. He had them picked up and delivered. The profit that he could realize out of that was limited, and he never had help outside the family.

GRADUATION AND FIRST COMMUNION

FOR 8TH GRADE graduation we got dressed up, and it was a bittersweet kind of time. You were really saying good-bye to a lot of your friends who were maybe not going on to the same school. At home it was kind of an important time, but not as important as when we took our First Communion.

That was more of a recognition of a special day when we took our First Communion. That's partly because you had a godmother that had to be entertained as well. I just had a godmother and my brothers had a godfather. Your godmother was the sponsor at your Confirmation, meaning that she promised that she would be responsible for seeing you would have a Catholic education if anything happened to your parents, and she put her hand on your shoulder when the bishop came by.

Your godmother gave you a present, and the traditional present was a wristwatch. It was more of an imposition on the godmother than anything else. You were allowed (at least I was) to pick whom you wanted, so I picked this girl who was the daughter of close friends of my mother and we remained as close friends. I always looked up to her as my godmother and she looked down to me as her godchild. Then she got married and moved away and had children and we didn't see each other any more. Now she lives in California and we correspond. Usually you select from a circle that's close to your parents. Most drift apart because they get married. If the godparents had money they would buy your Communion dress.

HULL-HOUSE

WHEN I WAS in high school Hull-House was really the catalyst for our activities and it gave us a place to go to. It seems to me that that's one reason young people get in trouble is that they have no place to hang out that gives them a sense of place. Hull-House offered us that. We were active in the little theater there and the dancing class, and there were groups for different age groups. In the groups that we formed, we were also linked together in friendship. When I went to Hull-House I started in the middle group called the Ballerinas; that was a group of kids about 10 or 12 years old. When I was a teenager our group was called the Harlequins.

Edith de Nancrede was the woman who led us in these activities of the dance and the theater, and she was a remarkable person. She was from France, she wore a cape, and she was really a Left Bank-type artist. We were really lucky because she was marvelous. She was the one that I think opened the doors to the arts. At home I was pretty much immersed in the music of opera because my father loved opera and we had records. At Hull-House that was expanded for us. We did lovely folk dances and and ballroom dancing and also the Isadora Duncan kind of dancing. We didn't use chiffon scarves, but we did use some scarves that she would bring. We knew how to dance very naturally as we got older. So Hull-House extended us, at least it did me. Music was important and music is still very enriching.

At first they had trouble getting the boys to go, but there was a kind of magic about it—"That's the place you gotta go to." The boys were hard to come by, but not for very long, as soon as two or three of them joined the group, then others joined. The nice thing about Hull-House, they were linked, not only in the dancing classes, but the same fellows were also on the basketball team. And all of the girls went to the basketball games. It was a kind of activity that took everybody in.

Edith de Nancrede held this diverse age group together and she was an incredible personality. Woe on you if you mixed up something, she'd get so mad, but then, once she blew up she'd forget all about it. She died later, and when she was sick, all of us were just devastated by it. We had a vigil in Hull-House for a whole week before she died. This was probably when I was about 17 or 18. It was a very great loss for all of us.

They didn't try to replace her particularly. Hull-House was

Edith de Nancrede who led the dance and theater programs at Hull-House was a special influence in opening new worlds to the young people in her classes.

going through some kind of change at the time when she died. They had another person come in to do the theater for a short time, but that didn't work out and I think it was because we just gave that person a hard time. Then another person came in who was much smarter and did not try to revive the theater with that same group. Instead they started a small theater group and brought in other people as well so that those who were interested in that could join. I joined that group, but it was nothing like Edith's group.

With Edith's group we would put on plays, maybe two consecutive weekends, and we'd do about three or four plays a year. We did contemporary plays and some classics. Most of her serious plays were done with the older groups. The middle group did *Midsummer Night's Dream*. She had help, she didn't do it alone. We met once a week on Saturday. Some from the group went into theater, but never got to be well known. One or two went into politics, and some became lawyers well known in their field.

The neat thing about the de Nancrede groups was that there was a mix; there were a lot of Jewish people, Italian, some Mexican, and Greeks. However, there were no blacks; blacks were not active in the Hull-House programs when I was going there. There were a lot of black families living over by 14th and Jefferson. In this particular area (Taylor-Halsted) there only a few black families and they didn't go to Hull-House. There were a few families that lived over on what was Blue Island Avenue, not far from here, and a few black families east of Halsted, maybe in one or two buildings. There were blacks who came to Hull-House, but not in any real numbers.

There was only one black girl who came to our classes, and she came from an educated family; her parents were sending her on to school. We used to call her "Bucky"; her name was Louise, she became a school teacher. And she was part of our group, and she'd come to summer camp, and most of the time she was the only black person there. She didn't seem to be out of place and she'd fit in and all.

You know I've often thought about that, about the fact that while I was going to Hull-House I was not aware that they reached out to blacks and brought them into the program. I know that they were surrounded by masses of people (immigrants), and they had all they could do to keep themselves above water, but I can't remember their ever reaching out to the blacks. I may be wrong on this, but I think that the people who were living in the area at the time when I was growing up, most of them, early immigrants, were not as apt to be prejudiced in the way that their children became later on. I do believe that. I say that because my father was never prejudiced. He was exceptional, but on the other hand, other people around here were not that prejudiced.

Everyone accepted their position in this geography. Blacks lived on Blue Island and there were a lot of whites that lived there too, but I cannot remember that there was a lot of hostility. There may have been, but I do not remember it. Kids had a territorial thing, and black kids would be subjected to that. I know that my brothers wouldn't dare get out of their territory. They'd get beaten up by other Italian kids, other gangs.

I still think they (Hull-House) could have reached out and had blacks coming to Hull-House in some way by participating in some of the programs there even if they weren't having black people at first in an integrated program. There should have been black people coming to Hull-House for all of us to see, and then if there was a way to blend in the groups either through sports or through the theater or whatever, that should have been done—even if there was a black theater group, apart from the white.

I have thought about that, not during those years, many years later. Right in our midst was the Jewish theater going on, and we knew it, we accepted it. Glickman's Theater was on Blue Island Avenue. We never went to it. We wouldn't have been able to understand it anyway. It's true, some of these worlds just never met. You were aware of them, you saw them, and where there was a difference in the language there was no incentive.

Early on I made the choice that I really wanted my friends to be the people that I met at Hull-House, the girls that I met there rather than the people I grew up with. There were some people from the neighborhood that went there, but my own girlfriends here on this block, and my dearest friends who lived across the street from me, never were motivated to go to Hull-House. What had a great deal of influence in their lives was the church, the Catholic Church, and the streets and Sheridan Park. They had their social activities there. I went there too, off and on.

Once I made the break and decided Hull-House was where I wanted to go, that was when my grade school teacher stopped in to see my father and said, "You should send the children to Hull-House. There's a lot for them to do there and they won't be out on the streets." Her family was one of the early Irish settlers and they had a bird store on Blue Island. My mother and father then said that I should go and register. And that was the beginning and then my brothers went.

At Hull-House I found girls whose parents were second generation, mine were first generation, so they seemed awfully different to me. Their families were different. I was so shy and they were more open. When I first went there I really felt very self-conscious, very self-conscious. I dressed differently, and people were not very friendly—you know how girls can sometimes be—but I persisted. Every week I went to these classes, to the dancing, and I joined the theater. And they eventually broke down. So, it didn't take very long. People that I began to chum with there were people that I spent the rest of my life with; they were closest to me. All of them are gone now.

OTHER TEEN ACTIVITIES

WHEN I WENT to McKinley High School I didn't really participate in any activities; social activities were centered around Hull-House. There was not much going on, and there more activities for boys than for girls. Also, high school was considerably farther away from home than I was used to being and I would rather come home. We took the street car to and from school.

I did date some when I was about 16. I had a date for my prom, but I didn't have a regular boyfriend until I was almost ready to graduate from high school. His name was Phil and we were dating for the whole year until we graduated. Then it just petered out slowly after graduation. After that I dated someone from our Hull-House group and that lasted less than a year. On dates mostly we went to the movies or we had group dates—rent a wagon and go on a hayride, dancing at the Aragon Ballroom, that sort of thing. We had parties in our homes, not extravagant parties, just get-togethers, dancing and pop and cookies.

I went to church regularly during that time, but I never got involved in the church activities. Most of us who were palling around together didn't do that, although a couple of the girls were pretty devoted to their religion.

I never did baby-sitting in my teens; there was no such thing. The thing I did while I was in my teens was that I cleaned apartments at Hull-House after school. I was a regular with a couple of women there, and I got a big $2 a week. And with those $2, there was another gal who did the same thing, and we used our money to go swimming, go downtown to the Medinah Athletic Club, or something like that, and spend 50 cents to get into the pool to go swimming and then go to Toffenetti's for coffee. That was a big night.

We went to the Maxwell Street Market regularly. At first, when I was in grammar school I used to go to the market on occasion because a girlfriend of mine sold shopping bags there. She'd sell the shopping bags for a nickel, so I helped her. There was a man who sold these bags and we would buy them from him; he was sitting outside. I think I did it for one whole summer. But we went to the market often just to walk around, buy things. My mother would take us when we needed winter clothes. More often we would end up buying the coats and things on the shops on Halsted. We'd start out on Maxwell, but what I think ruined it for my mother was the need to have to bargain. She was never sure that she wasn't being cheated. She'd rather shop Halsted where she might bargain, but not so intense.

Later when I was in my teens one of the girls in the Harlequins was always dressed so beautifully and we knew that her family didn't have a lot of money. Where did she buy these clothes? She finally broke down and said that she bought them on Maxwell Street, and she took us to this place. They were an outlet for some of the better houses on Market Street where they made very nice clothes. They were really neat things, because what you were buying were just the odds and ends of the wholesalers and whatever he could pick up wherever they were auctioning them. We went there often; as a matter of fact, we used to go there every Saturday. My mother didn't buy food there. We had everything in the neighborhood, but we bought our hot dogs there. We went there for jazz records, too. You knew just where to go for things.

Gangs, Crime, and Politics In the Neighborhood

THOSE WERE THE bad days for crime, I think. We all knew that the area was controlled by these adult gangs. Unlike the gangs today, they didn't bother or hurt the people who lived in the area all that much although some of the younger hoodlums would burglarize a local store or home. That was not uncommon, and yet it was not something that we saw happening that frequently. It was unpleasant because these hoodlums rather controlled the area; it was more a problem for my brothers than it was for me. But these hoodlums became the lieutenants who then graduated into the crime. The politicians were just awful; they never really helped anybody here in the area.

And the people that were seen as the ones you needed to go to if you were in trouble or needed help were not the police or these young hoodlums. The ones you went to were the Italians who had immigrated here who had developed La Societa groups that were organized around a town name or a saint name. And those people were kind of sub-lieutenants to what was becoming Al Capone-type of crime. You went to them if you were in trouble.

For example, I'm having trouble with so-and-so. He's making it impossible for me to conduct my business, and I want you to go and talk to him and tell him that he's got to stop that. Most often it would cost a little money. Sometimes it didn't cost any money if you were known to these people, if you were from their town. Then they would go to someone and they would be recognized right away and they would say, "Come on now, you got to stop that; we don't want you to do any of that." And the problem would be solved in that way— just the threatening presence.

So those were not good times. Remember that we were all aware of that hierarchy of power there. We all knew it and we kind of recognized it and had a sort of respect for it. My father had to recognize it because he was a tailor, and these men would come in and put their clothing down and say what they wanted done and just walk out the door, commanding, and he, of course, complied and he did what was needed to be done in the tailoring. I remember my mother and father talking about it in whispers.

The politicians were completely controlled by the hoods. That's what we heard, and we knew the families. One of the things they did right away was to try to control the courts and the police. They got some of the local people to get into the police department, and the police, some of them were corrupt.

We saw them getting money right on the street. Some of the precinct captains and some of the people who eventually got into power in a small way were related, so it was just one happy family. Gangsters and hoodlums controlled politics in this ward, absolutely.

As far as contributions to the party, that would only come if you had a political job. If you had a political job, every month you paid your dues; you just paid your dues as if you belonged to a union. The other way they got their money, they were able to control the insurance business; you had to buy your house and business insurance from the ward committeeman or the alderman. George Dunne still owns a big insurance agency, and John D'Arco; that's the way they made their money, in the insurance business.

And the interesting thing about that business is that it was established from the earliest days and passed on and on, so that when I became ward committeeman, while I benefited from that business, it was never mine. I couldn't will it to my kid or anything. I maintained it, I ran it, it was a corporation. Every year I had to send over the dividends from the business, and I received a considerable amount of profit from it as well by running it, so I became pretty wealthy. I could expand the business, and all the better for me, and in this area it was great because they had the Loop that they controlled in addition to all the little businesses along Halsted that they controlled. I must say though that they didn't force every single one to buy this insurance.

My father didn't buy insurance from them; they didn't come here. And too, all the businesses along this street were really small businesses. They got all those businesses, for sure, along Halsted Street because there was a lot of business there. They got the taverns in the neighborhood. They became extremely wealthy by getting that tribute from them. They'd force them to buy the insurance policies, and once they got the insurance, it was a set thing, because then you renewed your policy.

We can go all the way back to, let's say, when John Granata (Republican) was ward committeeman. Granata went on and on, and he was never drawn into the worst part of it because he was very smart. When he became state representative he was the one who was able to push through some legislation that they wanted. He was the leader of what was then called the West Side Bloc, and there were these West Side reps in different parts of the city who served the needs of the syndicate in getting certain legislation passed. It always had to do with how you can file a case or something like that, but they also controlled the legislation concerning insurance companies. They were deep into the insurance business.

We always worried at home about the effect of the gangsters. My father was always worried about that. There was one mean fellow, one of the meanest in the area. We called him "Irish," that was his nickname, and he came with a sawed-off shotgun. It was a gorgeous summer night, and he came down Miller Street, and everybody was sitting outside, and there was a lovely young woman from Sicily, gorgeous lady, who lived down right near here. She had a poodle and she loved this dog. Irish started to just shoot up the street and everybody was screaming and running around and her little dog was terrified. She was screaming for everyone to pick up the dog, and then Irish stopped shooting and walked away laughing and laughing. I remember how terrified she was.

I hated the hoodlums. There was a very nice man, Alessandro, who was gay, and he lived here on Miller Street. The Italians didn't torment him or anything. The hoodlums would grab him and jostle him and push him when he was on his way to work. Well, this went on for years, and the only protection he ever had was from the women. He went crazy and ended up in an insane asylum, and I think of him from time to time, how lonely his life was here. He probably left Italy because he was tormented there, and came here only to receive more torment, and mostly from these lousy hoodlums.

These guys strutted all over the place and they acted as though they owned the neighborhood. They'd sit on our front steps and make a lot of noise. My mother went crazy because she didn't like them sitting on her front steps. She would get out there and ask them to leave, and my father would yell at her for doing that. One time they did that at night and she went upstairs and filled a bucket full of water and she dumped it on them. Actually, what she did worked out; eventually, they just didn't sit on her steps anymore. At least she had that property sanctified for herself.

They would hang out in front of the undertaker's down the street, 10 or 15 of them in front of the store there. You couldn't walk past it, you'd have to go across the street. If you walked past them, you were just asking for it. But if you got off the bus at the corner, you had no choice, you were just right there. They were no good, and a lot of those guys were high up in the hierarchy (e.g., Sam Giancana). It was not easy living in that environment. And you know when people glamorize the neighborhood, they choose not to remember the way it was. I was glad when they began to get them off the streets.

Were there good politicians? I can't think of any. I can't imagine anyone holding public office that wasn't interested in terms of controlling for power. The mayors of that time were no good either.

Women were in politics only as precinct captains. Usually they were widows who needed a political job and they were usually the best precinct captains. But there were two I remember: Bessie Mazzoni, she was a Republican, and she was terrific. And then the other one, Mary Meyers, she was a Jewish gal who married an Italian. I never knew what her married name was. She was fantastic. They were so good and so skilled that they deserved to be aldermen because they knew their area so well.

First, they could get the vote out; and second, if you went to them with a problem, they would take care of it. I say, "My son's in trouble with the police, can you help me, or can you take care of a parking ticket." They would take care of it because they needed your vote. Third, if you needed a job, they weren't always able to help you, but they were a good first step. Fourth, if they knew that the family was in real need, they would go out of their way to help them get a job.

Jane Addams said in her book, the precinct captain and the alderman performed so many services that people needed, that their power was secured. Bessie Mazzoni was seen, you know, as an important person in this area and so was Mary Meyers. This was in the '30s.

My brothers weren't pressured to join the gangs, but they

were victimized by gangs; for example, gang members would break up baseball games. There was a group of fellows around here who had nothing to do with the gangs; they had their own little group. But they always had to defend their own turf as well. My brothers never got really hurt, but they got beaten up. One time one of the neighborhood toughs was beating up on my brother and I jumped in on it. Seeing it happen really just made me so mad, and he never bothered us again.

There have been problems between gangs of different ethnic groups, but I wasn't too aware of it, not in the way that we see a structured kind of gang thing, but a group of Italians might hit on a small group of Mexicans. Since they were going to the same schools together, that's where the conflicts might have been, but it wasn't part of the community life as I remember it. If there was a line drawn, it was in a very marked place. For instance, if people from our area went south of Roosevelt Road in the Jewish area they were likely to have some problems because that was really outside of our neighborhood. The guys liked to go south of Roosevelt Road to Stanford Park where there were bath houses. So if any of the kids here went there, there was going to be trouble. That kind of thing.

You know when we talk about gangs here in this neighborhood, we're talking about real gangs, junior gangs to Al Capone. That's a different kind of thing than I'm familiar with in the city today. The gangs that we had here, the Italian gangs, were not too turf conscious. They were thieves, and it was a business. Part of it was involved in alcohol. Then when Prohibition was repealed they got involved in busting unions and corrupting unions. And they were corrupting everything, and that's the kind of gang that was deadly, that scared parents. This was a structure, these were not just people out defending turf or flashing signs. This was an operation and it cast a pall over the area. They never bothered you directly, but that power was there and it just affected everybody's lives.

The Mexicans were nowhere involved in that kind of gang structure. Because they were new in the neighborhood, they were victimized. It took several years until they were accepted, so they didn't form gangs until many years later. I remember as a young woman thinking—wow, the Mexicans are starting gangs now. They've come up in the world.

After High School Graduation

When I graduated from high school (about '36) I needed to find work, and we were told that the government was hiring young people that were either still in school or just out of school for part-time jobs. Because we were part of the Hull-House Theater Group there was an opening in the Federal Theater Project, and some of us applied and we got jobs with the Federal Theater at $50 a month. The Federal Theater put on plays; it was a project that gave jobs to down-and-out writers and actors, dancers, musicians—a jobs program. Studs Terkel worked in the [Federal] Writers' Project during that time.

We were in plays wherever there was a rehearsal going on since we were part of this repertory group. The first play that I was involved in was at the Great Northern Theater. We were always in the mob scenes; we were the extras, and the people who were the players usually were all professional actors. For instance, they did *Abe Lincoln in Illinois* at the Blackstone and Walter Huston and John Huston were part of that production. All of them, in one way or another, were professionals.

There were hardly any theaters in Chicago or anywhere, which didn't have any resident companies at the time. In some cases the Project hired directors; whatever the case, they hired them at whatever the prevailing wage was in the Federal Theater Project. The buildings were owned by private owners, but the government rented them. There was an office here in Chicago which was the central office for these programs; it was kind of an umbrella office that oversaw the Theater Project and Writers' Project.

There was a dance group, modern ballet, they were marvelous dancers and they had been hired by the Federal Theater Project to give people in dance jobs, and I became part of that thing, but I was no dancer. We did that until WPA ran out, maybe two years, till just when the war started. That was one of the best times of my life.

I was living at home and I ate at home. It made a lot of

difference because I had money of my own then. My father was very good about not insisting that I give it all to them. He allowed me to decide how much I wanted to contribute, which wasn't very much, but it was a wonderful opportunity because it was the first time that I ever had money of my own. I could buy Christmas gifts; that was the first time I could do that.

There was no real encouragement from the family that I should go to college. There was no discouragement, but no real encouragement. The real problem came with, how could I afford to go, where was I going to get the money? And I thought that maybe I would go to the City Colleges, but then I soon found that I needed money even for that because you have to buy your books and all that, and I just couldn't ask my father and mother for that money. There wasn't anyone that I knew of that was going on. I wasn't able to go with any of my friends so I just didn't pursue it. I registered for a couple of months and then dropped out because I had to ask for money to buy lunch. I was at that age where I didn't want to bring my own lunch, I wanted to eat it in the cafeteria like the others. I wasn't motivated enough to sacrifice to do it.

I did a lot of odd courses later on. You don't have as much direction when you're young. I often compare those days with the present, and I often think, even at Hull-House we didn't get enough direction in those ways. No one said, "Well, you could just take a course." What was nice though was that afterwards my brother, who was two years younger than I, he did go to college. He went to the University of Illinois at Champaign. It was a great struggle for him, and he had to find work. My parents didn't help him much, but they sent a little food. My brother got a scholarship and my father gave some money to get started, but when he was down there he found work and that's how he worked his way through.

When World War II started I was already about 19 or 20. For one of our friends I had volunteered to write and do work in our community newspaper which came out twice a month. He had a connection with Roland Libonati, who was a congressman, who needed to form a draft board when the war broke out. I asked my friend if I could get a job in the draft board, and through him I was hired and worked there three years until they stopped drafting. I was paid by the government; that was a decent salary. I did just clerical work, signing up all of the men who came in, giving them a draft board number, and sending out their notices when they were inducted and had to appear.

I fell in love while I was working at the draft board. This was Charles (Chick), a man who was the uncle of a friend of mine. I used to see him when I was a girl and sort of had a crush on him. His family lived on the east end of the neighborhood on Clinton Street, and later they moved west. Many of the families were beginning to move from Clinton Street then. Those were the first immigrants that had come in and that area was beginning to become more factory and industrial. But at that time on Clinton Street there were no indoor toilets and things like that. Chick's father was a baker, the older brother had found work, and so they had accumulated enough money to consider moving, which is what they did, and they bought a house on Congress and California.

When his family moved over to the West Side, Chick's friends were still here. He would visit his friends and his older sister who lived here on Miller Street, so he would stop to visit Rose whenever he came this way. She'd feed him and that's how I became acquainted with him. So I knew him for years as my girlfriend's uncle.

You know as you get older that whole age difference changes very quickly; as I reached my later teens the 12 years difference in our ages didn't seem that much. It didn't bother my parents, partly because he was a very charming person, not tough and loud as some of the fellows from the neighborhood were. He seemed more refined, and he was a nice person. He liked to read a lot, so while he was very masculine and athletic, he had a lot of other interests that made him a more interesting person.

When they moved away I didn't see him for years, but the man who was the chairman of the draft board happened to be a dear friend of Chick's, and Chick would drop in to see him sometimes. That old feeling just came back, and I think he started noticing me. Of course, I was flirting, and then we began dating.

Chick was not employed at the time, but then he got a job

in construction; he became a carpenter's foreman. Those jobs weren't paying well because everybody was out of work at that time. It was before war production really revved up. Before we started sending boys over there it was very bad times for employment. Later it opened up.

So we dated and then we got married. We had a very small church wedding, and we went out for dinner afterwards with family and friends—just 20 people. We were married and then in just a few months he was drafted and he left the same year that we were married. That happened to all my friends though. They all left and went overseas at the same time. Chick was in Burma in the engineer's corps. The war was dreadful, but not as bad as in the European theater. They weren't fighting for cities and towns, it was more of an air war where Chick was, and they were building airfields and roads. He was gone until the war was over. When he came home it was summer of 1946.

We lived here up on the second floor. My mother was not well, she was getting ill, and my father still had his business here as a tailor. There are two apartments upstairs. My brother, Ernie, had married on a furlough when he was in the army so he was no longer living here. My brother, Mario, was still living here but had purchased a building over on Lexington just west of us here and was planning to rehab it and to move into it. So about a year after we set up housekeeping here, Mario moved out and my husband and I had this whole apartment to ourselves.

The first job that Chick could get after the army was on construction as a carpenter's helper. He'd never done that before, but they were building the Robert Brooks Homes, public housing south of Roosevelt at Racine, and he helped to build those. He did that until those were all built, and then he had a friend who had opened up a bar on the Near North Side, and asked him to come to work there at the bar. It became a very popular place, called The Storm. It was one of those little "in" places on the Near North Side near Rush Street, and he found he liked that job.

Chick loved it because people were friendly and you met all kinds of people behind the bar. Besides, you made good money, so he was very satisfied with that job. That's what he stayed in, changing jobs, maybe twice, because those people (The Storm) decided to close up when the owner became sick. He got a job just down the street in the same area and he stayed until he had a stroke, many years later, when he was in his '50s.

He enjoyed his work, and I enjoyed listening to all the stories that he had to tell me about people, especially if they were in show business and stopped in there after hours. The one thing I didn't like about his job was that the bars he worked in were always open until 4 AM. So that part I didn't like because it really limited the time that we spent together. We spent the daytime together when he got up—he got to bed about 7 AM. You can't go to bed right away, you either have to have a snack or be doing something—you can't go to bed right away.

So I found that I had to start doing something with my time. This was in the late '40s. I spent a lot more time with my girlfriends, for instance. They were all now beginning to raise their families and having little babies. From time to time I'd go to night school to pick up a course that interested me. That's how I passed my time. I didn't tap my resources; I wasn't using them. At that time Eri Hulbert was working at developing a community organization that would consider ways to renew and restore and hang onto this neighborhood. So I got into that. This was 1947.

6

FLORENCE SCALA

(CONTINUED)

NEAR WEST SIDE PLANNING BOARD

ERI HULBERT WAS Jane Addams's nephew, and when he came back from the war he became very interested in the condition of housing in Chicago. Previously, in the '30s, he had been the first director of the Chicago Housing Authority's Jane Addams project here. He served as director of public housing until the war and then he went overseas. When he returned he worked in Washington awhile with United Nations Relief Association. It was then that our young men got back from the war and found this neighborhood looking rather depressed. It was wearing down. Previously there had been the Depression and then during the war years when everyone was making money, you couldn't buy things because everything was rationed.

But as soon as they could, people began to do things for their houses. Sometime in 1947-48 about four young men went to Hull-House and said, "The neighborhood seems to be deteriorating, going downhill. What can Hull-House do to help us pull ourselves together as a community so we can become more involved in saving ourselves?" The Near West Side Planning Board was formed after months of discussion. At the same time Saul Alinsky was organizing on the South Side in the Back of the Yards community where the meat packing industry was located.

I knew Saul Alinsky. I didn't know him well, but I knew him. He was a very nice person. I didn't like his style because at that time I was under the influence of Hull-House, and I think that was detrimental to me when I look back on it. Saul's way of doing things was, as he said, " . . . to rub raw the sores of discontent." That's how you identify his work. Stir up trouble, attack people. I thought the marching was O.K., but not the attacking people and picketing certain businesses to the point of utter distraction for those businesses. Of course, at that time I didn't realize how important it was to picket the banks in the area.

But Eri didn't like that style, and I loved Eri, and anything he thought was good. I believed anything he thought. Eri said, "If we can't make these things work democratically, if we can't do it by telling people the truth and digging up the facts, and doing the research, and laying it out for them so they really understand it and then take ahold, get a consensus, then we're not advancing the cause of democracy."

Well, I ate that. I thought, that's so inspiring—how wonderful. It went against my grain to do it the way Saul wanted to do it because we surely should be able to communicate to people, and we ought to get people to rise up out of the goodness of their understanding. So many times since then I have almost resented the fact that I allowed myself not to think for myself, not to realize that Eri's way was the wrong way. It was not the wrong way, it was really the right way, but it was not going to work. That's where my conflict is within me, but I realize now that you've gotta play hardball from the beginning.

The men always had the more interesting things to do in the Near West Side Planning Board organization and the women were always worrying about the membership committee and all that kind of junk. Then I said to Eri, you know, I'm going to take pictures of the neighborhood, so when we have our meetings we could show these slides. "Look at this alley, it's filthy, we've got to do something about getting the city to clean this alley." And show these empty buildings with absentee ownership and so on. I ended up with most of those pictures, but the best of them were ruined in a fire that we had in this building.

So Eri saw the value of that, and he began to also take pictures. He did a special kind of slide for his presentations that he would give at say, International Harvester or our local bank, so he could raise money and get support from the business part of this community. Mostly he spoke about planning and how to plan space in an area of the city like this, that it could be configured so that it was a decent place to have people living and so that there would be a place for businesses, a place for commerce, and for green areas.

This was an old neighborhood that was in need of a lot of help. In the years immediately after WWII when the national housing program was instituted in the country, what the city and the social workers were looking at was the result of prior years of poverty, of growing out of poverty, and of the city's absolute failure in Streets and Sanitation in upkeep.

They never picked up the garbage, maybe once or twice a month. The young men in this neighborhood had a sport on Friday nights—every Friday night some of them would go out with BB guns and kill rats in the alleys. The buildings that were no longer occupied, perhaps someone had set fire to them. They just stayed in the block like gray, ugly hulks for years and the city never came to pull them down and never got after the owners to pull them down. That's what gave impetus to the idea of the Planning Board; we began to work on that stuff immediately. There was some absentee ownership, but it was spotted on the map.

When you came into this area, what you saw was a community that was crowded with bad land uses. There were trucking garages, there were little factories mixed in with the residential areas. Small factories on a residential block need not be a bad thing. For instance, there was one called Morand Bros. Beverage and they dispensed pop and later on wine and beer, but fortunately they were located on a street where there were just a few houses. That didn't seem to be very bad. You know it provided jobs for some people.

There was also a cigar factory, small, where people sat at tables. Those were not harmful; those were not a bad use. But if you had a factory where there was a lot of smoke or bad odors, that wasn't any good. And there were just a few of those spotted around in the area. Mostly, I think the biggest problem was that they had these cartage companies. We had a big trucking garage in the next block; big trucks would pull out with kids on the block and you had to live with a big trucking garage in the middle. Well, we'd take a picture of that and say, "This doesn't happen in other communities or in other cities, we have to zone that out. That can't be on a residential street."

When I was growing up almost every flat and store was occupied, but as time went on the overpopulation began to sort of correct itself because a lot of the families left the area and moved on to other areas farther west from here. The other thing that was important was that all during these early years, the local doctors used to live in the neighborhood. We had a lot of nice housing in the neighborhood. The druggist who had his drugstore in the neighborhood lived here. Lawyers who grew up here continued to live here. Over a period of some years, eventually they moved, but for a long time they lived here. And during those critical years when it was accused of being a blighted area, those people were living here. We always had a mixed population, economically.

And one of the things the Planning Board did was to encourage the alderman at that time to fight in the City Council to get the designation of this area as "Slum and Blighted" changed because as a Slum and Blighted area, if that designation held it would have been eligible for land clearance. Although I was so gung-ho in support of a program of urban renewal in city planning, I realized later that we really had tied that noose around our necks when it came to the city clearing land in the area and then selling it to the university. In other words, they double-crossed the whole concept of the program.

Planning in the inner cities at the time was so stupid; there was no zoning application that meant anything. So that the concept of thinking about what went into planning was what became interesting for the politicians because they could see that it was to their advantage if the community didn't interfere with their coming and going either. At first the alderman (John D'Arco) was suspicious, very suspicious of us, because Hull-House was involved and also because he didn't like the idea of the people being organized.

But Eri made it clear that this was not a political group in any shape or form, that the opportunities would be there for him as well as for us, and that we had to learn how to live together. The politicians finally bought it because they could see, in their own way, that they could make money. They had the money, they had the access to the City Council, so that they could see that their essential power was not being challenged.

We were rehabbing this neighborhood, and people were beginning to spend money on it, their own money, because at that time there wasn't all of this money available from the federal government. Congress refined and developed the urban renewal program so that moneys were beginning to become available to individual homeowners who could apply for grants to get their houses fixed up.

The decision (to build the university at Harrison-Halsted) came along when people had already begun to put money into fixing up their buildings, when we had gotten these tot lots in the various locations in the neighborhood so that children had a place to play with swings and sandboxes and all. It came when there was a real program of getting the city busy about getting rid of vacant buildings that were dangerous and when we were really getting the city much more involved in respecting the zoning laws and all of that.

We were really doing this our own way, which was different from the way Saul Alinsky was doing it. We were negotiating with all of the city departments, and Eri was going at it constantly, but his job was difficult. Not only did he have to do persuading, not only did he have to get the city officials to understand his position and decide what our goals were, he also had to worry about getting money. And the pressures were incredible on him always. Eri ended up committing suicide, but not as a result of the pressure, but I think he got a diagnosis of an incurable illness and his vision was already impaired. It was a tragic thing, he was such a terrific person. But the job did wear on him terribly, because he was not the kind of person who could be mean and tough.

I think when we formed the Near West Side Planning

Courtesy of Florence Scala.

The Miller Street Playlot, one of the first in the city, was made possible by the Near West Side Planning Board community program.

Courtesy of Florence Scala.

The Near West Side Planning Board. In the front row is Father Bieri of
St. Ignatius and to his right is Bernard Schwartz of the Hull-House Board.
In back of Schwartz is Florence Scala, the only woman on the board, and
second from the left standing is Ernest Giovangelo, Florence's brother.

Board here, it was the first time there was any kind of a real
community organization in this neighborhood which was not
being controlled by gangsters, by lousy politicians, by immigrant overlords, you know, *padrones.* Eri Hulbert believed in
people being able to form an organization. The only trouble is,
he didn't know how to arm himself against the thugs. And he
didn't understand it because he came out of a patrician background. He believed in the concepts that we all treasure, and
he tried so hard to be one of us.

It was easy for us to accept him and get to know him, and
for him to know us, but to come up against a Johnny D'Arco or
any of the people out of the 1st Ward political organization, he
was not able to confront that, which is one of the reasons, why
he hired my brother, Ernie, as a community organizer. That
was one of the responsibilities that Ernie had, not only as an
organizer but as a liaison between the 1st Ward and the Near

*Courtesy of
Florence Scala.*

A Near West Side
Planning Board
fundraiser in the
1950s. Russell
Ballard, director
of Hull-House, is
on the left and
Florence Scala
is center.

West Side Planning Board. The politicians trusted Ernie and they accepted the idea of the Near West Side Planning Board as being an organization they had nothing to worry about.

One thing is, that from the very beginning, the agenda was always clear to everyone; if it was a community meeting, everyone had a copy of the program. If it was a board meeting or a committee meeting, there was always an agenda, so the politeness of that procedure had a good effect on everybody. And if anybody got carried away with their own agenda, they could quickly be brought back.

Eri was salaried by Hull-House. Afterwards Hull-House got to thinking, you've (the Planning Board) got to take on your own life, we can't be responsible for you anymore. That's when things got tough. They pushed him off, and then we had to raise enough money to pay Eri, and pay the rent for a place in the neighborhood. We accepted the fact that we had to do that, but it came too soon, much too soon.

It was maybe three years after we were organized that we had to move. You never generate enough money through ordinary dues to pay for anything, and the dues were only $3 a year. The crunch came much later when the city asked the Hull-House board, "Are you with us or against us?" And the Hull-House board said, "We're with you." That was when it got difficult; when they sort of washed their hands of what we were doing.

So, I think it was all that experience, of how hard it was to achieve, to see it happening and living it, and also to discover that the thing that really hurt everybody the most, and Eri in particular, and my brother, Ernie, later on, was to be betrayed by the Hull-House people, the Hull-House Board. That was very hard, because you believed that they were untouchable. You thought these were the cream of the crop; that was very disillusioning.

Because Ernie's job with the Near West Side Planning Board had to do with community organizing and participation, he was the one who visited all of the meetings, made special trips throughout the neighborhoods, visited the churches, visited the social centers; and he had the link to the communities officially better than anyone else on the NWSPB. Some of the members themselves were associated with different agencies, but Ernie was meeting with everybody all over the city. Because he knew the area best and had a sense of what they accepted, and also because he had a good rapport with the local politicians, which is critical in these cases because you need ordinances passed, he could go to city departments. If the department knew that the committeeman and the alderman were solidly behind you, it made it easier for you to get a commitment from the department to send over staff to say, study a particular block.

After Eri's death, of course, it was a real down period for everybody, but Ernie's links were invaluable and we voted to have him assume the post of executive director. But the Planning Board was on its way out at that time. Only a couple of years later when the mayor announced that they were thinking of using this area for the University of Illinois, of course, by that time the Planning Board just was kaput, the interest in it, the value that it had, people thought, oh, the university's a done deal.

Those members of the executive committee who were influential in International Harvester, the railroad, and people like that, they just pulled back. The only group that remained loyal to the Planning Board during that critical period was Central National Bank, our little bank here, and they remained loyal to the very end. So as you can imagine, an announcement like that, pitted against all those years of planning that went before really was a depressing thought. The people in general thought, wow, what's ahead now?

It took a couple of years for all of that to happen after Eri's death. But Ernie was trying very hard during those years. By that time the money was running out. Unfortunately, Russell Ballard, of Hull-House, decided that Ernie didn't have the stature necessary to be the executive director. He was more neighborhood, my brother, he was more ordinary. Even though he had been to the U. of I., he was not one that had a silver tongue. He was just neighborhood. So Ballard began to sort of undercut him.

Ballard was brought in from outside. He was the superintendent of St. Charles Correctional Institution. Why they hired the superintendent of a boys' jail to be the director of Hull-House, I'll never know. But he began to give Ernie a hard time. Sometimes Ernie would make presentations where he might not have made himself too clear, and Ballard would call him on it.

As a result of all this dreadful stuff that went on over a couple of years, my brother suffered what he thought was a heart attack. And that came partly because he never thought that he would receive that kind of below-the-belt treatment from people at Hull-House. Because he loved Hull-House and spent his childhood there. If it had happened with the D'Arcos, with the people with a bad reputation, he would have known how to fight against that. He loved what he was doing, and he believed in the idea of planning. I think his health was not good because later on he did have to have heart surgery, but I'm sure that that stress just aggravated his condition.

What he tried to do was to continue the program. He held onto it, you see, till we got our final approvals for the federal monies. All of that had to go through City Council—the acceptance of the program—as an official city and federal program. He'd shepherded all that through to create the conditions of conservation and urban renewal. That program of urban renewal was dreadful; it was just a beautiful opportunity for politicians to make money out of it because they would be able to have control of land.

So he was able to do all of that, and we were in a fallow period because we always had to wait for things to get official designation. So it was during that fallow period that Hull-House decided that it wanted to go on its own and pulled out the small grant of money that they had allocated to the Planning Board, and they engaged in a program of their own. They made an application to the Wieboldt Foundation for funds to do their own little program, which was to develop low-income and medium-income housing in the vacant areas around the Hull-House building.

And the interesting thing is, the Wieboldt Foundation, which had strongly supported the Planning Board, rejected Hull-House. They said, "The plan we supported, the Planning Board program, we wonder what's gone wrong with that?"

They invited Ernie to a meeting and he explained what was happening. Then they just didn't give Hull-House the money. The money went to a foundation of which we were also part, but all monies in the foundation were then funneled through Hull-House, and after that were allocated by Hull-House. And there we were, just waiting for the final approvals to come through from the City Council, waiting to put some of the sites up for bids so that we could show progress. This took time, and this collided in 1961 with the announcement that there was going to be a University of Illinois in our area.

Before 1961, maybe in 1960, we had heard rumors that the area was one of several that was being considered as a potential site for the university; that was our first inkling. Ernie and Father Etalo Scola, who was the pastor of Holy Guardian Angel, discussed the matter. Daley had officiated at the opening ceremony of Holy Guardian Angel only three or four years prior to that. Daley had said, "This is where we will have a new community; this church will be the nucleus of a new community."

THE NEIGHBORHOOD AND THE UNIVERSITY OF ILLINOIS

AT THE TIME we (the Planning Board) were meeting, it was in the wind that the University was considering five sites for their new campus. What happened was that the University was designated to find a site in Cook County somewhere. About 1947 there was a bond issue for the university. But what happened was that some of the businessmen heard about that idea and persuaded the mayor to get the legislature to change it so that the University of Illinois would have to build, not in Cook County, but in the City of Chicago. They would have to find a site in Chicago. So that was already in the wind.

One of the reasons the Cook County thing was important was that Riverside Country Club and some of the forest preserve areas were sites that the University was looking at. So that became a subject of conversation among some of the people who were interested in planning. Eri was aware of that so he, together with an organization of business people, the West Central Association, just north of us (which takes up Madison Street to the north and near the Loop), were involved in talking about where the university might go in Chicago. So it was in the wind. It was just part of the discussion.

Goose Island was one site, Meigs Field was another, Garfield Park was another. But our site was never one of those considered. I know that. So all of those sites that I've mentioned just now, except for Goose Island, were not involved with any clearance of any buildings at all; they were vacant land.

So, hearing these rumors, Father Scola, Ernie, and John D'Arco, ward committeeman, went to see Daley to find out what was going on. But Daley said, "Oh, don't worry about it—there's nothing going on. It (your area) happens to be one of several sites within the city that are in the urban renewal program, and therefore, we can present alternative sites as a place for this campus since they're having a hard time locating themselves in the areas where they want to be—Garfield Park, and all of these places."

So they left his office reassured because he said, "If anything happens, if they do anything that I worry about or am concerned about, I'll get in touch with you immediately." So they came home and told us the story and Ernie said, "Well, you see he didn't tell us that it was not going to happen. He left us wide open." They didn't challenge the mayor.

That was in the summer of '60. By early February of 1961 Daley had already made his decision and he made the announcement on television. So that effectively ended the Near West Side Planning Board as a body for planning, for renewal. What happened was we had to organize a different kind of organization to fight what was going on. The Planning Board decided to dissolve. You know, the whole thing just died. It was just so demoralizing to everybody.

Ernie became so knowledgeable about how communities work, what the laws are, how the city departments work, the role of local politicians, what role politics play in every facet, he became very knowledgeable. But you see, in a city like this, what good does that knowledge do you? You could be St.

George and you couldn't slay that dragon. It's too much; there's too much going on out there playing against your interests.

When Daley made his announcement, he designated the Harrison Halsted Renewal Project R-10 as this area from the Congress (Eisenhower) Expressway to Roosevelt Road and Morgan Street to Racine. This Harrison-Halsted program under urban renewal was easier for Daley because renewal programs gave him the right to totally clear land. The Conservation Area Program did not give him the right to totally clear the land, only to take out the bad parts. But the power he had, anyway! That's how much land they were given then, just the 40 acres, but how they've expanded that! The city has allowed them to jump over Roosevelt Road. Later on they acquired a lot of land on Van Buren. They're spread out all over.

Daley made the announcement so quickly and without any warning or consultation with us, but a core group of key people organized themselves and the group became the Harrison-Halsted Community Group. What happened was, people knew I was active with the Near West Side Planning Board, and one woman came and knocked on my door. This was when I was in the middle of mopping my kitchen, and she said, "Florence, what are we going to do about our houses? Are we going to fight? Are we going to do anything?" I was mopping my floor and not thinking about anything except finishing the mopping.

I said, I don't know, Lee. She said, "We got to get together; we got to get together." So I said, O.K., let's see what Father Scola at Holy Guardian Angel thinks about it, because he's directly involved. That church, that new church that Daley had blessed, is going to be forced to go. Lee belonged to another parish but agreed. It almost happened simultaneously because Father Scola decided that this could not happen in our country. So he sent the Catholic kids home from school one day and said, "Tell your parents to come to church tomorrow night; we're going to have a community meeting."

So up and down all these streets that's what was happening. And, at the same time, Father Scola called St. Francis of Assisi on Roosevelt Road because many of his parishioners lived in the area and told them that we were going to have a meeting at our church if they wanted to combine with us. The priest there said, "No, it would be better if we had our meeting here and then we can come together." So that's what happened.

On the night in question we went to that meeting, and that was the first meeting we had. And Lee Valentino, the one who shook me alive, came to that meeting, and everybody was just so aroused. And out of that came the decision that we weren't going to be pushed around like this. The city promised us so much, we got involved in it, we gave them so much in our relationships over the year with the program, we were going to let Daley know. So we set a date to picket City Hall.

And it was at that meeting that Father Scola told us, "I became a citizen, I just got my papers, they can't do this without consulting the people first." And that was the thing that shook us up, too; why did they do it without letting us know? Father Scola died recently. He was transferred to a church in Roseland, all Italian at the time. The neighborhood began changing, but he remained there till he died.

Most of these people were homeowners, but not all of them. Like Lee Valentino who didn't own the building that she lived in, but she was a resident for a long, long time. Most of them were either residents or owned their own homes or had their own little businesses. The actual working committee was small, about 14 or 15 people, the larger committee which met once a month had a lot more people. These were people who actually committed themselves; they also were smart. They also instinctively thought in ways of battle, they thought we've got to picket. All of this was very new to most of us.

So the initial strategies were instinctive—fighting back. Where we lacked the skills in the beginning was in recognizing the political nature of it. Later we got somebody that had the political savvy to help us, but not in the beginning. In the beginning we did the traditional things, but we instinctively did the right thing in terms of picketing. We didn't know, for instance, that you've got to get in touch with the press right away. It was almost a month before the press paid any attention to us. We had petitions. We didn't write letters to the paper so much, but we did the petitioning, and we realized that we needed lawyers and that we needed advice. That came a little later too.

Then there was a planner who had been involved with the Near West Side Planning Board—Tibor Haring. Tibor had spent about a year or two developing preliminary plans for redeveloping this area. He was hired by the Near West Side Planning Board on a part-time basis. He came from Europe and is a Jew. He had suffered through the Holocaust in a way. He was not in the camps, but he was on that ship (the *Exodus*) that was turned away from our shores. I'll never forgive President Roosevelt for that. So then that ship went down to South America and that's where Tibor and his wife disembarked. After a while they made their way up, getting in through the border. That's how they got to the United States. He had to wait for legal entry.

Tibor had an innate sense for political strategy, and he was the one that started us thinking in political terms. Unfortunately, Jessie Binford at Hull-House didn't have faith in Tibor. Jessie came to Hull-House as a young woman and was head of the Juvenile Protective Association when Jane Addams was there. She wanted to conduct business on that high diplomatic plane. I loved her, but I could never could get her to understand the political strategy. Tibor said, "Florence, they're going to make hamburger meat out of you if you try to play with them with white gloves on and appeal to their sense of honor. These men have no sense of honor."

But you know what happened. In the end I had to make a decision; what is it going to be, Jessie or Tibor? We chose Jessie because, first of all, at Hull-House she had the name, a reputation. She came from the community; you couldn't ignore her, it would go against us if we did. It was a bad thing. And in the end we told Tibor that we couldn't go on together. And when he left he was heartbroken, he was crushed. He said, "You know, Florence, I never thought you would do that. I never thought you would figure it out that way." I said, I don't know, maybe you ought to go home and think about it and why I'm doing it, and maybe you'll understand.

It was Tibor who made it possible for us to understand.

Not only was he sharp about how to fight, he was not identified with the group as an activist, so he maintained his links with City Hall, with the professional community there, before they got onto the fact that he was working with us. He was really able to steer us correctly, but I couldn't ever get Jessie to see that. She was a headstrong woman. See, she didn't want to be involved with anything that was not 100 percent kosher in her mind. She was a personal friend of Gov. [Otto] Kerner, and she made a useless trip to Springfield to talk to him. He sent her right back.

The people who rose up to fight were the local community small businesses, the church (excluding St. Ignatius and Holy Family), and the people, the property owners and the renters, the little people. Afterwards when we began to scream and holler and picket and do those things, then the city began to put some pressure on the small businessmen along Halsted Street. So these small businesses were visited by inspectors who were finding lots of faults. You know you're going to find dozens of faults in these old buildings, and the businessmen started to feel the pressure. That's how the city did it. Then they started to make offers to buy. However, the city had no intention at that time of clearing the business area. They were on the slow track; what they needed to do was get into this area and stop our uprising. That's where they did their thing.

At one point we put out a pamphlet explaining our position. Riley Printing Company donated the pamphlet and

Redevelopment meetings held in 1957 and 1958 to present plans for requesting federal money for the improvement of the neighborhood, such as this one at Our Lady of Pompeii Church, drew huge crowds.

The University of Illinois at Chicago, The University Library, Department of Special Collections, Italian American Collection, IAC Neg. 189.14

stupidly we recognized them in the pamphlet, and the next time I went in to thank him, he said, you made a big mistake giving us recognition because the city people came in here. They went all over the printing plant (looking for code violations). I learned something then, never to give recognition in writing.

Riley had to move out; they were going to move anyway, but they did it as quickly as they could and they left. You know, a major small business, a printing company, now, they located themselves not too far away, but they never, never identified with us again. Never gave us any money or anything.

When we testified at hearings we had a lot of support. June Dolnick was a wonderful woman in Hyde Park who came to our aid. She was very active in an interracial group called The Citizens' Housing Committee, and they were one of the groups in the city who actively decided to support us in our fight, and they came forward. They came to City Council hearings, the marches, and the thing that was so impressive was that these black people primarily, and the few whites, they were supporting us when they were having this dreadful time on the South Side with their own fight.

The Taxpayers Federation also came and supported us. There was no organization speaking against us. The city might have brought in some professionals to sit before the housing committee of the City Council to talk about the value of having a university there, but there were no people who actually came to speak on behalf of the plan.

I think even if there were some neighborhood people who agreed with the plan to build the university here, they wouldn't have dared to testify because City Hall chambers were always packed. It would take a lot of guts to get up there if your neighbors were sitting in the gallery. But you see, even with all of that display of strength and solidarity, the power was not there, in the people, to stop it.

There was all that activity all the time, in one form or another. We kept the community informed, either by newsletters that we posted around or by having meetings and even in the critical times when they were taking down these buildings

The University of Illinois at Chicago, The University Library, Department of Special Collections, Italian American Collection, IAC Neg. 140.4.

A typical street (1000 block of West Polk Street) in the Harrison-Halsted area in 1957 before it was demolished for the construction of the University of Illinois at Chicago. These trees had been planted by the Near West Side Planning Board one year before they were cut down.

and we knew the end was coming, what we said was, O.K., we're going to stay until the end. There was a kind of acceptance of what was happening; and of course, by the time it had ended, they had cleared almost all of the land, which was a terrible thing to do.

While we were still in court litigating, they're taking instead of waiting. Daley was able to do it, and he got away with it, by what they call a "quick-take technique," which means that you can take land, even though you're litigating, and that if the public entity loses the battle, then the community or entity instituting the suit would have to be appropriately compensated. It's ridiculous. So that technique of quick take is rarely used nowadays. It is a way in which powers can assume their powers of eminent domain, especially when whole communities are involved. Anyway, they just devastated my feelings of patriotism, and my belief in the system was incredibly shaken.

The newspapers always characterized the protests as being mostly women, but that was because whenever they photographed any event that took place during the day downtown, it was always primarily women. A few men might be around on the marches and the picketing, but most of the men were working. The organization, the committee itself, consisted of men and women, and in the evening meetings or the community meetings, the men were there. As far as demonstrations, they were mostly women because they were the ones who were available. The City Hall meetings were mostly women in attendance.

Alderman Vito Marzullo said we were "a bunch of crazies." I remember reading that in the paper. Yet when he saw us he was always so nice. See, he was so close to Daley, and so loyal to him. When it became evident that this group was not going to give up, and our own ward committeeman, John D'Arco, didn't have any control over soft peddling us, Marzullo began to get nasty. It seems odd that he would say that because we've got our neighborhood right next to his. Sure, it was a real male chauvinist thing because it was the first time in his memory since he got off the boat that any bunch of women stood up to them.

There hadn't been anything like it in this area, never, and really in the city. There was only one instance that I remember since the days of Jane Addams, anyway. The Amalgamated Clothing Workers strike was largely women because the Garment Workers Union was mostly women. But in the neighborhood setting where they were protesting on community issues, it was rare that women protested in this way. In this community, which was predominantly Italian at that time, it never happened. Even during the worst days.

Women were more used to keeping quiet, and all of the people were conditioned to accepting authority; there was the *padrone* system from Europe. That's why politicians succeeded so much here and because the gangsters were here. You know, the gangsters who came here and set up their little hierarchies, they acted as judge and jury over any community dispute. People didn't take it to the police. The decisions made, when they went to these people, were quick, and it was absolute. This was instead of going into the legal system which was so corrupt at the time anyway. It was ugly and awful; it worked because it was based on fear.

We were never intimidated when we went to see Daley; we treated him respectfully, but we were not intimidated. And if we were angry our voices showed it. As these battles go on you get so exhausted, physically and mentally. We were always near the edge, and you have to have control of yourself emotionally so that you don't break. If we didn't agree with him, and if we decided we were not going to go along, we told him we're not going to do it. The time before the last that we had a meeting with him was when they had already torn down a lot of the buildings. They were going to tear down Holy Guardian Angel Church and they were already starting to talk about tearing down the Hull-House building.

We decided they were not going to tear down Holy Guardian Angel Church and school then. We were in the month of April and they decided they were going to tear the building down just before school let out when the children had to graduate and get ready to go to another school and all that stuff. That goes to show you how they were just using that bulldozer technique, not stopping to think about what they were doing. Because the law was on their side to go ahead and do it, they started.

So we asked for a meeting with Daley on this school issue. Sitting at his table in the outer office was Daley, the corporation counsel, and another man. As we came in Daley said, "Where are your lawyers? I've got my lawyers here." We said, "We don't need any lawyers, we're going to tell you exactly what we want, and you're the landlord, you can decide exactly what you want done here." We happened to have an example of a very nice home that was on Indiana Avenue, near the Glessner house, that was purchased by a black couple. They had renovated it, and they (the Land Clearance Commission) wanted to tear it down. Well, it was such a ludicrous thing and Daley stepped in and stopped that, so we used it as an example.

We said, we know you can stop this. He said, "There's no

way I can stop this, and we have to talk to your lawyers about this." We said, we know you can stop it because this is what you did in this other case. To come to the point, we told him, these kids have to graduate, they have to pass, get their certificates, make arrangements, and all of that. He didn't tell us that he agreed with us, but in effect, what happened was that they didn't tear the building down until after the graduation ceremonies; *immediately* after that they tore it down.

The University of Illinois at Chicago, The University Library, Jane Addams Memorial Collection, JAMC Neg. 3041.

At a Hull-House special events gathering, c. 1960, Hull-House board members cordially greet Mayor Richard J. Daley—an irony given the nearly total destruction of the Hull-House complex within a relatively short time.

At that time Daley was always saying, "It's not me, it's the University that's to blame, they're the ones." One day I recall that a reporter from the *Daily News*, a very good reporter who went to Washington later, drew me aside and said, "Don't listen to what he's saying, he's (Daley) the one." That reporter straightened me out so quickly. There we were, beating our gums on this thing with the University when we really have to focus on this other guy.

In other words, our strategy has to be twofold: we have to concentrate on the University, but we have to make it clear that Daley was the guy who was the boss. You're really dividing your attention, and your strategy, and your strength. Look at the resources they have, and they've got it all figured out.

We didn't have an obvious fringe that attacked us or that was obviously working against us. We knew it was there, but it was not something that we could say, that group on such and such street, or that group that belonged to so and so, we only knew that the people we depended on for moral support as well as for physical support (St. Ignatius and Holy Family) did not join in our struggle and never even mentioned it at mass or anything. Therefore, the people who went to church there never felt the intensity of the battle here. Strange to say that, right on their doorstep.

When I think of how St. Ignatius pulled away from us, I'll never, ever forgive them. Sometimes if you're on the losing end people will have nothing to do with you, especially if you're a political operator like the Jesuits. Daley was close to the Jesuits and his kids were going to school there. Still, that was something we couldn't understand then and I don't get over it even today. It's helped to make me a cynical person.

We went to Cardinal Meyer to ask him to support us and we found that some of his advisors were sympathetic to what we were up against and some were not. Then we went to see Monsignor Egan because we thought since he had been active on the South Side he should be able to do something for us. I went to see him one night in his office on the Near North Side and asked him to support us and to help us. He turned me down flat. He said, "You're not going to have any problems in relocating; you're not black. Black people have the problems in relocation; you're going to be able to move anywhere and everywhere you want." That's what he said. I had a friend with me at that meeting and she really sailed into him; she really gave it to him. I didn't do it in the same way because I had to be able to communicate with him later. But I never communicated with him again. I felt utterly betrayed and I lost respect.

As the years passed he went to Notre Dame for a while and eventually came back to Chicago. When I had this restaurant open he came to the restaurant and he became a fairly regular patron. We sort of resumed a loose relationship in the way that restaurant people sometimes develop a relationship with their customers. So all of that animosity left me. But I never, I would say, could totally embrace him with my heart, but I like him now.

Recently there was a big anniversary celebration for Monsignor Egan at a downtown hotel. About 400 people were there from all different backgrounds. People from the community were introduced and we just stood up and sat down. Then Studs Terkel asked him a question, "How much impact did community people like Florence Scala have on you and in the way you took up your fight against City Hall?" He, at that point, confessed and said, "I must say that I'm sorry that I didn't support Florence in those days. It was a mistake." He said it right there. I wanted to go under the table, but then he went on with answering the question.

I waited for Studs after that meeting and we walked out together and he said, "Wow, I didn't know that about Egan and you; I wouldn't have asked him the question." I said, well, it's good you asked him because I've been waiting all these years for him to say that to me. If he had said it to me privately that's one thing, but he said it to me publicly!

Saul Alinsky managed to interest and excite the cream of the crop in the various universities and then he found a way in Back of the Yards to get the Catholic Church involved, so I went to see him at one time. When we got involved in trying to stop the city from taking this neighborhood, I thought, I've got to go and see him. What would he do in my place?

When I saw him he was really charming, really understood what we were up against, but he kept shaking his head, saying, it's not going to happen, and I said, "Saul, is there anything you can do to help me? What can you tell me that I should do?" He said, "Florence, I'm not going to tell you anything. You're cramping my style right now." He said this kindly, but he said, "I have a big thing starting out in Wood-lawn. We're going to blow up the city with picketing and marching and getting down and fighting for schools, and you are grabbing all of the radio and television and newspapers."

He was very friendly, but I could see that he was holding back and that he was not really going to level with me. See, I knew of him when he was a younger person and he worked for the Institute of Juvenile Research. They formed community committees in different neighborhoods, and they focused on delinquent youth and trying to save them from prison. They formed one group called the Near West Side Community Committee. And Saul was central to organizing that part of the program—that is establishing these community committees in the various neighborhoods in the inner city of Chicago. After he left the Institute of Juvenile Research, some years later we heard of him organizing communities.

I always wondered about why he didn't want to join our fight. You know what, I think that he saw that he couldn't win here. I thought of that several times that this was a situation that was so political that he couldn't win. The only thing I could figure out was that he had too much on his plate; he could see that this would be an incredibly difficult battle, totally political, whereas in the Woodlawn area he was really stirring up what had not been stirred up before, so he thought he could make his name and reputation better there. And it turned out he was right as far as his own situation was concerned.

Those people of this neighborhood that we couldn't go to for assistance, who we realized were either neutral or on the other side, we never knew whether they worked against us. Our psychology was, let's not argue with anybody who wants to sell their building and leave because they're people who have been planning to go anyway. There's no use fighting with people you've known all your life; let them go if they want to go.

But there were some political people. When they set the bomb here at our house it made me realize, wow, there's somebody out here that doesn't like me. My mother was in bed upstairs in our apartment where I could look after her. My husband was at work. It happened about three or four in the morning, and it woke me out of bed—a horrible noise! It was in our back hall and it blew away all the steps that led back upstairs. My father was still living downstairs in the rooms behind the store, and his door was blown in. He was terrified. He told me, "If you don't quit, you've got to leave."

So we sort of talked about this and we knew it had to be political or it was some really disgruntled person who was against what we were doing. They might have thought that we were standing in the way of getting rid of their property or something. After the fact the city placed a police car in front of this building for about a month. A policeman was detailed out here and the cops were out there all night long. They did

Antoinette De Salvo and Mrs. Mascione, old friends, meet on the terrace at Hull-House during its waning days.

superficial detective work, and they collected the evidence of the pipe bomb.

Earlier there was a bomb that someone had placed in front of our building on the steps. It made a noise and it woke up my father. He asked me the next day if I heard an explosion of any kind. I said, no, I hadn't. I was so exhausted after our picketing and sitting in the mayor's office all the time that I slept through it. I went to look out there and I found the fragments of this bomb and gathered it up—and I was terrified.

I said to my father, oh, it was nothing, Pop, but I took it to the police station that day and they told me what it was. So I said to the policeman, without making too much of it because I don't want to frighten my father, can you give me some protection? The policeman said, "O.K., we'll have a patrol going by regularly during the night." A couple of nights later the bomb went off in the back, and it was a stronger bomb. We never found out who did either of them.

What happened was that, although we were not on good terms with the Hull-House hierarchy because they had decided to cooperate with the city (although they didn't do this openly), Russell Ballard, who was the director of Hull-House, offered for me to have an apartment there at Hull-House if my apartment was damaged here. So, I took him up on it.

We talked about it among our committee members and we all thought that it would be a good idea to go there, so my husband and I and my dog moved into an apartment at Hull-House. They were already emptying out the building. I had to come here to my house during the day because my mother was not well and upstairs by herself, and my dad and my brother were busy downstairs.

We felt the bombers would never do it again because they were able to accomplish what they wanted to, so after about six months at Hull-House I came home. That's when they were beginning to knock Hull-House down. I asked my father if I could come back and he knew the situation was just untenable with my mother in bed and me coming in every day, so he agreed. My main concern was that she wouldn't eat properly and that she would have bedsores. She wasn't suffering from some debilitating disease, but it was her mental condition.

Jessie Binford lived at Hull-House when we stayed there; she was part of the fight and she stuck it out till the end. She stayed in her apartment while they were tearing down all of the buildings around her. We had to put blankets on the windows because of all the debris, and it was summertime and it got so dangerous. We said, "Miss Binford, you've got to get out of here." So we forced her by saying, "Why don't you go to a hotel, and then come here during the day so they can see you around. Just as long as they see you around, then they won't tear your building down."

She wanted to make that point even though she knew it was lost. So for a long time she did that. She went to the Blackstone Hotel, and then that bastard, Tom Foran (city corporation counsel), caught onto it. So early one Saturday morning when she was on her way back to the apartment, they knocked the building down. She got there just in time to watch the building go down. After that she went to Marshall-town to live and I don't think she lived more than a year.

On issues, Tom Foran was like a hit man; he'd get an

assignment and he'd carry it out. He had a certain kind of technique in which he appeared to be affable and friendly and open and then he'd snap. If you attacked him or fought him or didn't agree with him, he was vicious. He was tough and vicious and opportunist.

There was one thing that we did with Foran that he couldn't stand. When we knew that the fight was lost we told people, O.K., we've lost, they want your property, don't negotiate with Foran. Go to court because you're going to wind up getting much more money than you would if you didn't. A lot of families did exactly that; he would offer them as little as possible (about $9,000 for each building) and these people went to court. All of these cases on condemnation are adjudicated by a jury. So if you ask for a trial, we knew and also a lawyer told us, there was enough publicity on this issue that the jury would be sympathetic. So when we did that Foran could have killed us because he just liked to count his scalps.

When we were in our battle there were so many fronts on which we had to fight and we were so inexperienced, but fortunately there were enough good brains around that we tried to think things through. We had an election coming up in our area here in the 1st Ward when one alderman got sick or died or something and this new candidate was running. He happened to be related through marriage to Sam Giancana and the newspapers got onto that and said, "We don't want this guy representing the 1st Ward."

He was an interesting character; he was a state representative, and he was picked by the mob. They said, "Well, you're going to

The University of Illinois at Chicago, The University Library, Jane Addams Memorial Collection, JAMC Neg. 963.

The Hull-House demolition. Of the whole complex, none of the neighborhood outreach buildings remained; only the original manor house and dining hall were left as museums.

leave the legislature and you're going to run for office." He, himself, was not a person that was involved with the gangsters. He was just a thing they used to represent them. He was their emissary, so he just did what he was told. He then left this great job on the state legislature to run for alderman, and the papers just hounded him out of it, so he never got to really run. So they had to have another candidate and they picked some guy from Winnetka or Wilmette or something, another Italian, and they brought him into Chicago.

So I said to our group, why don't we run because it will be our way of letting the city know that our politicians have doublecrossed us and are playing ball with Daley. So I ran for alderman of the City Council. But before I did that we didn't know what to do so I went to the Independent Voters of Illinois (IVI) and got advice from them. And then later with the Citizens Poverty Committee I joined IVI, became part of the group, that was when IVI was in its heyday. I wasn't able to do much work because I was so involved in our fight here, but I did go to the meetings.

I lost the election. It was a write-in because I decided to run when all of the petitions were already submitted to the Board of Election commissioners. The names of the candidates were already printed so anybody who wanted to run after that would have to do it as a write-in. Very tough! We lost considerably; we got some votes but I can't remember the percentage, but there were big write-in votes against us.

We were still involved with our neighborhood and our struggle was still in the courts when we went to Washington with June Dolnick and the Citizens' Housing Committee when Martin Luther King marched on Washington. We thought we would also use that as an opportunity to visit the Housing and Home Finance Agency. We got an appointment with them and we talked to their top, Mr. Reber, who headed the agency, and they all came to this meeting and sat at the table with us. I think it really impressed them.

They knew about the Chicago story, they knew that they had this problem with Daley, that there was a conflict. They certainly knew about the University of Illinois struggle and the failure of urban renewal, and they listened to us. But that doesn't mean we won. You don't get any commitments from them, really. If you're strong enough you might get commitments, but nobody is ever strong enough in these struggles that I'm always involved in.

When we got back home, then it was time to plan some really strong action, you know. We knew Daley needed lots of money to always be able to purchase the land to offer to the University of Illinois. So they had submitted a bond issue to the voters, and it was for a $4-million bond issue, a pittance today, and it was earmarked for housing in particular and acquisition of land.

So at our Citizens' Housing Committee we decided that we should fight that bond issue. We knew what was going on by looking at the amount of money and the areas that were designated. They said that they needed the money to expand their urban renewal programs in Lincoln Park, in Lawndale, etc. See what Daley had done was he had taken all of the money that was allocated to him for acquisition of the properties here in the Harrison-Halsted area, so there was no money left to expand the programs that had already been designated.

So we formed an unholy alliance with people who were called The Chicago Taxpayers Foundation (not an exact title), but they were people primarily who organized themselves to see that their neighborhoods didn't become black. So they were against urban renewal and they saw the threat to their areas of this project.

We called them over to a meeting and we sat down and laid it out and said, "You are fearful of blacks coming into your neighborhood (we had blacks on the committee). We don't want urban renewal because we don't want blacks to be uprooted without having decent housing to go to, thrown out of their neighborhoods. So we have to come together to make it impossible for the city to expand this program by denying them the money that they need in order to be able to apply for the federal funds."

So we all agreed. But we had some very nasty meetings at first because they couldn't trust our motives, but after we met for several months, it became clear that we were on the up-and-up, that we really wanted to fight this program of

Courtesy of Florence Scala.

After the final mass before the destruction of the recently built Holy Guardian Angel Church on June 16, 1963, and the subsequent demise of the parish. Left to right: Constance Varelas, Mary Diggles, Jessie Binford, Sr. Mary Filibert, Joe Diggles, Gloria De Laurentis, and Florence Scala.

urban renewal that was being misused by the city and they wanted to stop urban renewal because they didn't like to see what was happening as a result of it.

Where we met was interesting. We met at Hull-House, and Hull-House was not very friendly to us one way or another. They had already betrayed the community, going along with the city and not joining the fight at all, but they could not risk getting bad publicity and denying us any place to meet, so we had all our meetings there.

So what we did then was we divided up the city because these people of the taxpayers organization came from the North and the Northwest Sides, and we were the central area. The housing committee was primarily made up of people from the South Side. We planned leaflets and then we flooded all these neighborhoods with the leaflets. We survived without money and then when it became necessary for us to go to court, we had fundraising. The Citizens' Housing Committee had a treasury, so we paid dues to the committee and we shared the cost of it.

And we beat the bond issue. We beat it! That was the first and only defeat that Daley ever suffered, and it really threw him for a loop, so for two years, he had no access to money. What he was paying for here in this area was the clearance of the properties, condemning and buying up the properties.

But that was all challenged in court, and we never got to first base on that. It's terrible, it's terrible, we never got to first base in the federal court because we didn't have standing to sue because there was no other case that had been before the court on this particular kind of issue.

But we defeated the bond issue, and that put him back a

couple of years insofar as being available for more federal funds to come into the city. While it did hold up programming in those other areas of the city, it didn't hold up whatever he needed to do to make this land available to the University of Illinois. It slowed him down just a little bit, but not much.

THE AFTERMATH

AFTER THE PERIOD of the fight with the city I think I just wandered. I tried to get my life together. When I moved back here for a long time I did nothing except walk around that whole campus area with my dog. It was just like going to a wake every day. I couldn't get over the fact that all of those buildings were down and nothing but little fires here and there. And then I'd walk past Hull-House and it would be the only building still up. That building looks very different now because what she (Addams) did was she built a lot of buildings around it.

Courtesy of Florence Scala.

Florence Scala walking her two dogs outside
the gated site of the new university.

So I really didn't do anything; you know those years are kind of like a blur. I tried to get back to where I was, but I never did get back. I mean I just never got back, and my friends were all dispersed. They were all living out in the suburbs or the near suburbs and they were trying to put their lives back together again.

My dad still had the store, my husband was working tending bar on the North Side. It was the '60s that I ran for City Council and lost. This was the second time. When President Kennedy was killed, and I thought, my God, it's so awful what was happening here, and I thought I was going to run for public office. I didn't know what way to turn and I was really upset about his death and I thought, I've got to do something. Actually, I was just trying to work out the frustration of not having to fight for that neighborhood anymore. But there was nothing left in the neighborhood. I couldn't rally any troops or anything.

So I went over to friends that I made over on Roosevelt Road, a black church, and asked them if they would be interested in helping me do a campaign. They were looking for a cause to embrace, so they said yes. And so I got involved in this campaign to run as alderman of this ward, and it became quite a cause célèbre.

The IVI decided to support it, and we were able to raise some money (not much), and the young people from the church helped. In those days, most of the people who came to volunteer were white although the area that they served was black and the church had white ministers and black ministers. These were people who had been dedicated to that community for a long time. What was left of this neighborhood was pretty much controlled by the local politicians so we knew what we would be up against would be the regular organization, and they would be a considerable foe. The machine controlled the neighborhood and Maxwell Street was controlled by the machine.

We had a terrific campaign. When I did campaigning down in the black precincts, some of the precincts were very threatening, but I never provoked them. When I saw that they didn't care to talk, I thanked them and said good-bye. I knocked on doors, went to the church services on Sundays. I picked up a lot of allies and some good friends doing that. I really didn't have that much of a spiel except to say, we've really got to get rid of all this stuff, we've got to change it all. And they were familiar enough with what I had done here, that I kept fighting against the city, that I really didn't have to explain my motives that much to them, except to suggest that it was time for us to take it in our hands and do it ourselves. But, of course, it wasn't possible, and I lost that election.

I ran against three different candidates. One man that they brought in from the northern suburbs who was a clean jeans, very nice guy, no bad reputation, but had nothing to do with the neighborhood. So when we challenged that, when one of my lady friends challenged it they had to remove him from the ballot. Then the newspapers got onto it, and they quickly brought in a very credible young man whose father was also part of the machine in the older days. He was president of a local bank, and I ran against him.

We did get a lot of attention, from the press and from Len O'Connor in his day, but even he would say, "Yeah, she's putting up a good fight, but she's not going to make it." When it was all over with all he could say was, "Well, she did put up a good fight, to get a third of the vote, and I bet she got more, but we could never prove it." Anyway, I lost that so it helped to sort of deflate my need to get involved in things a little bit.

After the election my sisters-in-law lived in a house on Ashland and those buildings were going to be coming down, and they weren't ready to move yet and they were one of the few people living on that street, so my husband went to stay at one of the apartments so that when they came home from work they were not alone in the building through the night. So my interest shifted to that and I simply took care of my mother.

The time of the Martin Luther King assassination riots was so disturbing to me because I had friends there that helped me in the campaign. Nothing happened on Taylor Street or in the Jane Addams housing in our area. Most of the rioting was south of Roosevelt where the Robert Brooks homes are.

That's where it began, as a matter of fact. Some kids were fooling around in the summertime with an open hydrant;

policemen came to turn it off and they had a fight about it and the policemen dragged the kids out of the way, and this started this whole conflagration. So it was awful, and it all seemed to tie in with Martin Luther King, but it wasn't the civil rights movement that precipitated it here. It was that incident. Then it just ignited all over the city—on Madison, on Roosevelt—it just got all over the place.

I remember I was washing my windows on the stairs and I just heard all these cars going up and down the street with their horns honking and people very upset, everybody with their lights on showing identification with the fact that they were protesting what was happening. I got in the car and went over near the Shiloh Baptist Church, and some of the people came up to me and said, "Florence, go home, don't hang around here because all of a sudden white people are not wanted. Just go home." And I had brought my dog with me. I always took him along with me. I decided I should take him with me, but I knew that that would be a challenge as well; someone might identify with the dogs of the south. But I did go home and I never went back after that again. And everything changed considerably.

Earlier when Martin Luther King was here in Chicago he came to a meeting of the West Side Organization. Some of those people had been helping me in the campaign, and they were right across from the West Side Christian Parish Church. Martin Luther King was going to come to talk to people and we all came to listen to him. What struck me at that meeting was the young black males who belonged to the West Side Organization; heretofore, most community organizations were either church-related, or groups that were dominated by women. This group was completely all male, no women allowed as members. And they were not all that friendly to Martin Luther King. They questioned him very carefully about what he wanted to do there, they made it clear that he was coming into their turf.

I went to that meeting because it was a special occasion because he was coming. King was quickly put on notice that, sure, he would be able to get cooperation from this community, but he would have to understand that they would have to work together as equals in this setup. He accepted that; he said, "Oh yes, I do understand that I'm coming as a guest, I understand that." He was smart about that.

I didn't participate in the movement except as I did occasionally with the West Side Christian Parish if they were going on a march or something. But eventually when this became a movement that I just didn't want to be active in, I attended a lot of those meetings, but I must confess, I was too scared to go into the neighborhoods. I didn't have the guts to do that. I really didn't. Especially Marquette Park. I attended the meetings in preparation for it and all of that, but I couldn't go. I was scared.

I didn't become part of the hierarchy of the civil rights movement. I got to know everybody in a sort of peripheral way. Many of the real leaders in the civil rights movement were from the South Side, Hyde Park and all, and people from the West Side were just awakening to this idea of community action and exerting some leadership, and it was being done through the West Side Organization. A few of the churches on the West Side, like St. Agatha's and some of the great priests who were there, were involved, but it was fledgling, you know. Not strong in the way that it was on the South Side.

And so, South Side people were smart, they were all college educated, many, most of them, like Al Raby and others. And I had no real link there except with the Citizens' Housing Committee. So anyway, I was just very peripheral in the movement, but I identified with it.

I attended Citizens' Housing Committee meetings at that time, even though at that time, there was hardly any decent reason for me to be going because our neighborhood was already changed so much and all we could do during those years was focus on the issues of real interest such as the failure to provide low-cost housing in the city and the failure to do anything about public housing. So what we did was we wrote letters, we attended meetings, we attended park board hearings, we communicated with politicians; in other words, we were a group like any other civic group that made ourselves known, but we were not being too effective.

On the South Side it was a disaster because they cleared a lot of land they shouldn't have cleared. Some of the people on the Citizens' Housing Committee lived in very lovely neighbor-hoods on the South Side and they lost their homes. So I wasn't doing much, I was just trying to find myself again.

But anyway, I was the only one of my group in this area that got involved with civil rights. One day, somebody, evidently knowing that I was involved, put sand in my gas tank. It was at the height of the movement and there was a lot of agitation in the area and I was over at the West Side Christian Parish a lot. It was one day that I decided to get in my car and I saw something funny. I don't know what made me look there, a guardian angel, I think. As I was walking to the car I saw sand. I didn't get in, and went over to the gas station. He said, "Did you start the car?" I said, no. He said, "It's a good thing you didn't, just leave it there." And he towed it to the gas station and they flushed out the tank and drained all the gasoline and it didn't get in the motor or anything.

My brother, Mario, was living at home then; thank God for him because without him I would not have been able to do what I did because he helped take care of my mother. He had bought his own building on Lexington and he announced that he was going to be moving one day and so he stayed until he got his building in shape. I would go there every day to kind of help him scrape walls and do things. My brother Ernie went over to help him. And eventually Mario moved out. He was working for the Pullman Company. And Ernie was still working for the city, the Department of Conservation in the Building Department. Ernie was living in the first floor rear here until he moved to California.

I worked at Encyclopedia Britannica for a time as a picture editor. Then I left Britannica; they were downsizing at the same time, so I was let go because I was one of the last hired. And then I got another job, and for the first time in my life I used a political connection. Walker was governor at the time and I had a friend who was high up in his administration, and I said, Barbara, I need a job, you've got to get me in here. And through her and through Al Ronan I was given the job of volunteer coordinator for the Department of Mental Health. This was nice because I sat in the downtown office and kept in touch with all of the volunteer coordinators in the district hospitals throughout the state. So that was O.K. for a while but

I wanted to get out of it.

This all happened at the time that my mother was still alive and my father was still alive, but they were sick and then they died. Both my parents died in 1976. My father was 92. He had kept working until he was in his 80s and he just kept getting weaker and weaker and then one morning he just didn't wake up. My mother died two months later, but she wasn't aware that he was gone.

Then Mario lost his job, and I began to think how we could make use of this store that my father left us. What could we do? Now that the university was established, how could we make a living here? That's how it all started. I asked my brother, would you be willing to help us? We could fix up the store and we could have an Italian deli, just a deli, nothing fancy. Just sandwiches.

Photo by Carolyn Eastwood.

Well, he began to fix this up, and every time I came in here I'd say, Mario, this doesn't look like a deli. And finally I began to see that he was making it into a nice little place, and then I began to study Italian cookbooks. I didn't know a damn thing about it. I didn't know a damn thing about what to do so I had to learn. There's a lot of work in any restaurant, to set up the kitchen and all of that stuff. So that is how we got into the restaurant business.

Florence Scala stands in front of the mural painted by her brother, Mario, in the Florence Restaurant they opened in the former tailor shop of their father.

I continued to work and it took about a year, almost two years before we were ready. Some of the woodwork came from Hull-House, some of it we accumulated, some of it we made. All of it was old wood, some came with the building. Some came from buildings they were tearing down on Ashland. And Mario did the stained glass. He put it together and he painted the mural on the wall. It's always a pity that he was never able to follow his own star. He should have been a real artist.

I bought the chairs at Toffenetti's Restaurant on Randolph Street. They were closing down, and I got the nicest tables at Toffenetti's. I had them delivered and they just stayed in the basement until we were ready. You could find stuff like that, a little at a time. I'd look in the *Tribune* and see which restaurant was selling dishes and silverware, and that's how I bought all of those things.

It took a lot of money, but it didn't take half the money that most people would need to open a restaurant because we did all the work ourselves, mostly Mario did all the work. The major amount of the cost went into the kitchen, the refrigeration and a real stove, the electricity and the plumbing.

I never figured out how much it cost, but it didn't get too much beyond $50,000, and I know you can't begin to even look at a restaurant without having about $300,000 today. Chick was kind of passive; he didn't think we would be able to do it, but he was interested. What his job was, we'd have a little service bar back in the kitchen and he'd sit down on a stool and with a little table and just mix drinks or pour wine.

Chick died in 1986. One Saturday I sent one of the boys up with something so he could have something to eat and he was dead. He was watching a ball game. Again, he had a nice death. God, you know what was so awful about my life when I think of it was that instead of spending more time with my family I was always caught up with things that had to do with the outside. The best years of my adult life were spent fighting this Harrison-Halsted thing.

And then working on this restaurant where really, Chick had to pull his own weight. I couldn't pay attention to him at all, I had to neglect him. I feel badly in that he had to be up there alone so much except for the company of our dog. Our dog was great company for him because he was alone most of the time. People say, aren't you sorry you gave up the restaurant, and I say, oh, no! If they only knew how I'm not sorry. The only pleasure I remember is the pleasure of knowing that we were able to do it.

My brother hated it, he liked it and hated it. He's not an

Courtesy of Florence Scala.

1985 views of Mario's Italian Lemonade stand (above),
a popular seasonal attraction on Taylor Street, and two
satisfied customers from the neighborhood (below).

The scene outside Mario's is much the same today.

outgoing person, kind of shy, until you know him. When you know him, he's a son of a gun, but he's not an aggressive person, and it was hard for him to handle the dining room. Especially when the place was crowded and he needed to seat someone and he couldn't seat them, and the customers were leaving and all that stuff. That's hard, and he never liked it. And it takes a special kind of person to handle a dining room. You have to be a little tough while at the same time being gracious. And he was unable to be the two. It got him all nervous, you know. He did the dining room; I could never get out of the kitchen.

So I decided one year to close, and he was so happy. Then I changed my mind and said, oh, we'll go another year. Then I was sorry, the minute I said that I realized I was pushing it. We closed every summer, the way the Europeans do, we closed in August. So then we decided that we weren't going to come back. I used to go on a guilt trip about my employees who were very nice and stayed with me because I knew they would be out of work. But I just thought, hey, I can't do it anymore. So that was the end of that.

About three and a half years ago I joined a very small group called The Friends of the Roosevelt Library. Somebody called me and asked me; I joined very reluctantly because I didn't want to be a part of any group any more. But it didn't seem like this was very time-consuming. So when I went to the first meeting in this building which was so utterly un-suited for a library and located where it is on Roosevelt Road at Blue Island where children would have to cross major streets to get to it.

That's when I looked at the building and I thought, this is a terrible building, if we don't work on getting this library relocated, it's never going to have circulation; people will not come here. We began to make applications to the bureaucracy and we also got in touch with the alderman at the time who was Ted Mazola. When we told him it was about the library, of course he couldn't ever refuse that because it's always such a good project to support. But of course, like all these politicians they have to have control of it, you know, how, where, when this is going to become a fact. So it became our business then to keep prodding him.

Then we shifted emphasis a little bit saying, why don't we meet with Mary Dempsey, head of the Chicago Public Libraries, and that way we were dealing directly with her rather than dealing with Dempsey through Mazola. I would have to say, that with Ted Mazola's help, his wanting to be part of that thing, and our own pushing for it, it was finally accepted. We put together a wonderful plan and we also made some recommendations as to the site. And that's when they settled on a site on Taylor Street.

At this point now we're waiting for them to do the interior work that needs to be done. The staff feels good about it. They know that circulation will improve. I hope our group will continue but it's a difficult situation. It's important to have really good people on the committee, true professionals that have a sense of community, and everyone of those people is very busy.

CHARACTER AND CONVICTIONS

I DON'T KNOW why I responded to so many fights and issues, but my mother used to do that; she would respond. My father was the intellectual; well, he really wasn't, but I mean he read a lot, he could have been an intellectual. It was wonderful to listen to my father. But my mother held the thing together and she fought for us and she fought against the hoodlums who would sit on the stairs. She was restrained more by custom because men didn't allow their wives to do those things.

I always remember her as being the person who fought for things. So who knows, maybe I have more of her genes in me. She was idealistic and uneducated, but smart. She could cut a dress pattern; she just took the cloth and just cut it. Whenever my father and mother argued, it was so rare that I can remember the times, it was very disturbing to me. I always took her side. One time I went up to him, I just challenged him and I told him, "Get out of here—leave her alone." Because he wasn't physical, and because he was quiet, when he got mad, we all ran. I can remember my father hitting me just twice in my life, and then it was just a whack, no beatings. Pow, that was all. I ran whenever he got mad. You never saw him angry.

I think what gave me different interests than many other people in the neighborhood was the Hull-House influence, the selected Hull-House influence, because I chose my friends and the activities there. But even with those people my interests were different.

Prior to the Near West Side Planning Board I became interested in the ideas of a young Hull-House staff person, Walter Johnson, who felt that Hull-House was too insulated. You know, it wasn't really reaching out like it was in its early stages with Jane Addams. He wanted to build an outpost in our part of the neighborhood. He had observed that a lot of people were not taking advantage of what was going on at Hull-House, and he presented the idea to the board.

That old fashioned board turned him down, absolutely turned him down. They had wonderful traditional programs, but they weren't challenging new problems, they weren't out conquering new worlds. He was challenging Hull-House to reach out at no great expense. And he proposed that they should rent an apartment somewhere and start a little outlet there.

They turned him down, so he did it on his own with the measly salary that they gave him. Some of us from our Hull-House group were very friendly with him and we helped him get that place going. He rented the first floor of an old Chicago-style building, and he kept that outpost going for about four years out of his salary and our help with fundraising. But then things got worse and worse. This was a time when everybody was poor. We had to heat the place with a coal stove and eventually he started to get sick.

Another reason that I could pursue my interests and feelings was that my husband was very tolerant, very laid back. He loved to read, he was just great at history. When we were driving around he would tell me all about these things that were going on in Chicago. But he didn't have the same drive that I had, it was just different. He never stood in my way and that was very helpful; he was very supportive.

But you know, I hate all that; I hate what we do to our families, how we sacrifice time for that thing that we get so wrapped up in. It's like people who have careers and get so involved in their career, they have a difficult time saving time for their families. Well, it's almost the same thing with these causes, it takes up all your time. It just demands that kind of time. You feel you're committed to it and you can't let it down. So, it's a conflict, it's really a conflict, and in my old age, I regret a lot of it.

You see where I lived and the kind of life I lived, I was always isolating myself from where I came from and finding things to do elsewhere. I don't regret it; what I do regret is the time that it took away. I suppose if you won, you would say, it was worth it. The people who fought in the civil rights movement have got to say it was worth it. And it opened up so many things; it did change things. I think our fight stays in peoples' minds because it was such a strong fight. You'd think politicians at that time would have been smart enough to realize that there were winds of change. Things were changing in the city.

I really did believe in how a community of people dedicated to a belief that if everybody has the information and everybody is fully informed, then the rules that you live by in this country will work in their behalf. I think I'm still struggling with it. The belief in our way of life as I saw it, as I thought it was written, and my father and mother believed in it when they came to this country, was that no matter what happened, in the end, right was going to prevail. It's just hard to come to grips with the fact that it isn't always so. It isn't.

The neighborhood and the Maxwell Street Market didn't need to be destroyed because there were all kinds of alternatives for the problems that the city faced at the time. These alternatives would have been just as beneficial to the health of this city and to the needs of people wanting to go to a university. There is the failure to understand the importance of continuity in your family relationships and in the community. You know, that continuity is part of the historical fact of this city. They destroy that and I think it's so wrong to do it.

And Maxwell Street, more than almost any other place, represented continuity in a very condensed way. It never moved, it expanded. It struck home to me when I was listening to Andrew Patner on Public Radio. His grandparents had a business on Maxwell Street and though the years had passed and the father and the grandparents didn't have a business there anymore, Patner's father, would take him, as a little boy, every Sunday to the market. They used to go early in the morning when the grandfather was still there, and they used to spend time with him. And then when the grandfather passed on they continued to go there. So, in telling the story, it is remembrance of grandfather and father, of the market, of his father taking him every Sunday, of their stopping to eat together.

You know, he's recounting this today, and I was really transfixed by his recounting it. It was not playing the violins; it was straightforward recounting the history. But it's all going to disappear because when he gets old, he's not going to be able to tell it. And it evolved. Mexicans came in, and blacks became part of the market, the fact was that all these different people found their way to make a living, to work there. There must have been some friction, but the acceptance, and the tolerance, was much more important than anything else.

CONCLUSION

I'VE MEANT TO write the library people at the University to see if they'd like to come over and take a look at the records I have, Near West Side Planning Board minutes and records of our struggle to save the neighborhood. They have some things in the archives that have to do with this land acquisition. They wrote to me some years ago and inquired about these records, but I was so upset by the University then that I threw the letter away and never responded to it. Now I think I'll contact them.

I don't get mad walking through the university grounds anymore. I always feel as though the place is alien, alien territory. Sometimes I've gone to Hull-House because they have had something going on there. The last time I did that was in the evening and as I left the building, there was all of downtown lit up in front of me and for the first time in many years I felt teary-eyed. I thought, you bastards, you took it all, we don't have anything. I'm an alien person here.

I've seen every building go down there. Every building that was taken down on that street took something out of me, it really did. Because I've been there all my life, and I've seen them tear down buildings that should not have been torn down.
—NATE DUNCAN

Courtesy of Nate Duncan.

Milton (far right), Nate Duncan's father, and his three brothers and one sister (seated right). The other two women are Milton's sisters-in-law.

7. THE BLACK NEIGHBORHOOD

8. NATE DUNCAN

9. NATE DUNCAN (CONTINUED)

Photos by Carolyn Eastwood.

Above: Gethsemane Missionary Baptist Church, formerly the Roumanian Congregation when the neighborhood was Jewish, had been a center of community life in Black Bottom. Church members now travel long distances to services, as their community no longer exists on the Near West Side.

Below: Piano C. Red is a popular band that frequently played on Maxwell Street during the Sunday market.

7
THE BLACK NEIGHBORHOOD

INTRODUCTION

BY THE TIME the Maxwell Street Market was removed from the Maxwell-Halsted area, much of the black neighborhood surrounding it had already been removed through urban renewal and the construction of the Dan Ryan Expressway. Yet at the time of the closing, approximately one-third of the vendors and thousands of regular shoppers were black. The black shoppers came from public housing adjacent to the market but they also traveled from other parts of the city and from outlying areas. Shops along Halsted Street, many with black owners, were still doing a reasonable business weekdays and were thriving on Sundays.

Prior to the destruction of homes, businesses, churches, and schools that took place over several decades, there was a small vibrant enclave—a black neighborhood—that former inhabitants remember with great enthusiasm, but which is virtually unknown in the literature and by other Chicagoans. The community was known as "Black Bottom" by residents, but even the origin of this name cannot be traced with certainty.

During the course of my discussions with Nate Duncan and with other former residents of Black Bottom, I felt that the community had a Brigadoon-like quality. It was very real to the people with whom I talked. They could describe vividly daily life and relationships among residents of the community, and certainly they would wish to have their neighborhood back in an instant. Outside the neighborhood it was an area "where the blacks lived" but nothing more.

What has been called "the Black Belt" began about a mile to the east and was completely separate from Black Bottom. Black Bottom extended eastward only to Jefferson Street, which is west of the Chicago River. The perceived western boundary for Black Bottom was Union Avenue, one block east of Halsted. The northern boundary was Roosevelt Road and the southern boundary was 16th Street.

One of the reasons for exploring the life of this community, apart from the fact that it was the home of Nate Duncan and is described in his oral history, is to understand what is lost when a community is demolished, for whatever reason. To a city planner, these may be just a few city blocks indexed by several lines on a piece of paper. They are easy to discount because the buildings may be somewhat more decrepit than others, but mainly because the residents and business owners have absolutely no power—no "clout."

THE MIGRATION

ALTHOUGH MUCH HAS been written about the "Great Migration" of blacks from the South to Chicago, this movement was notable for the numbers of people coming to the region, and not because they were the first blacks to establish residence in this northern city. Apart from Jean Baptiste Point du Sable, part French and part Haitian, who was the city's first settler, there were a few other black residents as early as 1833 when Chicago was incorporated. The black population remained small, however, until the decade from 1910 to 1920, when the number of black residents increased by 148 percent.[1] By this time these new residents were more likely to come from the lower South than from the upper South and border states.

The major reasons for this influx during World War I were increased needs for steel and foundry workers and greater demands on the stockyards. At the same time, unskilled immigrant labor to the United States was cut off during the war.

Labor agents, sent south first by the railroads, then by the steel companies, helped to spur the migration.

Later, independent migration clubs formed around leaders who organized groups and made all the arrangements for the trip. Because Chicago was a major railway terminus, it was a natural destination for blacks from the South who could board the train and travel north to friends, family, and work in Chicago. The *Chicago Defender* newspaper was also a great force in popularizing Chicago and furnishing information with its articles and "help wanted" advertisements.

The fact that Sears Roebuck and Montgomery Ward, the two great catalog companies, were in Chicago and that people were used to writing to them for goods also gave the city an edge. Another source of information for migrants came from the thousands of visitors Chicago that traveled to Chicago every year for religious meetings and other conventions.

Apart from family and friend networks, there were also professional networks; prominent among these were jazz and blues musicians who passed the word about opportunities to play in Chicago. As a result of migration to the Maxwell Street area, black "blues culture" sprang up in the neighborhood and established it as a place where blues could be heard, especially at the Sunday marketplace.

Hound Dog Taylor began playing his guitar on Maxwell Street when he first arrived in Chicago from Natchez, Mississippi. He described the scene to Ira Berkow:

> "We were all down there, Muddy Waters was down there . . . Howlin' Wolf was down there . . . Little Walter was down there . . . I'm over there . . . and Jimmy Rogers, too. We were all in Jewtown. I'm tellin' you, Jewtown was jumpin' like a champ, jumpin' like mad on Sunday morning. And I had the biggest crowd there was in Jewtown. All them cats would beat me playin', but I, you know, put on a pretty good show."[2]

Hundreds of books and articles have been written on the subject of segregation, and some have characterized Chicago as more segregated than any other northern metropolis. Obviously, segregation was a fact of life for residents in Black

Bottom just as it was in other parts of the city, but in that neighborhood it may not have been quite as stringent in some ways.

In 1928, the sociologist, Louis Wirth, wrote that the "Negro" had drifted to the Near West Side for precisely the same (economic) reasons that the Jews and Italians came here. But, he claimed that, unlike white landlords and residents in other areas, there was no appreciable resistance by the Jews of the area. One landlord answered "some fellows" who questioned his renting to blacks by saying:

> I told them it was none of their business whom I rented to. The property in the neighborhood is in such poor shape that if you didn't rent to anybody that comes along, you would have it stand empty and pay your taxes out of your pocket. I asked those fellows whether they would pay my taxes or rent the building themselves, and they took to their heels.[3]

Census tract data for 1930 shows that by the time Nate Duncan's story begins, Black Bottom was either in a temporary state of transition with a population that was 44 percent black and the rest a mix of white and other races, or it was a relatively stable neighborhood with the kind of exceptional integration that many city and suburban dwellers could envy. His story of the neighborhood seems to imply the latter.

Although origins of the name "Black Bottom" are obscure, interviews with former residents indicate that there is no doubt that this is what they called their community. Two long-time residents, whose family members moved to the area in the late 20s or early 30s, said that they called it "Black Bottom" because the lights were always dimming or going out in the neighborhood, especially in the summer. Because the streets were dark at night, they called it "Black Bottom." Larry Strong, one of the early residents, said, "Blame it on Edison. Lights would go out at any time, and everyone had kerosene lamps in the house to use when the lights went out."[4]

Michael Flugg, a library curator, suggested the name might be borrowed from the early neighborhood in Detroit called Black Bottom.[5] A musical influence has also been proposed for the name. One source suggests that in the 1920s a popular Jelly Roll Morten song and dance called "Black Bottom Stomp," named after the waterfront district of Nashville, Tennessee, inspired the name.[6] Another source claims that "Black Bottom" was a song and dance routine introduced in the "George White Scandals of 1926," and that the phrase "black bottom" probably referred to the muddy bottom of the Suwanee River (a river in Georgia and Florida), "the dance movements apparently suggesting the dragging of feet through the mud."[7] Perhaps the musical inspiration for the naming came first and the streetlight brownout explanation of the name came later.

BLACK BOTTOM, THE NEIGHBORHOOD

"EVERYBODY KNEW EVERYBODY—people took care of everybody, and most of the people were family and friends," said Larry Strong about his old neighborhood of Black Bottom. John Walker, another former resident commented, "Growing up there you knew a little bit about everybody—you loved all people. Everyone lived in the same community, everyone lived over their shop or under it. You won't find anyone as fired up about their upcoming as we were. I'm 61 years old now and I've traveled the length and breadth of this country and I've never found anyone anywhere with the enthusiasm for their neighborhood that we had."[8]

There were hundreds of businesses, large and small, in the Black Bottom area as former residents remember it. Larry Strong's family members, in the hauling and cartage business, settled first on the South Side, but then they wanted to be closer to both the Maxwell Street and South Water Markets, so they moved to Black Bottom.

In those days, horse and wagon was the main mode of transportation and cattle were still driven down Halsted Street. Horse-and-wagon cartage and peddling continued until about the late 1940s, when such businesses made the transition to trucks. Strong remembers this as "a good time between old Jewish merchants and black merchants."

There was an abundance of businesses in the area, as

John Walker describes, "When we were little kids we'd go outside the matzo factory and shout, 'We want matzos!' and they'd give us some matzos. Then we'd go by the bagel place or Jay's Potato Chip factory. Afterwards we'd go over to the International Harvester factory where they had ice water in a cooler—that was something in the summer time for black people to get a cold drink of ice water! All the candy factories were there too. Leavitt Bros., the 'corned beef king,' used to buy all our baseball uniforms."

Yvonne Watkins Kyler, who also grew up in Black Bottom expressed another aspect of their everyday living, "One thing about growing up in the Maxwell Street area was, you ate everything; you had Greek food, you had Italian bakeries, and you could live on what was thrown away after the stands closed."[9]

She described her father's cleaning and tailoring business, first on Union Avenue where they lived in the back of the shop, and later in a more spacious shop on Maxwell Street. "He would do alterations for the whole street, so all of them knew Billy Watkins." As mentioned by Harold Fox, Fox Brothers Tailors also sent out work to Billy the Tailor.

Four major institutions were important in the lives of

The popular Billy the Tailor's shop at 1345 S. Union. The building was eliminated when the Dan Ryan Expressway was built.

Courtesy of Philip Albert.

Black Bottom children as they were growing up: Foster Elementary School on Union Avenue, Stanford Park, the social service agencies, and the churches.

Foster School children were a mixed population as Nate Duncan will describe, but there was a continuity too, and a strong feeling of loyalty still exists as evidenced by the reunion every autumn that draws 150-200 people from the old neighborhood. Yvonne Watkins Kyler explains that at Foster there were blacks, whites, Hispanics, and Gypsies. There were many Gypsies in the Maxwell area, and a troop of Gypsies even came to her father's funeral. All of these children were used to each other and got along well even though there were economic and racial boundaries to cross. Yvonne says that she and Dorothy Chernin (a white girl from a family of shoe store owners) even had a friendly competition for honors that continued through the upper grades of elementary school.

Larry Strong recounts that the same 8th grade teacher had taught both his mother and himself. After school this teacher walked by their house and would stop, sit down, and talk to them for a while. If it had been a bad day at school for Larry, this "talk" might not be so pleasant, but it is an indication of the connections that existed among people of the neighborhood.

John Walker describes how, as kids, they would rush home from grade school, do their chores, and head for Stanford Park. "It was organized and there was always some type of activity. Your competitive juices were allowed to flow and your character was built and there was nothing that you felt that you couldn't do. You had the 'I cans'—I can do it, I can do it."

Stanford Park was demolished for the Dan Ryan Expressway, but everyone I have spoken to has positive memories of the park. It was an after-school center of life for children of the neighborhood. In that place and at that time the Park District seems to have found the right formula for making this little one-block park important in the lives of local residents. Situated on a block bounded by 14th Place and Jefferson, Union and Barber Street, the park was dedicated by Jane Addams on February 22, 1910. In a neighborhood where children usually played on streets and alleys, this was really a green oasis.

Courtesy of John Walker.

Above: The Stanford Park field house in the park that was a
center of activities for many in the neighborhood, particularly
the young people. The park, bounded by Union, Jefferson,
Barber, and 14th was eliminated by the Dan Ryan Expressway.

Below: The day began at Stanford Park with
the Pledge of Allegiance each morning.

Not only was Stanford Park a playground and a place for athletics, but it provided a library and outdoor concerts.[10] Another feature of Stanford Park was a shower house where records show there was an average of 4,000 bathers a day. Most of the houses in the neighborhood had no form of shower or tub so many residents would either use the Jewish bathhouse or the Stanford Park shower house.

CHICAGO PARK DISTRICT

Stanford Park

NEWS & VIEWS

Courtesy of John Walker.

A Chicago Park District Stanford Park program booklet showing Yvonne Watkins helping a younger child. The motto of the Stanford Park Youth Council was, "Forget self, serve others, and contribute to human happiness."

Other activities at Stanford Park included Friday evening dances and a park vacation school. Boy Scouts met in the park and, after a 12-hour work day, adults often met for lectures and discussions.

In Black Bottom there were also a number of social service agencies and settlement houses. Reviews of them are mixed compared to the unanimous acclaim for Stanford Park, but generally they seemed to have provided various useful services to the residents of Black Bottom. Henry Booth Settlement House was across the street from Stanford Park, and Kyler recalls, "What you didn't get at the park you got at the social settlement where there was programming, there were social services, and they had residential summer camps. They had these marvelous athletic programs, and you got a lot of other cultural kinds of things."

Photo by Carolyn Eastwood.

"Mother" Hughes, who has turned 90, is a long-time and faithful
member of Gethsemane Missionary Baptist Church and a
contributor to the potluck dinners between Sunday services.

Larry Strong said that he went to Hull-House for the doctor
and the dentist. However, as he put it, "The activities were for
the Italians and the Greeks. Adults and kids (black) could go
during the daytime, but not at night." Most of Chicago's
settlement house executive boards typically did not have black
members. Settlement house staffs were recruited from outside
the neighborhood, and services were separate and far from
equal.

One of the most important institutions in family life in the
black community was the church. In the Black Bottom neighborhood the Gethsemane Missionary Baptist Church, still
standing and functioning at 1352 S. Union at the edge of the
Dan Ryan Expressway, played that role. Virtually all members
have left the neighborhood, but they come back for the enthusiastic, friendly service where they say they find a spirit that
they do not find elsewhere. They have traditions in the church,
and, indicating an elderly member of the congregation, John
Walker said, "I've been eating Mother Hughes's chicken din-

ners here for 60 years."

Adults in Gethsemane also remember that when they were children there was still a synagogue next door. On the Sabbath elders would pay them a small amount of money to go into the basement and turn off the lights, a forbidden chore for orthodox members of the synagogue.

Most of the land surrounding Gethsemane has been acquired by the University of Illinois. When University spokesmen discussed their plans on television and in print, Gethsemane Missionary Baptist Church did not even appear on the map, apparently wished away. Gethsemane members have also been disturbed by unidentified strangers counting the cars in the parking lot, and by city inspectors in excess numbers arriving to "check the structure," all familiar harassment tactics.

Even though the Maxwell Street Market had been a viable market from the 1880s onward, and the neighborhood supported hundreds of small, single-owner shops and many larger businesses, it was always viewed as a run-down, expendable area. When the Maxwell Street Market area was turned over to

Courtesy of John Walker.

An interior view of Gethsemane Missionary Baptist Church
soon after it was purchased by the congregation, c. 1942-43.

Photo by Carolyn Eastwood.

Police barriers across Maxwell Street after the market was removed
discouraged customers from patronizing Nate's Deli, which was still open.

the University of Illinois, Chicago City Council members fell in
line with the mayor's proposal. Most politicians of Chicago
either dismissed efforts to save the market as misplaced senti-
mentality or embraced destruction of the market as a kind of
slum clearance in the name of "progress"; they never really
faced the fact of its economic importance in the lives of poor
people.

After the market moved, Nate's Deli was in limbo; loyal
customers still stopped in for a cup of coffee and a kosher
corned beef sandwich, but for several weeks they had to walk
around the police barriers at the corner of Halsted and
Maxwell. It was a sad ending to a deli that had been flourishing since it was opened in 1921 by Ben Lyon and his wife.
Agene Beach, a retired Maxwell Street policeman, who
worked the surrounding neighborhood at one time and who
went to Nate's every day, commented:

Nate always had a unique atmosphere in that place—people
were always comfortable. I've never seen a fight down there,

and I've never seen a loud disturbance—unusual for Maxwell Street, but I've never seen one at Nate's. It never made a difference whether you were black, white, or where you were from.[11]

Nate Duncan's oral history tells the story of his family, their move to Chicago, and his childhood and adult life in Black Bottom and the rest of the Maxwell Street area. He recounts his experiences in the work world, in the army, in the tense times surrounding the riots after Martin Luther King's death, and the good times at Nate's Deli.

NOTES TO CHAPTER 7

1. Allan Spear, *Black Chicago: The Making of a Negro Ghetto 1890-1920* (Chicago: University of Chicago Press, 1967), 140-41; James Grossman, *Land of Hope: Chicago, Black Southerners, and the Great Migration* (Chicago: University of Chicago Press, 1989), 33.

2. Ira Berkow, *Maxwell Street: Survival in a Bazaar* (New York: Doubleday, 1977), 424.

3. Louis Wirth, *The Ghetto* (Chicago: University of Chicago Press, 1928), 230.

4. Interview, 1997.

5. Michael Flugg is curator of the Vivian Harsh collection in the Carter Woodson Regional Library of Chicago, interview, 1997.

6. Eric Townley, *Tell Your Story* (Chigwell, England: Storyville Publications, 1976).

7. David Ewen, *American Popular Songs* (New York: Random House, 1966), 43.

8. Interview, 1997.

9. Interview, 1997.

10. Nathan Kaplan, "Stanford Park: Garden in a Ghetto," *Inside Chicago* (March/April 1990): 31.

11. Interview, 1997.

Courtesy of John Walker.

Nate Duncan (standing) at a show at Stanford Park,
with John Walker performing a gymnastic leap over him.

8

NATE DUNCAN

CHILDHOOD AND NEIGHBORHOOD

I WAS BORN on March 8, 1930, in West Virginia. My grand-mother was born in Virginia, but she wound up in West Virginia, and that's where my mother was born too. She was born in 1912. I don't remember my great grandfather or my grandfather, and I don't know what my grandfather did for a living. I do remember my great grandmother though. She was tall like I am; that's where I got that height from. Me and my sister went there to visit when I was 14 or 15 and that's when I saw my great grandmother.

My father was born in Alabama and probably came to West Virginia to work in the mines. He lost his arm in the mines; when I knew my daddy he had one arm. I remember him telling what happened to him. Well, it was a cave-in. Back in those years you used to have a lot of that kind of stuff. The way they put up the mines, they weren't secure. They pulled him out and he lost his arm. I'm pretty sure my father saw John L. Lewis because he's the one who organized them. I think my mother might have had a little compensation from my father's accident. Some people got money. I know my auntie got money because her husband ended up with black lung.

When my father came to West Virginia, that's when he met my mother. They probably married in the late '20s. My mother had a baby before me, but the baby died. My mother came to Chicago in 1935, but I stayed with my grandmother in West Virginia for a year and came to Chicago in 1936.

I went to school for a year in West Virginia in a one-room schoolhouse. It wasn't a country schoolhouse either; there were a lot of houses around. I remember this hill and that hill and a place where the miners used to bring out the stuff they called slate and they'd dump it there. My grandmother didn't want me to come here to Chicago; she wanted to keep me. My mother told me that. My grandmother came here in later years and lived with us.

When my father got here he was an elevator operator for years. I used to go with him; it was behind Montgomery Ward on Chicago Avenue. It was a factory that made mirrors and frames and stuff like that. It was fun to ride the elevator; I used to pull the ropes. Pulling the ropes with one arm was no problem with my father. He was strong, and he was a very independent person. He didn't let that bother him at all. He was like a guy who didn't have just one arm; he did everything on his own. Nobody did nothing for him. He had no handicap whatsoever; he was not a handicapped person. He'd light a cigarette and all that stuff.

My father used to be a gambler, they tell me. He'd been in every state in this country when he was a young man (he was much older than my mother). He told me he used to have $6-7,000 in his pocket when he rode the freight train. He used to tell me he'd go from state to state gambling, good gambling too, with one arm!

I don't think he ever quit until he got to be an older person. They used to arrest him for gambling and take him to the Maxwell Street police station, keep him for the weekend, and then let him out. The police would raid where they were gambling. They'd take the money and put it in their pockets; that's what they did in those days. Nothing that big. When I was a youngster they had a lot of gambling houses in that area, but they were different than now, life was different then. They were just gambling houses; people gambled, that's all, nothing else.

My mother was a very fine person. My mother had a tough time when she was coming up in West Virginia. She told me she used to fight practically every day during the time she was going to school because she was so light skinned. She had a lot of problems when she was young. She had problems with black people and white; the white people would call her "nigger," and the black people would call her "honky." She went through life like that; it was tough on her. When my mother worked in the store, people used to come in and start talking Spanish to her.

But my mother was a tough woman. She worked in restaurants, and she was a great cook; she worked in Pixleys and all the restaurants downtown. She used to do Jewish cooking and worked in the Jewish homes. During World War II she worked at the torpedo factory somewhere out west. She always had a job.

My mother and father separated when I was a teenager or something like that, but my life was always fairly comfortable.

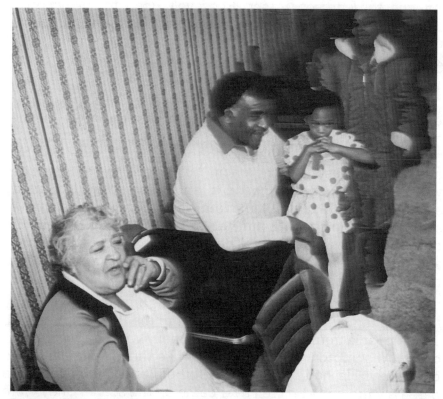

Courtesy of Nate Duncan.

Nate Duncan in his deli with his mother, Roberta, and his grandchildren.

This is the way I feel about that; I didn't really know that we were poor; we were poor, sure we were poor, but we got everything that we needed. I didn't lack for anything when we were youngsters. For the area that we were in, everything was reasonably easy to get. It was no problem. We didn't know we were poor; when I got older I found out.

I'm the oldest in the family, then Patsy is two years younger, and then James was born in 1941, 11 years younger. I used to take him everywhere. (Young) people don't take care of younger ones no more. I don't know what's happened to them; they don't want to be bothered with them no more. On Sunday we used to go to the park, me and my sister and my brother, to Lincoln Park and to Grant Park. Occasionally my mother went too.

We lived on Jefferson Street, Jefferson and Maxwell, in that area called Black Bottom at that time. That was Union Avenue to Jefferson Street, Roosevelt Road to the viaducts (15th Street). It was a lively neighborhood at the time. I never wondered about the name. It never crossed my mind. All I knew was it was Black Bottom and that's the way I grew up with it, and I never did find out what that was.

My mother used to go to Gethsemane Church on Union between 14th and Liberty, and she got baptized in that church. I went to Gethsemane when I was a kid. It was just a regular church. I didn't like going to church; I'd say, I've got a headache. I wasn't in the choir, but I used to say speeches when they had special holidays, and I had to go to Sunday school every Sunday. My mother would give us a quarter or something, and I would put half of it in there and spend the other half on the way home. They used to have church picnics, and my mother would make big barrels of lemonade. Most of my father's family went to that church too.

Most of my father's family was in this area, but none of my mother's family lived here. They went to the Philadelphia area. Those people from West Virginia normally wind up on the east coast, Washington, D.C., and places like that. My father had a big family. He had four or five brothers and two sisters. His parents were gone before I ever came on the scene. They were born in the 1800s, but I met most of my father's brothers and sisters. One still lived in Alabama and one lived in Dayton, Ohio, and when I was a youngster I'd go with my dad and one of his brothers to Ohio to visit.

In later years we had family get-togethers. We were always together anyway, to be honest with you. We used to go on picnics with the church and things like that. We were just like one big family. We didn't have no special place to eat at, nothing like that. If I came home from the swimming pool I wasn't going to walk all the way down to 13th Street to go home and eat. I would go to my auntie's house that was right there at 14th Street. You don't see that no more either. The closest place you come to, that's where you would go and eat for that day. Everybody knew everybody.

I had a cousin and my birthday was on the 8th of March and her birthday was on the 4th. Her mother used to have a big party every year when we were kids. It was pretty big when someone had a birthday, and they'd have a nice big party for them. We'd have a big party at people's house and back and forth, dance and talk and eat. We had a birthday cake and lots of food. Everybody cooked cakes and pies, and ham and chicken and stuff of that nature. All I know is, there was always a lot of food there, potato salad and all that.

I never did do anything in the preparation. I had too many aunties come, older people. Most of the older people would set up stuff like that. Even as I got older I never did any preparing any food in my life, nowhere for nobody. I can't cook. I never saw a Christmas where we didn't exchange gifts in my family. For most of the holidays we'd get together—especially Christmas.

In Chicago I started at Foster School at O'Brien and Union. It was built in the 1800s and later it was a police academy. The school had two parts to it, the vocational side and the elementary side. The vocational kids were the high-school-age kids. I was just a regular, normal student, nothing spectacular about school for me. My mother had to get on my back. My sister was a good student in school, much better than I was. That's why I got out of school. I didn't really care for it that much when I got in high school, and I quit about the second year.

In those years nobody pushed you to go to school, especially blacks. Nobody pushed me to go to school when I was a kid, you know. I could have been a bad kid. But my mother, being the type of mother that she was, I had the fear in me not to do anything that was wrong. I had to do everything that was right; that was the fear that I had from my mother, by the type of mother that she was.

My dad used to beat the hell out of me with the one arm. He gave me some good beatings. If I did something wrong he'd put me across his knee and hold me with that little hand (his arm stump), and he used to whup me. For instance, I used to go to Grant Park and be there, you know, quite a ways away; me and the kids used to go there. This was during the summertime. I never used to skip school. I knew I wasn't supposed to go unless I told them that I was going, because in those years you just couldn't fumble around and do things like that.

I was with a bunch of kids and my auntie happened to be on the bus coming home from work and happened to see us coming across the street bridge, and I never will forget that as long as I live. I didn't see her, but she told on me and I got a good beating. I did a few things. But, like I said, the neighborhood then was just like one big family; you didn't have to go home and eat, you went anywhere, everybody knew everybody and everybody knew his neighbors. Today if a kid would do that (go to Grant Park), it don't mean nothin'. There's a big difference then and now.

There was the principal and two male teachers when I was going to Foster School. One was a Jewish teacher and his name was Kaplan. One other left while I was a kid and went on the police force, an Irish guy. The women teachers were really mixed, and the neighborhood was mixed when I was going to school. At Foster you had Spanish, you had Jewish people, you had blacks, and you had Gypsies. People say Gypsies don't go to school, but they do. Gypsies lived all down Maxwell Street (the 600 block) and all up Union Avenue, and on Jefferson Street. A lot of them lived there. If you don't live around here you'd have a completely different opinion of them. If you don't know them you just form your opinion by reading history.

There were a lot of Gypsy families there when I was a kid.

They were just like anybody else. I got along fine with them—I used to go in their house just like I'd go in everybody else's house. Their house was always in a store front, they never lived in no apartment, they always stayed in a store front. They didn't have a business, but the women used to tell fortunes. I remember that too.

I remember there was a king of the Gypsies down in the area at that time, and he was a wealthy man. He had a lot of property downtown, this particular man. His name was Eli. Everybody knew that he was king. Everybody in that area would know him. He was not a poor man; he was a very wealthy man. Where the money come from, I couldn't tell you that.

You talking about parties, you've never seen a party in your life like the parties they used to have. You know the parents used to sell their daughter. The guy would have to buy their daughter. That was a tradition. And they would have parties for someone that got married that would last for two or three days. They had pigs, barrels of whiskey, barrels of wine, I don't know, that was their tradition and it was something! I went to school with Annie; she used to tell fortunes on the street until five or six years ago.

When I was older, most of the guys (Gypsies) used to be roofers, and they used to be car mechanics and body men, doing that work during the whole time that I was coming up. They used to go around and if they'd see a car with a fender dent they'd say, "I could fix that for you right away," and right on the spot they would knock the dent out. I've seen them do that many times. I used to see them on the roofs all the time. And they also used to sell stuff on the streets back in the old days. I don't know where that stuff came from. Some of them were involved in carnivals, and a couple of them on the streets used to sell jewelry.

The kids in the neighborhood, when they were little got along fine. Lots different than it is today. Nobody could steal, everybody would holler "thief" at that time and nobody could get out of the neighborhood. There was no such thing as racial stuff when I was growing up in the area. One big family is what the area was! When I say my "area," I mean *my* area. At that time older people could go anywhere, but a youngster could not go out of the area.

Let's say, I couldn't go on Taylor Street; they would beat the hell out of me. On Newberry, on the corner of Roosevelt, all the way to Taylor Street was Spanish. They would beat you; it was nothing serious. There were no big gang wars, nothing like that. They would take you unaware, beat you up a little bit, nothing compared to now. Even the blacks, we couldn't go across Halsted. Certain guys, when we were youngsters, would take your money or beat you or something like that. They would beat you up with their fists—there was no weapons involved in that. There was nothing where no one would really get hurt.

We had a Park District (Stanford Park) where we went to play. That was on Union, 14th Place on the south, Jefferson on the east, and north to Barber Street. It's gone now to the Dan Ryan Expressway. The Park District at that time was very effective, they were good, all kinds of tournaments they had. They competed all over the city, everywhere. Very good top ball players. I don't understand why they can't go back to that. When I was growing up we had no problems. We didn't have no time for nothin' else; that's what I don't understand. I mean, the horseshoe tournament, that really was big; you played in each park until you got to the top.

Marble tournament, I was in one of those. I got a medal because I was in the finals, 1941; I won champion of Chicago when I was a kid. Yeh, I won the Marbles Championship, 1941. We had a runoff; they got it down to two people. The final was in Douglas Park. I was great at marbles, man, never bought one in my life, and I was bringing hundreds of them, and my mom said, "What are you going to do with all of these?" I used to have them in a pillowcase, just loaded with them, loaded! They were just so pretty at that time. I don't have any of them; they got away from me.

We had tournaments, handball, I used to play good handball. I used to play in the fire department. You know we had a fire department on Maxwell Street, but nobody really knows about it. I've had a lot of arguments because nobody really knows about it. It was at Jefferson and Maxwell between

Clinton and Jefferson. I used to go there and play handball.

You changed sports with the season. I even played soccer with a soccer team. We had a guy that came from the old country that taught all of us how to play soccer. We competed with most of the Spanish kids and the Polish kids over at Ford Park over on 26th Street where you have the Spanish people living. We had soccer teams when I was a kid.

I didn't play sports that much in school. I really wasn't there long enough. I did play basketball; I was a good basketball player. As a matter of fact, when I was a kid at Washburne High School, I got a letter to play with the Harlem Globe Trotters farm team. Yeh, and I was supposed to go for a tryout. My biggest basketball playing was in the Park District, and it was big too! At that time we played all over the Chicago area, Evanston, all over. I was a good basketball player when I was coming up.

When I was a kid I used to go to school, and when I'd get home from school I'd have things to do. Before I could go to the park I used to have to get the wood together and get the coal together. Before I could do things, that was my job. I didn't have no time to get into mischief. That's the big problem today. They have to be kept busy. You see these guys standing around on the corner because they don't have anything to do.

I always used to work too during my school years. I used to work for a Jewish fellow on Jefferson Street. He had a used clothing store, and I used to work there on the weekends. I've probably worked all of my life. I guess I was put on this earth to work. I used to put the stuff out for him and make the stands and wash them. Then we'd sell stuff on the stands. There were shops on Jefferson, most of them were used shops, used clothing, furniture, Jewish restaurants there, I remember.

When I was growing up the Jewish store owners lived in the Douglas Park area, Central Park, etc. When I started working there were still a few Jewish families living there, but they were really living in the Douglas Park area. There weren't any black store owners, there might have been one guy, he had a shoe repair shop on Maxwell, that's about all. There was one lady I know that had a restaurant on Jefferson Street.

In the years I'm talking about, Jefferson was the big street, it wasn't Maxwell Street. The bulk of the people in those years were on Jefferson Street, straight down Jefferson. They had stands set up on each side of the street. There were always people on Maxwell Street. They had the stands out there too, but it was nothing like Jefferson Street as far as the crowd of people was concerned. The 16th Street streetcars would park on Jefferson, sometimes 20 or 30 of them, all the way from Roosevelt to 14th Street when they had events at Soldier Field.

The market on Maxwell really ran from Clinton Street (there was also merchandise on Clinton Street) all the way to Blue Island. You could only make one trip. They didn't have the market on 13th Street, O'Brien, Barber Street. You didn't have the market on those streets; they were in between the markets (people lived on those streets). So you had the market on Maxwell Street, 14th Place. The biggest part was on Jefferson Street. So when they cut it off and put the expressway there, then the flow went back west.

I used to shine shoes when I was very young. I always made my own money; I never asked for money from my mother. When I earned money, I took it home, put it on the table. Whatever my mother gave me I was happy with, whatever it was. That's what I did with my money in those years. I was just a guy who wanted to work and have whatever I wanted to have at that young age. I wanted to work and I wanted to have my own. What I used to do, I used to take that money and take my sister to the show and the parks.

I used to shine shoes on Sundays on Maxwell Street, and I used to make a lot of money. You know everybody had shines in those years on the weekend for church and going out. I used to shine shoes for Mr. Redd; we both shined shoes, me and him. It was his stand and I used to make good money. I don't remember how I got paid, but I would get five or six dollars. That was a lot of money. But don't forget, everybody got shines in those days. It was a lot of work, but people made that kind of money.

Then there was a matzo factory; I worked there for a while when I was 14 or 15. I remember I worked there during the summer months. The matzos were made on a lower floor, and then they came up on a belt to the third floor. I used to have to bend over and spread them out to dry. The matzos were hot from the oven and they had to be spread around to cool off. It was hot on the third floor; you had to be young to do that kind of thing, boy, you had to be young!

When the matzos were dry I used to have to put them down in a machine where they would grind them on the next floor and it would be like matzo meal. The matzo meal was something like cornmeal. They made that in a particular section, and there was a machine they would put the matzos in and it would grind them up like a cornmeal. They use the matzo meal the same way they use cornmeal, for battering.

There were two factories like that, one right next to the other right off the corner of Jefferson and Maxwell. There were quite a few back in those years. There were a lot of little industries around; oh, boy, at that time it was just loaded with them. You didn't have to worry about getting work at that time.

There were so many stores, big ones and little ones, and people kept moving. The people I worked for in my teens (Ben Lyon) moved to the store on Maxwell Street in 1921, but before that they had a store on Jefferson. Before that they had a store on 14th Place. Their store on Jefferson was across the street from where Barney Ross's (the prizefighter) father got killed at. His father had a grocery store and someone came in there and killed him.

L. Klein's and the 12th Street Store were big department stores when I was growing up. Across from Klein's on Halsted was a doctor's office, a Filipino doctor, and a haberdashers and a theater. It was just there when I was a kid and then was gone, but I remember the lady who used to play the piano; she just passed away five or six years ago. Just east of Halsted was a place for people to drink water and on the other side was a water trough for horses. There was a stable for horses, a big stable with two floors of horses, where people could go in and rent horses and rent the buggy or cart to go with it. Then they'd go through the alleys selling watermelons or collecting rags or whatever. Later that place was a gas station.

On Maxwell was Mackevich; that was a general store that started out selling railroad salvage, but you could buy everything from a can of soup to a sofa. The block that went for the Dan Ryan Expressway was a very popular block, the 700 block. They had a big department store there and everything, Robinson's Department Store. There was a big grocery store at 701 Maxwell, a nice store, with families living upstairs. I knew everyone that lived up there. They were black and Hispanic while I was coming up.

On the corner of Union and Maxwell was my buddy who had a hot dog stand. There were a lot of places to eat, six hot dog stands along there. There were enough people in the area at that time to really support all those hot dog stands. He did a lot of business because of the school. There used to be a candy store near the school, too, for all the kids after school. There were homes along Union near the school, and a Chinese laundry, and also a factory. One day the roof caved in, a horrible sight for the kids to see.

TEEN YEARS

I WAS 17 when I started working for Lyon (Lyon's Delicatessen). I wasn't out of school too long when I started working for him. An auntie of mine used to work for them doing housework, and she told them about me and told me to go down there and talk to them, and that's what happened. They lived out west on Adams and Pulaski. I was very friendly with Ben Lyon's mother too.

Some of the stories I know are like I'm 100 years old, but when I worked in the store they didn't close until nine at night two or three times a week and most of the oldish Jewish people would come there at night. They used to sit at the tables and talk. My hours were from seven o'clock in the morning to five o'clock at night, but I used to stay and just listen to them. They talked for hours at night, and that's how I go back much farther than I am old; that's how I know the history.

When I first started working I did cleaning and waiting on customers and that sort of thing. I learned about preparation by watching. I was just working there, at that time we had four or five workers, all Jewish. When I first started working there I was the first black guy, and there were four other workers. Most of them were older. They all worked together for years.

I never had to do heavy lifting. Most of the time you had companies that brought supplies, meat, canned goods. Earlier we sold all the Jewish things, the chickpeas and the matzo meal, matzo flour, farfel, we had bags and bags, big sacks that they used to roll down the steps. And they had herring and all that stuff in big 50-gallon barrels.

I used to make all the kosher pickles and the tomatoes and chopped liver and herring. I used to make that myself when I was a kid. I used to watch Ben Lyon's mother and that's the way I learned to make all those things myself. We never bought prepared pickles; we used to buy them and I put them up myself. They had kosher suppliers, lox and sunfish and shad, all kinds of fish, everything. In later years the Jewish customers were fading out and we didn't have a market for them.

There was a bakery right next door on the east side. I used to go there and get all the bread and rolls, called Paul's Bakery. On the west side you had a meat market, right next door a kosher meat market. Then you had a chicken market next door to that. You had all that stuff there. And I used to go next door every morning and pick up the bread, and it was hot; all the rolls and things, they'd just bring it out of the oven. What a big difference!

Often at five o'clock when I got off I'd go play ball at Stanford Park. I'd do a lot of swimming, I was a good swimmer. I played football; I played everything during those years when I got off work. During that time they had dances at the Park District every Thursday night, 15 cents, and they went up to 17 cents, when 2-cent tax came in. They had nice bands there. Hal Fox (Jimmy Dale) played there; that's where I saw his band practicing. You met girls there, in later years you probably took some.

Plus they had gym shows that were very big there. Once or twice a year the Park District had gym shows, gymnastics, boxing, a little of everything. They were very nice and everybody used to come in those days, they were big time. And the ball games, they don't have them any more the way we used to have them. When we had ball games everybody in the neighborhood used to come, young men, young women, whole families, older people, too.

We used to have house parties. We had a lot of that when I was a kid. Every week somebody had a party. But it was something, I don't know if they could have that type of thing now, but we had parties every week. We were very active. It depends on the age group whether you had dates or not. Sometimes I had a girlfriend and sometimes I didn't, not that often.

THE ARMY

THE KOREAN WAR was just about ending when I was drafted into the army. I was a medic in the army. When I first went in I was in Fort Leonard Wood, Missouri, and I was there for a week. From there I went to do my basic training in Colorado. It was real nice there, I really liked that. I always thought I'd go back, but I've never been back for a visit. The camp was outside of Colorado Springs.

My medical training I got in Fort Sam Houston, Texas. When I first got there I didn't like it at all. When we came there on the train I met two fellows from New York and they were two Jewish fellows. They were going there for medical training also. When I first got to town I stopped in a restaurant there, Walgreens, as a matter of fact. We were sitting there and little did I know; I didn't know from this kind of thing. They sent a young lady over to tell me that they didn't serve blacks. But me coming from here, you know you hear about this all your life, but to experience it!

This was a hell of a way, to go somewhere and start out like this. This was the way it started out with me in Texas. From that point on I just did not care for it. I'd never seen this, but you know you hear about it all your life. They came and told the two fellows from the train that were standing there. They didn't tell me direct. Those fellows were going to fight too, they were really mad, they were from New York. They were worse than I was because I had to get them out of the place. Boy, I was really down, all the time I was in Texas; I was down. And I saw these signs on the bus, "To the rear of the bus." Spanish and blacks had to go to the rear of the bus. And I'd never seen it. That was in '55.

When I first got off the train I saw these signs with two water faucets, one for white and one for black. When I first got off the train this is what I saw. And I was never happy. I was there eight weeks for medical training. I didn't care for it. These two incidents, one right after another right away. Colorado was gorgeous; they were two different places.

Perhaps the officers were all white, but I can't quite remember. There on the base, that was one of the prettiest places I've been, there at San Antonio Medical Center where I took my training, it was so pretty there. But when I got time off I had a good eight weeks I didn't do nothing. I didn't like it; I went to the zoo there, I did a few things, you know, but it was always a funny feeling with me, "go to the back of the bus" and all that crap. And by me coming from here in 1955, that was pretty late for them to be doing that type of a thing.

I went from there to Washington, D.C., Fort Myers, right outside of Washington, sort of behind the Pentagon. I stayed there for a while; I was unassigned, I had to wait for an assignment. There was a lady that was attached to the WAACS and she was in charge of us for a while.

I really had nothing to do so they used to send me and two other fellows up to Arlington National Cemetery. We used to just pick up paper and stuff around there and they used to shoot that cannon off up there in that cemetery at four every day. We used to go up high there where those homes are—it's just like walking into the past—all those beautiful homes up there—all those retired colonels, etc.—beautiful! The homes were just outstanding up there. We used to go up there and look around.

I did that for a while and then I was assigned to Fort Dilworth, Virginia, and that's where I did most of my time in the service. I got attached to a field hospital. Most of what we did was train and I worked on the medical wards. As a matter of fact, I saw Eisenhower's granddaughter there; she had cancer real bad, and I used to see her. If you were in the service your family could go there.

So I worked there, I worked in the babies' ward. I did a lot of things; I enjoyed it. I enjoyed the service while I was in Washington. I had a good two years in service. I worked on a lot of OJT (on the job training) and we had to go out with people that did two weeks reserve training. We had to set up the camps and the field hospitals for them, and the equipment and all that stuff. We had to watch them do it. We did it up in Maryland and all around there.

They wanted me to go to school and train to be a nurse when I got out but I had enough. But I enjoyed the service; outside of Texas, the service to me was just great. I had two good years in service, and with me being so big, I was always in charge of something. I was always watching somebody or something like that.

9

NATE DUNCAN

(CONTINUED)

BACK IN CHICAGO

I GOT OUT of the service in 1957 and went back to working at Lyon's again. Then I got caught up in that thing, which was the most terrible thing, that active reserve thing. When I got out I had to put in two years active reserve, every week, Wednesdays. From work I had to go all the way out, all the way out to 79th and Jeffrey. There was an armory out there. I had to go out there for two years. I was training, that's all, it was very nothing. But I guess it was like you see these National Guards, probably it was that type of a thing. That was harder than being in the army for two years.

After that it had to be real bad for them to draft me again, recall me in the service. That was terrible, it was lousy, it was a waste of time. I had to catch the El and then catch the Illinois Central train every Wednesday. And that used to be my day off my job. I got tied up for two years, and you had to go, if you missed so many then they'd put you back in service to make up the time. So I went! There was really nothing that you could learn or anything. We had to go to camp once a year for two weeks, and there's your vacation. I went to a camp in Kansas [Fort Riley] and Fort Leonard Wood.

There were two apartments upstairs above the store, and I lived there and my mother lived upstairs too. My daughter was with me when she was a little girl. My mother really raised her.

When I went to the army my mother got the care of my daughter when she was just a year old. My daughter's grand-mother wanted us to have the baby because of the type of person the baby's mother was; she didn't think that she was a good mother. My daughter went to private school and went to college and everything else. She did very well; thank God, she had a good life. My mother was a strong woman, and she just took over.

In those days I went to all the clubs. I used to go every weekend when I'd get off work. I used to go to the dances out south to the Pershing Ballroom. I've been to the Club DeLisa; that was a special occasion when some of my people would come from Ohio. They would come in and we'd go there for the entertainment. You couldn't go that much; how much money did you have? George Kirby I saw there. I've seen all of them. I've seen Sarah Vaughan, Charlie Parker, Ella Fitzgerald, Dizzy Gillespie; I've seen everybody. Billy Eckstine I used to see at the Oriental Theater.

I used to go to the Regal all the time, that was a big thing, we had a lot of places to go. I used to go see Redd Foxx down on 47th Street. As far as entertainment is concerned, I've seen them all. Billie Holiday, I used to see her all the time, she was one of my favorites. I've seen Sarah Vaughan downtown at the Blue Note. George Shearing, I used to see him at the London House.

I used to go to all those places. I've been to just about every club that was in the city of Chicago one time or another. At that time you could go to them—you didn't have to worry about it—it was not expensive at most of them. Each one of them was unique in their atmosphere. I used to dance a lot, so I had the most fun when I went to the Pershing Ballroom (64th and off South Park). They had dances there every Sunday. Every Sunday they had a different band there, or entertainer. I used to love to go there because I liked to dance.

Next to the Regal Theater, at the Savoy, they had a big dance floor, huge, and I've seen Nat King Cole there. They had the bands there, but I've seen him there when they had the trio. The Savoy was just gorgeous, boy, was it nice. They had dancing in there, and skating, they had all that in there. They had amateur shows there too. A guy by the name of Al Benson was one of the first who had a radio show that played black music. He was the guy that because of him they flew over Chicago from the southern states and dropped all that confederate money over Chicago. He was a very popular guy. He started a lot of things in Chicago.

There were so many clubs then. I could name clubs for an hour. There were so many of them downtown at that time with top entertainers. It wasn't that expensive at that time, nothing that would really hurt you if you were working, it wouldn't bother you. They'd have a cover charge, but it wasn't that high. The only place that I couldn't go that often was the Club DeLisa. I wasn't aware of any policy of seating white customers closer to the bandstand, not one bit. I was a young guy, I didn't pay no attention to that. I didn't notice that whatsoever. It wasn't noticeable to me. At Club DeLisa they may have had people up to the front, people that had money.

When I was a kid I was too busy to get myself really involved in any kind of trouble that was very serious. Thank God, I've never been to jail until I got a little older, which was stupid! Every time I think about that I get mad. It was nothin' really; it was just funny. Me and a friend were in a place where they drink beer and whatever, and one of the policemen come in there, and the lady didn't have no license for the tavern. He made her mad, and she made him mad, and he called the wagon and had everybody in there hauled off to the station.

That was in the neighborhood, and that was the most embarrassing thing that could happen to me, and people could see us. It was embarrassing to me, and I'll never forget it, when the wagon passed Maxwell Street going to the Maxwell Street station. My mother was in the window and she said, "My son is in there." She didn't see me—it was just that intuition thing. She knew I was in there, and I'd never been in trouble in my life. I wasn't in trouble then.

I got down to the station. They was putting us out of the wagon, and I saw one of the bailiffs I knew. Steve Blue, I'll never forget his name. He said, "What are you doing in here?" I was working at that time. He said, "No, you're not going to go in there, I'll be right up in there before they fingerprint you. I

Photo by Carolyn Eastwood.

The Sunday market on Maxwell Street with the Maxwell
Street police station in the background. This station, familiar
from the opening scenes of the popular television series
from the 1980s, *Hill Street Blues*, was built in 1888.

don't want them to fingerprint you. I'll get you out of there
before they fingerprint you." So he went in there and got me
out. I would have been fingerprinted for no reason at all.

Irv Gordon, the Market Master, said, "Nate, don't worry
about it, when you get the court date, I'll go down to court
with you." When I went down to court with him, me and my
friend, we're scared like a son of a gun. I've never been in no
court, and when we got down to the court he went in the
chambers with the judge come out he said, "Just go home."
Oh, did I have friends back then too, right?

ACTIVISM

I WAS A Scoutmaster for 10 years. I was into that in the '70s. I
had a very good scout troop. We used to go camping in
Michigan and in southern Illinois. Every year we used to go to
camp. I've even gone camping in some of the parks here

during the winter months. I spent so much time with those kids and so much money. The area that I came from, they didn't have the money, so we'd have paper drives and this drive and that drive, but it would never come up to the amount of money that you'd really need to get the kids to camp. But I enjoyed it, me and my brother, we'd send him sometimes to camp with us.

A few of the members of the troop turned out to be very successful; one of them is a heart specialist. Some of them, as they got older and got out of the troop, went astray. But I still see them and I'm very well respected by them. The problem was to get the parents involved. "Take my kid, go ahead." They were just glad to get them out of the house; they didn't have to worry about them. But I went quite a long while with those kids.

I had my meetings down at the Newberry Center; that was one of the places, and at the First Congregational Church. The Scout Council of Chicago was broken up into regions. They were very good; they used to come out and work with me pretty good. Matter of fact, we kept up with a couple of them in recent years. The troop is no longer going; after they got older the replacements just weren't there.

Boys Club was around the corner from me. I used to go there. That's the same Boys Club that's on Racine and Taylor now. It was good. My mother was there, she was Mother of the Year from that Boys Club. She was on the Senior Citizens Auxiliary and they did a lot of work there; they raised a lot of money for that Boys Club and the Newberry Center. She was involved in both of those clubs. They did a lot of work back in those years. They're very active now.

I was on the board of directors there at Newberry Center for about three years. I didn't like it though. I was really the only one on the board that lived in the neighborhood. I really felt most of the women and guys were on there just for their personal selves. And I got out of there. They really wasn't into it, I got out of there, I couldn't deal with that. United Methodists was the one that supported them; that's a big, rich organization. I used to go to meetings at the Chicago Temple. I've been through a lot of things; for a guy that's not educated,

I've been through a lot of things. I was there for the kids, to help the kids. I got out, these people ain't doing what they're supposed to do. I got a plaque.

I didn't have anything to do with civil rights activism—I used to keep familiar with what was going on, but I wasn't involved with any of it. I used to hear about how they'd march in and they'd hit them with heavy rocks and things. It doesn't seem that long ago (Marquette Park, etc.), but I didn't get involved in that because I knew that I wasn't the type of person that could be hit upside the head with bricks and stuff and didn't do anything. I don't think that I was that cool about things. When that was going, at the end of it, I was old enough to realize what was going on, but when that stuff first started I wasn't too aware.

After the Martin Luther King assassination I was there on the West Side. You get a little involved in that. That was such a dangerous day. I'll never forget that as long as I live. We had to close up the store. They were setting the store on fire and they were setting all these buildings outside and setting everything in these other streets.

They were on the streets, on Maxwell Street. They tried to set the building I was in on fire twice; I put the fires out. They were going crazy because it was a Jewish owner. But they (the police) came in there and stopped all of that before it really got started. The police academy was over there (on Union) so they come in there and closed that street off for three or four days.

I couldn't even go home half the time. We couldn't get in and out of there because they had it all blocked off. Down Maxwell was the police station and then you had the police all up on the roofs when I was there. We had a bad, bad week or so there. The Lyons left; they got out safe and everything, but I'm sure they were terrified, everybody was terrified.

Terrible, terrible time! It was a thing that really happened that gave the burglars, the thieves, the not-so-doing-right people a chance to loot and take advantage of that. There were mixed emotions on that. There were people that were scared and there were people that were taking advantage of that.

Lyon's to Nate's

In 1973 Ben Lyon was getting up in age and his wife got real sick, got real, real sick; she had a stroke. I used to go to see her quite often; I was real close with them. Ben and I talked a long time about the store and he was showing me a whole lot of things. When she got so sick he just figured, he asked me if I wanted the store and I told him that was a tough decision for me to make, to have a store. He was a hell of a guy; you rarely saw people like him.

And he helped me out, and he did everything for me. All the arrangements with all the companies, he did that for me, and we made arrangements for me to pay him. He wanted me to have it. After I got a good footholding I paid him off. I knew most of the business. The business (financial) side I had to get into that more because I didn't know too much about that. I went through it real smooth. I didn't have any problems; everybody was nice that I did business with.

I had no idea what sort of money I would make. Because with me being black and going into a business, at that time mostly 60 percent was Jewish. There was not many black customers when I went into that store. At that time there might have been a couple other black owners in business there. There was a clothing store, I remember. I was there with only two or three others at the most. I had a few problems with some Jewish owners when I bought the business—trying to buy it from under me and stuff like that, and things was getting around that I wasn't going to be there long. That they'd give me six months.

People that was friends of mine, when I become the boss, it was a different ball game. They did things to me; you know they were very friendly to me when I was working for someone else, but then they were putting things out on the street that I'd be gone in six months and that I'd start having hamburgers and french fries and all that stuff, change the menu, which I never did. But they said I would and that I wouldn't be there long, but I tricked all of them!

There were some friendly people there, too, that would tell

you that these people were talking about you. It didn't mean nothing to me, they were customers too, they were my customers. Once I chased out two Jewish brothers, they were just harassing me to death. I was behind the counter one day and they put salt in the coffee, and then they'd go back and say there was salt in the coffee. These two guys were really bad characters. They were very friendly when I was working for Benny, but they changed, and I finally chased them out of the store.

They were giving me a tough time trying to buy the store from under me, and all that stuff, trying to buy the building and all so they could charge me rent, but Benny held firm. He wouldn't budge. I paid him off, and then I had enough money to buy the building. I worked it out until I paid him. I paid him everything I owed. And they were trying to pull all that stuff. A lot of Jewish people on the streets was trying to do that. I was doing fairly well, see, and they wanted to buy the building from him.

It was gradually changing in the neighborhood, but when I took over the store there was no Koreans there at all. They were all Jewish-owned stores except for the few people I'm telling you about; 90 percent of them were Jewish.

When I first got that store it was busy like hell, busy like hell! I used to have to close the door until I'd let a bunch of people out and let another bunch of people in. Mostly it was Jewish customers at that time; not all, but basically it was Jewish customers. They got over my owning the store, and they would come, even the guys that said it. They kept coming, they just thought I wouldn't last, they thought, hey, this guy ain't going to make it, you

Courtesy of Nate Duncan.

During his early years in business, Nate Duncan kept the shelves stocked with a full line of delicatessen items.

know. They just thought that way about it. I don't know why. I tricked them all. I hung in there, and I was busy. We had some busy days down there.

I had a big stock at that time. I used to sell a lot of groceries then, but basically it was corned beef and lox and all that stuff. I had a full line of Jewish products. It was busy; basically they used to come in and take it back to the stores. I worked hard; we had a busy store there, until later years, you know, the last five or six years I was down there it started fading. When the university come in, I was on my way out. So they changed my business, the university did.

When the Koreans came in (on Halsted), that really affected my business. They don't patronize, very, very few. Don't forget when the Koreans come in to the street, Jewish people had all these workers, blacks working for them. They were customers of mine. But when the Koreans came in they eliminated that a little at a time, and they had their own people in the business. But the way they operated at that time was they would then let a person stay until they get familiarized with the business and let them go, and they would bring in their own kind. Eventually they eliminated a lot of people there.

And don't forget 14th Street and Halsted all the way back to the viaduct, those were wholesale houses. All those were my customers, and the houses, those were all my customers.

There was the black customers out there that lived there in the area. They supported the streets during the weekdays. Gradually, they were taking away people, a little at a time.

There was some competition; in fact there was a deli right across the street from me. But that didn't bother me. There was enough bus-

Nate Duncan's sister, Patsy Webster, who helped out in the deli on weekends, with Al Perez, whose book stand was set up in front of Nate's on Sundays.

Courtesy of Nate Duncan.

Photo by Carolyn Eastwood.

Nate's Deli on a Sunday market day with
Al Perez's book stands and tables in front.

iness to go around. There was no problem about business
then; business was good. Saturdays and Sundays you had to
work from the moment you got to that store till the moment
you got out of there, you worked. You stayed behind that
counter, there were people standing in line, twos and threes,
all the way in.

I couldn't get away on Sunday to walk around the market,
even though I had quite a few people working for me at that
time. I had my mother, my brother, Kenny, me—I had about
five people working there at that time. On a weekend my sister
would help me out. I had kids working for me. Kenny was
working there. He was a young man during the time that the
Lyons had the store, and he continued to work after they left.
He worked there for years and years. He knew the business as
good as I did. As for my leaving the business to go out for a
while, I had my mother. And all my brother's kids worked
there; six kids and they all worked in my store, one time or
another, every one of them until they got to a certain age.

FAMOUS PEOPLE AT NATE'S

SOMETIMES SOME FA-MOUS people came in the store too. When Jerry Lewis was in town, they used to get stuff from the store— when he appeared at Chicago Theater. Red Skelton was in my store; he sat in the corner there. Yeh, I talked to him; he was

Courtesy of Nate Duncan.

Crowds surround Nate's Deli for the filming of *The Blues Brothers* in 1980. For the movie, the deli was renamed the "Soul Food Cafe."

my size, 6'4". I didn't realize he was so big at the time. He was a hell of a guy. He was just on the streets at that time and he came in.

Sheldon Leonard was in my store, the producer of the Desi Arnez show, and he made a lot of the "B" movies during those days. But that wasn't during the time I had the store; that was earlier. But Senator Dirkson was in my store, I remember that. There were a lot of people in there. They were very friendly people. I used to laugh and talk with them.

The Blues Brothers, that was pretty exciting when they decided to do a scene in the deli. A group of them was on the streets, looking, I guess, at the location. They had the spot next door and I was in the store doing some bookwork, and they left some kind of message for me to get in touch with them. And they came in and talked to me about they wanted to shoot something there. I think it came basically from that book (*Maxwell Street*) that Ira Berkow wrote. When they looked at the store, they said, boy, this is perfect for what we want. And I talked to them and they said what they would do was, they would get in touch with me when they wanted to shoot the movie.

It was a couple of months or more before they did the shooting. When they came down there, oh, God, did they have the equipment. We knew one of the fellows that was working with that crew. He went to school with my brother. He did that work, camera work. He went all over; he told me he just worked six months and then was off six months, and he was working everywhere. Evidently he must have made a lot of money. When he was in Chicago, every movie they made he would come in my store and tell me about the movie they were making.

Courtesy of Nate Duncan.

Dan Aykroyd and Nate Duncan's mother, Roberta, during the filming of *The Blues Brothers* in 1980.

They did a lot of things out there in front of the store that they didn't even show in the movie. I imagine they took so much stuff that they just cut out what they wanted. 'Cause they were there all day from seven in the morning until seven at night. They paid me; I wasn't supposed to have any customers, but I did. They'd get in there. They was coming through the back and through the side. The only thing was, when they started shooting they wanted it just like it was at that point, it had to be the same people, because I remember my mother took off a sweater or something she had on, and they made her put it back on. They had a lady there looking at these things and she noticed.

They were very friendly. They stayed down in my store for hours laughing and talking, telling jokes, just cracking everybody up. Just down there like people. They were drinking a lot of beer. I had to go out and get them beer because we didn't have it in the store. Oh, they were drinking beer, especially that one that passed (John Belushi). We never knew at the time that he was the type of person that he was; he was just constantly drinking.

John Belushi was from the Chicago area, and he said, "I used to be down here and used to steal stuff." He was funny, he was really funny. Yeh, he knew about the streets; he was familiar with the area. But the other guy [Dan Aykroyd], he wasn't from here, he was from Canada. He did a two hour television special in front of my store on blues. It was a thing that he covered all the blues that was being played in Chicago, especially on Maxwell Street.

MAXWELL STREET

THERE WAS SO much music on the streets in those days. There was a man called Stovepipe and he played on the streets on Sunday. I remember at one time he was across the street from us. You know that the area across the street from my store was where a lot of those guys started out and they became very, very famous.

The blues band that played out of a blue bus started playing in back of my store when they tore all of the buildings

Photo by Carolyn Eastwood.

Outside the "blues" bus where musicians played
every week during the Sunday Maxwell Street market.

out of there. Behind my store, years ago, there was a big pickle factory, Manhattan Pickle Factory. During my time there was a Baptist church back there. They tore that building down in the '80s. They tore all that area down in the '80s in that particular block.

You had homes there. Where the bus with the blues band played there used to be a home, and the bus was sitting in what used to be their backyard. When they tore down all those homes it just left the tree there. And then they started gathering under the tree. There was a big apartment building on the corner of 14th and Newberry. They tore all that down and all that was open land. Before that the band used to play on the streets. In those years there was nowhere that had open space like that. There were a lot of individual musicians playing a lot of places. They had about four bands there, four bands in that little area there at one time. There was a blind guy with a guitar that played religious music. He was very famous—he was in papers and things.

They used to have carnivals there every year on Newberry. They had carnivals from Maxwell and Newberry all the way to Roosevelt, big carnivals. In those years they were big and they were very successful back in that time. They were all over, different streets through that area. The first one I saw when I was just a kid was at 14th and Union.

On the streets—they had what they called the "Strong Man," a very strong person, and I've seen him with pipes in his mouth and he would bend them. In those years they had that type of thing on the street. He used to take a nail and put it between his hands here and put a rag around his hand and take a two-by-four board and put the nail all the way through it. He was a very strong man; I can't believe how strong this man was! He was mostly just beyond my store. He could do a lot of things. I've seen him pull cars with his teeth, very strong man.

Then you had an Indian, he didn't have no legs, and he was on a piece of wood with rollers. He was a medicine man. And with his wife. He had snakes and snake remedies. The most fantastic thing that I saw was a foot doctor and they had a stand, and on a Sunday they used to cut calluses off peoples'

Courtesy of Nate Duncan.

> Some vendors were well known on Maxwell Street for years, such
> as the "Chicken-man" who walked around with a chicken on
> his head, the "Strong Man," and this familiar seller of plastic toys.

feet. Corns and calluses, right on the street.

I've seen more in my later years of people preaching on the street than I did back in that time. Don't forget, back in that time they went to church on Sundays. They used to come down on the streets and get a shoeshine but then they used to all go to church. I see more of the people (preaching the end of the world, etc.) in the last 10 years. I didn't see it then.

When I was able to get out on the streets I talked to the vendors I knew. I just knew the ones that had been there for years and years, I knew them as personal friends. Even at the end of the market I talked to them about what the situation was. In the old market, you could spend a whole day on the streets; but with this new one, you go down one side and come back on the other. God knows, what they were selling; they

Photos courtesy of Nate Duncan (right) and Carolyn Eastwood (below).

Right: The intersection of Halsted and Maxwell Streets (looking west on Maxwell Street) on a Sunday morning in the 1950s.

Below: The same intersection in 2000 with the Sunday market removed and most buildings in the area shuttered or demolished.

Photo by Jeff Fletcher.

Near the end of the Maxwell Street Market, these Chicago mounted policemen rounded up protesting vendors and bystanders on Halsted Street for a night in jail.

were selling everything from shoes to rusty tools to everything.

I guess people would buy those rusty tools, what's rusty doesn't make any difference. Most of that rust doesn't bother that stuff and they'd buy it so cheap that if you'd buy it in the store, it would probably cost a lot of money. If it's something that they see that they need, the rust doesn't matter. It rains on it and it rains on it, and it gets rusty and people buy it. Guys buy it, you know, in the plumbing business, and carpenter business and this and that, and that stuff is very useful to them.

The vendors were customers of mine. They would send a helper in for food, and I knew who that was for. I knew most of the vendor owners that had been there for a long period of time. I talked to older people, younger people. I knew them very well. I don't have any contact with them since I left the street. I might know a few, but I've lost contact with them since I left the street. I just know them from being on the street. I don't know nothing about the other jobs they had, stuff like that. I never knew what most of them did.

I didn't talk to that many of the produce people. I just talked to one produce guy, Herbie. He was Jewish and he had a hearing aid. I'd

445   Form 100B   10M   1-70

CITY OF   CHICAGO

Maxwell St. Market

—

MARKET PERMIT

Nº 7428

GOOD THIS DAY ONLY

___

Fee 17 Cents

THIS PERMIT MUST
BE DISPLAYED
PUBLICLY

Courtesy of Nate Duncan.

A Maxwell Street Market vendor's permit from the 1970s, when they still officially cost just seventeen cents.

Photo by Carolyn Eastwood.

Nate Duncan seated at the third table, of three in the delicatessen,
where the Market Master Irv Gorden liked to collect fees and conduct
other market business. In 1976 this position was eliminated.

known him very well. But the other vendors, the Spanish
vendors, I really didn't know them that well. Most of them
didn't speak English, so I just knew them by seeing them after
we had got that organization together. I didn't really know
them personally. I would go by and make a purchase, but I
didn't know them.

Me and Irv, the Market Master, was very close. He was a
friendly guy with me. A lot of market people said a lot of bad of
things about him right at the end, but he helped me in a lot of
ways. People said he was on the take, but he wasn't as bad as
people say he was. They wished he was on the take now like
he was then. If there was a guy on the street who made
$3–4,000, Irv would probably take $150 from him. But after that
that guy would have to pay no taxes; all that money was tax
free. But don't forget, some guy that made himself $50–60 a
day, Irv wouldn't take nothing from him. The fee was 17 cents
at that time. That was just the way that was.

But the guys that made a lot of money didn't want to give
him anything, so they hated his guts. At that time he was

splitting the money with the 1st Ward Alderman, John D'Arco. But nobody got hurt, don't forget, those guys were making so much money they didn't know what to do with it. The more money they made, the more that he asked them for.

There were a lot of poor people that didn't make no money, he never took nothing from them. See, they never tell you those things. He was the controller of the streets, there was no problem like this then. He never even bothered with guys with little things. He wouldn't even take the 17 cents from those guys that were making very little money. They don't tell about him that he did those things.

He died. They pressured him right out of there and he died. A lot of complaints, a lot of heat, a lot of this, a lot of that, and he died not too long after that. Irv didn't last too long after that. I knew him real good; I was a real close friend of his.

URBAN RENEWAL, THE EXPRESSWAY, AND THE UNIVERSITY

WHEN WE FIRST heard of urban renewal it was quite a few years back, and there were the neighborhood people that were having meetings. It was a long-term plan that they were going to take the streets out, but Lyon's wife always said, "Nate, don't worry about it; they're never going to take the streets out."

This was going back 30-35 years ago. It had been targeted that long. It was an area that they had let go down and it was such a valuable area. I believe that's why it had really been targeted because it was a valuable area. Look at how close it is to the middle of Chicago. They let the area go down to do what they did. They never maintained it. The city didn't do nothing about the area, just let it decay. They could have stopped that. They could have maintained it the way other areas are maintained. They never did nothing. The streets needed paving. I don't know if the owners complained about it enough. They never cleaned things, never cleaned the alleys, never repaired the pavement.

I didn't know about urban renewal as such. They were talking about putting the university in there south of Roosevelt

Road before the university come in there. There was no connection between urban renewal and the university at that time, because we used to go to meetings at the YMCA. Urban renewal was trying to get the area, and that was before anything was in there. All that stuff that you see wasn't there.

They used to have meetings at the YMCA, which at that time was on Miller and Maxwell, and they used to have some pretty strong meetings there. The people in the neighborhood were there, just the people that lived there, and the churches. The people that had the churches there, and stuff like that, they used to have meetings. There weren't city or government officials there, just the people that lived in the neighborhood with the YMCA staff and the ministers in that area were there. It wasn't held at the Newberry Center because they just sold out. I don't think they was interested in the subject because they wanted to move their building. It was a smaller building. They were glad to get out of there and move down where they're at now, but then they were at Maxwell and Newberry, right down from me.

They had meetings at that time, but as I recall, most of the people that had homes really wanted to sell them so it was really just a 50-50 thing. A lot them were absentee owners. It was fairly easy for the city to get what they wanted when they first took it out in the area because these were old houses. At that time the residents didn't realize how valuable the area was and for the type of people that was living there, poor people, I guess, it wasn't hard to get them out of there. At that time they had not got organized, and they had a lot of factions there. They were all blacks. The ministers were definitely against it because if you have to move a church you're going to lose most of your congregation.

I didn't think this would happen. No, I don't think nobody ever felt like that would happen, what you see now. They never figured out what to do. When the city took that area they had no foundation or nothing. They just conned the people out of all their land and went in there and stripped it all away. There really wasn't that much; there was no big fight. The people didn't know about the things that they know about now. They didn't know what was happening to them.

The alderman was John D'Arco; so that was your alderman. That's the 1st Ward, and that's the thing there. Whatever they decide to do they could do it easy in those days, like the YMCA and all those people. They said, "We'll move you here, we'll move you there."

The Dan Ryan Expressway came in there so fast that I never really knew what happened. I don't know what happened; it just looked like I was sitting there and it was there! They got those houses out of there and tore that down and built it up so fast it'd make your head spin.

It seems to me, after they bought all that land, they started building right away. There's really nothing over there, all fields, two fields from Newberry all the way to Morgan and down Morgan to 14th. And then I believe the University acquired it. At Newberry and 14th there was a school, Garfield, my daughter went there. The year that she graduated they tore it down. Those buildings were solidly built, those on 14th Street, they were pretty solid like the buildings on Halsted. 14th Street had the same kind of buildings; they were good buildings. I'm sure there were some bad ones, but these were mostly big buildings there. So they stayed there for quite a long while.

From Maxwell and Newberry to Roosevelt Road they took that right out of there, they took all that out of there. You had homes on the east side of the street on Newberry; on the west side of the street from Maxwell to Roosevelt, you didn't have that many homes there. You had a building on the corner of Maxwell and Newberry; then you had a factory there, the next building over, a mattress factory. Next to that was the Boys Club. Then you had the school that was connected with the church. Then you had a building where the nuns lived. Then you had a building on the corner.

I don't know if the mattress factory was still going. I think they had made a trade school out of the mattress factory. It could have been the type of kids that they were rehabilitating. There were a couple of teachers that used to come to the school that I knew, with the big hats, black guys, and they were teaching the kids skills, mechanics and things like that, at the time that they tore it down. So evidently that must have been owned by the Board of Education or something.

When people got mad, most likely it had to be against the city; I don't think the university's name popped up too much during those times. It was like the city was talking about buying up all that land back when that first started. The only thing that we had to go by was what they did over in the Italian neighborhood on Taylor Street with Florence Scala. This is what they were going by at the meetings, that this was what would eventually happen over here. 'Cause she fought so hard and lost.

That could have been the way a lot of the older people thought; they didn't know about what really was going on. So maybe this had a connection with that. How they got in there so fast and took that land; because she failed, worked so hard and failed, so I guess that's what it was. After that time they figured the city was so powerful and that Daley was so power-ful, if that's what he wanted, he'd get it, even though they did fight. I guess they have that hopeless feeling.

There were some meetings that Friends of the Market had; the vendors were there, and Florence Scala was there, and I was there, and lots of other people. Oscar D'Angelo was there too, and that was when people from the Maxworks (a green organization) exposed him. We were trying to save the streets, and D'Angelo was infiltrating the organization, and he was getting information. How he got in there I don't know. He was really with Daley and those people. They were talking about what a phony he was, and they told him he didn't have a care for what we were doing and was just infiltrating our meetings, and there was a big argument about it.

That was when we gathered up all the information about the market, who the vendors were and who the customers were, and sent it in to the University and the city, and they rejected everything we had set up. We worked hard to get that together. They were telling the city what they wanted, what they deserved, at that time. That was when they had the sanitation people come in and the department from the city. We were trying to keep them from coming south and had all those meetings and they turned it all down.

The city people made a special trip in my store. They

didn't ever give me any citations. They never did give me any problems with that, never. And I don't think they did any of the stores in the block that I was in. They begin giving citations when it starts getting real hard and they know they can't get what they want.

The city did make mistakes as far as my building was concerned, and when you showed them, sorry! I had a big problem with them once; they made a mistake on my property taxes. They billed me for $6,000 and it should have been $600. But I had to pay it; they made me pay it. And I got a lawyer because I knew there was a mistake somewhere; I knew there was a mistake. What the hell are you charging me $6,000 for property taxes? I got a good lawyer, he was supposed to be a good lawyer, but he was a piece of garbage, he couldn't find nothing.

But my sister said, "There's got to be something wrong here," and we went over to City Hall together. We met a man in the hall that went with us and he searched and searched and finally they found the mistake. It was an extra zero. But it was two years altogether before I got my money back, and they didn't pay any interest either.

When we fought to save the market I didn't feel hopeless about that fight. I never looked at it that way because I thought times had changed and people was a little more smarter, and they could make some more connections, and they could get it together a little more. I didn't feel that it would happen that fast like it did before because I figured the times were different times, and I just figured we had a better chance.

But that opposition that we formed, the [Maxwell Street Market] Coalition, it wasn't 100 percent right; it didn't set right. There were so many people there, that it wasn't right. There was one guy we had on there; sometimes you get people infiltrating those organizations and they're really not right. I don't know, at the meetings he wanted to have so much power; he just wanted to be the power of everything.

Another fellow, every time someone would try to say something or make some changes, he got furious about it. I mean, he got furious! I went to a lot of meetings with him, and he was very effective. You know, we were on radio programs he was doing swell, he was sharp. But, even as sharp as they were, and they did as much as they could, but still the bottom line was that they were looking for something for themselves. And I don't care to deal with those people.

I'm an organization worker. I work for whatever I'm working for and I'll work for it hard and I won't look at it as an individual thing to me, which I never did, even when I sold the store. I worked just as hard to save the market as I did before when I sold the store. Because when I sold the store I was really out on a limb. I imagine a lot of other people got pressured like I did.

There were so many people in the Coalition that didn't want to get together. I knew that and I worked so hard. I tried so hard to get the people in the housing project to come out of there and help out. And the Halsted Street merchants organization was not working for us either. If they had come out with the people in the market we would have been a really strong organization. That was the only thing that could have made a difference with what was going on. They would have still been fighting. I feel that they would still be fighting.

This is the difference between me and what I was really seeing with those people. I had my mind on one thing, to save the streets, and fight like hell to keep them. Keep the streets, the whole thing; not Nate's as an individual, but the whole thing. I always said that, and I'd go to meetings about that; people come in for bickering and it's not going to work. You got to come in on one accord, everybody's for the same thing, but they didn't do it that way. You're not going to do it on your own, you got to come in as one organization. I tell people that all the time.

All you had to have was some numbers, and I know that this meeting we had at the YMCA that was arranged by the city to present their plan, so many people showed up that they couldn't get in there. That was the big shock of the whole thing. It shocked them (city and university people) because they never expected that.

Then they started changing the meetings around to places where they knew working people couldn't be there—during the week in the afternoon. They didn't have no more of those night meetings because they would have this huge amount of people coming to it and they couldn't take that, so they broke that up. That was the last big meeting they had at night. So they started having them during the week when the people was working. They started pulling those tactics when they couldn't be there. Then they started having them downtown and here and there where you never knew where they were at.

One of the first clues to what the University was doing was when the Submarine restaurant on the southeast corner of Roosevelt and Halsted burned down six or seven years ago. They were having it rebuilt and the University stopped them. It might still be in court. They said, "You can't build nothing here." That was the key, the cue, what they were going to do. People just couldn't see it. Then the University don't want to have to pay them for nothing, for the rebuilt building, so they went to court to stop them from rebuilding.

I didn't know anything early on that the University was going to take my building, but I knew that eventually. The owner of the big building on the corner of Maxwell and Hal-

Photo by Carolyn Eastwood.

Chain link fences and "No Trespassing UIC Property" signs became increasingly prevalent in the Maxwell Street area in the early 1990s.

sted, he got a letter from the University. And the other two buildings behind him, they got letters before I did from the University that they were interested in getting their property.

You know, that's the way it started. There was no offer there, it was just a letter from the University that they were interested in the property and they would call you and talk to you about it. That's the way it started, and here I am, got this letter and don't know which way to go or what way to turn.

I had my lawyer and he explained a lot of things to me about how they're eventually going to get it. At that time he said, "You don't have an organization here, you're not strong enough to have an organization. Just go down and talk to them and find out what they have from there, what they have in mind." And we did that. We went up to their office; my lawyer went to the lawyer's office that represented the University in the Sears Tower. Big law firm, big law firm, 79th or 80th floor, had the whole floor.

I was just there as an individual, not with other shopowners, nobody else but me, and they told us they wanted the land, they wanted the property. I didn't have no intimidation from them, like we're going to do this or do that, they didn't get that far down the line. They gave me three or four years to get myself together. They made an offer, then that's why I had to go back up there four or five times. What they offer you, forget about it!

They negotiated with three or four offers and they kept going up and up. It was low to start with and naturally you turn down the first couple times. And then I talked to my lawyer, and he still wasn't satisfied and he got everything he could get over what they had offered me, which at that time was pretty decent. He was getting a percentage of it, which wasn't the big percentage that he wanted, so he worked at it for months. He got more, much more than I thought he would get. The amount that he got was more than he thought he would get. I had to give him a percentage of it. So that's the way it happened. We didn't have no organization so I felt that way at that time; heh, this stuff is being torn up around me, there's no organization here, so what are my chances?

One thing that hurt us was the politicians and another was

Photo by Carolyn Eastwood.

Many old friends stopped by Nate's Deli before the final day, including Jerry Portnoy (left), harmonica player with Eric Clapton's band, whose father had owned a carpet shop on Maxwell Street.

that the Halsted Street merchants would never come in with us, and I could never understand why that was. And I went down and tried to get the people that was living in the new housing. I tried to get all of them, but it wouldn't work. The Halsted Street merchants thought they were safe; they were stupid. I kept telling them they were stupid. They thought they were going to be safe another 10 or 15 years. What must have made them feel that way, I don't know. That's why they never got in the Maxwell Street organization, they thought they were safe for another 15 years. If all of us had gone in together it would have prolonged it if nothing else. With St. Francis too. If we had gone in as one big whole we might have gotten some place.

Then the Halsted Street organization started having meetings down at the Holiday Inn. People were coming out from the city to talk to them. I was at a couple of those meetings, and the man from the city he made it sound so good like they're really not interested in getting the Halsted property. I don't know what become of it, but they had got an organization together.

Last day of the market? That killed my business anyway whether they had my store yet or not. They closed me out with barriers and they had me blocked off like I was a foreign country. That's what really got me. That was the worst part for me, being on that street when they did that. When they closed

Portnoy Carpets, owned by Jerry Portnoy's father at 658 Maxwell Street, disappeared with the building of the Dan Ryan Expressway.

the market down I was out, my business was shot after that. I just felt pretty bad about that, the way that they did it, and it lasted for two or three Sundays having those barriers up. Maybe they were afraid we would do something, but what could we do? It was done already.

The media coverage of the market closing, it stunk, a lot of it did. The story that you would tell them was never printed like you told it. I didn't like that; that used to irritate me. At the end they would say things that really weren't true and that would hurt in the streets. On the evening news, I couldn't stand those things, just some little shot at it and then they would make comments that didn't sound good at the end. But there were a lot of them that were pretty O.K.

My store was just something I loved. I just loved going to work, to meet people like I did and the assortment of people and the conversation and everything to me was just gorgeous. I loved it. It had a lot of value to me. I looked forward to my work.

Now I know why people liked it so well, because there's really nothing like it now. There was a friendly spirit in that store. It was just a comfortable feeling for everybody. It had nothing to do with race or religion; it was just a place where people could come and they could feel the friendliness in there no matter who you were or what you were. In my store you had the richest and the poorest right next to each other, and they all got along. It was something that life don't do that way now. It just doesn't go that way.

You couldn't explain to the politicians why it was important, only the ones who went down there like Alderman [Robert] Shaw. He knew that area and he knew how important it was. You could talk and get in conversations with anybody about anything. This went on for many, many years, even when the Lyons had it, so this little place went on 50, 60 years that same way, same atmosphere. Although when I was first coming there, there weren't that many blacks coming there because they probably didn't eat that type of food at the time or didn't know that much about Jewish food. But later years they began to come in and get acquainted with the corned beef and the different types of things.

So that's the way it was, it was just a thing where you could sit at a table with a strange person and get into a conversation. You don't do that in restaurants today; you sit by yourself. Everybody that would come in my store would tell you about that feel, that atmosphere, they loved it.

There was the Market Master with his little office at the back table, and then there were all those jewelers. There's no where in the world where they could come into a store and do what they did. They always stood at the back part of the store trading back and forth and showing their jewelry to each other. I remember my mother, when it got too busy (at that time we were busy). She would get the mop and start mopping the floor and mop them right out the door. They knew they were in the way at that time and they would leave. Years back there were a couple of them that were really good customers, they'd spend $30-$40 and would feed all of them.

The last day of my store came, and I had a lot of mixed emotions at that time. It didn't really hit me yet that that was my last day and I would never be down there any more. And the outpouring that I had was just tremendous. I really enjoyed that day. But the next day I knew all about it; I knew they took me out of business, and I knew I had a lot of adjustments to

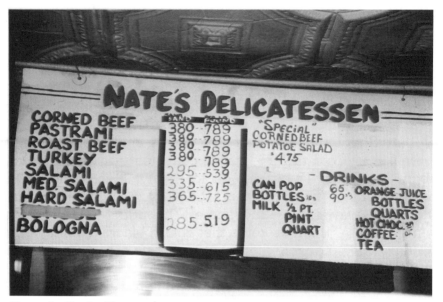

Photos by Carolyn Eastwood.

Above: The bill of fare at Nate's Deli, with
the vintage pressed-tin ceiling in view.

Below: Hundreds of well wishers came to see Nate Duncan on the
last day in his deli, and he was kept very busy slicing corned beef.

make in my life. I'd been there most of my life. It was a sad day. That's why I don't go down there much now. It's still very sad for me so I've only been down there once or twice. It's something that I try to control, but it's hard for me to control.

To see what they did, a parking lot there—incredible— to destroy the whole market. They did leave a part of Taylor Street, but they didn't leave any of Maxwell Street. That's one thing that's always bothered me. They could have left Maxwell Street alone. What they've got there now is nothing. And people came from all over the country, all over the world, to Maxwell Street.

Now I do a lot of work around the house, in the basement. I go to church a lot and I relax and take it easy. Occasionally I go out and eat with a couple of friends of mine. I keep myself busy. I don't have too much idle time. I just don't have that feeling to start up another place. The process of getting things set up is a lot of work and then location and this and that. When I had my own store I didn't have much free time, but being in the area like that, it didn't make any difference. It was really free time for me when I was there. I'd do whatever I wanted. In a business like mine you have to work two or three years to see any profit so it would be hard to start up again.

The business I was in you had to be physically in condition. I walk around now, but that doesn't mean anything. I had to get up early in the morning, but now I don't do that much. I'm beginning to adjust myself to that now.

*St. Francis of Assisi—finally I had a wonderful, wonderful place,
and nobody could ask for anything better than I had there.*

—HILDA PORTILLO

The University of Illinois at Chicago, The University Library, Jane
Addams Memorial Collection, JAMC Neg. 856.

A view of rooftops near Hull-House in the 1930s. The steeple of
St. Francis of Assisi Church can be seen in the background.

10. THE MEXICAN NEIGHBORHOOD
11. HILDA PORTILLO
12. HILDA PORTILLO (CONTINUED)

Mrs. Ramos and her family were among the many Mexicans and Mexican-Americans living on the Near West Side in the vicinity of Roosevelt and Halsted in 1951 when this photograph was taken.

10
THE MEXICAN NEIGHBORHOOD

FOR MANY MEXICANS living in the Halsted-Roosevelt neighborhood and for others living all over the Chicago metropolitan area, their spiritual home was the Spanish-language St. Francis of Assisi Church, located at the corner of Roosevelt Road and Newberry. The story of their migration to Chicago and the intensity and meaning of their struggle to save this church is the focus of this chapter and background for the story told by Hilda Portillo.

For the sake of simplicity the term "Mexican" will be used to refer to the immigrants and parishioners from Mexico, even though they might be naturalized Mexican-Americans of long standing or Americans of Mexican descent. This is an acknowledgment of the bond they have to each other through cultural associations and the Spanish language.

This is not to say that there are not differences among St. Francis parishioners in their cultural experience depending on their state of origin and its customs. But the bond that distinguishes these parishioners from those of many other parishes is the shared and unique quality of the St. Francis heritage and the impact that it has made on their lives.

IMMIGRATION

SPANISH-SPEAKING IMMIGRANTS HAVE come to Chicago in substantial numbers since the beginning of the twentieth century, and for many of the immigrants from Mexico, their destination was the Near West Side. The first large-scale Mexican immigration began as long ago as 1916, when railroad workers traveled to Chicago; but Mexicans were also drawn by the promise of work in the packinghouses in the Back of the Yards area and in the steel mills on the South Side. Even though many had possessed their own small farms in Mexico, harvests were uncertain and threats by the military were always a possibility. So they took a chance on Chicago.

A report from Hull-House notes that the settlement house workers had their first contact with a Mexican family at the turn of the century.[1] This family had come to the St. Louis World's Fair where the father exhibited feather work. After a short stay in Boston they came to Chicago where their young child entered the Hull-House kindergarten. Other members of the family served as interpreters when Mexican immigration to Chicago grew.

By the end of the 1920s there were 7,000 Mexicans living on the Near West Side. Although there were some housing restrictions in the sector of the neighborhood that was predominantly Italian, actual exclusion was less likely to occur there than elsewhere according to some research.[2] Other authors consider that it was a "volatile" mixture: ". . . the Italians feuded with the Mexicans and both groups attacked the Negro."[3]

Many of the Mexicans living in the Hull-House area had first come north to work in the beet fields of Michigan, but instead of going back to Mexico at the end of the season, they came to Chicago. Unfortunately, they found that their money would not sustain them for long, work was scarce, and Chicago winters were cold.[4] Those who were already established lent a hand to the newcomers and formed a helping pattern that was later repeated hundreds of times at St. Francis of Assisi Church.

The Mexican settlement around Hull-House and St. Francis of Assisi grew to such an extent that at one time it stretched from Harrison Street to 18th Street on either side of Halsted. Housing was poor in the neighborhood of Hull-House, and according to research in the 1920s, the Mexicans lived in

*The University of Illinois at Chicago, The University Library, Jane Addams
Memorial Collection, JAMC Neg. 144*

Mexican dancers in the Hull-House courtyard during a dance festival.

the poorest houses in the area.[5] They were often found in the
rear houses or in basements, and families often complained of
the rats in these houses. However, they tended to leave these
conditions and would move on as soon as they became established.

In spite of the poor housing, a number of small-scale
Mexican business enterprises could be found in the neighborhood at that time. Along Halsted Street, north and south of
Roosevelt Road, were 14 restaurants, five pool halls, five grocery stores, one barber shop, one shoemaker, four bakeries,
one meat market, one print shop, two sign painter shops, one
photograph gallery, one tailor shop, and one music shop—all
owned and operated by Mexicans.[6]

During this period of the 1920s, there were two active
clubs for young Mexican men at Hull-House and two Mexican
music bands in the neighborhood. Both Mexican children and
adults in substantial numbers were drawing books out of the
branch of the Chicago Public Library at Hull-House. Although

there was obviously some participation by the Mexican community in the activities of Hull-House, it may have been somewhat constrained because the Hull-House approach was a little too intellectual and middle class for these working-class immigrants.

According to the anthropologist, Robert Redfield, a stated purpose of the Mary Crane Nursery School of Hull-House, for example, was to make sure that "imitative children will not start imitating some of their parents' untrained and possibly undesirable habits." As late as 1948 no Mexican had ever served on the Hull-House Board of Directors and there was only one Mexican staff worker.[7]

Just as the Mexican laborers were recruited to come to Chicago when they were in demand to work the railroads, stockyards, and steel mills, many of them were deported when work was scarce during the Depression of the 1930s. Then, with World War II in progress, industries were again recruiting Mexican workers.

Many of the relationships of Mexican immigrants and other Chicagoans were colored by the legal status of the immigrants. It was only in 1924 that Mexican aliens were first required to register. Therefore, even when they had entered legally prior to 1924, they might have found themselves classified as illegal after 1924. If they entered or stayed illegally they ran the chance of being deported. It was only natural that they would tend to avoid contact with mainstream institutions and to rely on their own families, friends, and institutions. It also helps explain the importance in their lives of their own Spanish-language parish.

Another offshoot of the immigration status question was that Mexicans were vulnerable to harassment and intimidation by policemen. Rev. Peter Rodriguez of St. Francis of Assisi observed that policemen often stopped motorists in Hispanic areas and asked for immigration papers rather than driver's licenses, and that Mexican motorists were sometimes afraid to leave their homes for fear of being shaken down. At one point this priest risked his own status and stood up to INS officials who were harassing parishioners inside the church.[8]

One reason that this harassment continued in the 1970s

was that Mexican residents of Chicago were powerless politically. Even though Latinos were 10 to 15 percent of the city's population, there was only one elected official with a Latino background. Near West Side Mexicans were dependent on Alderman Fred Roti (1st) and Alderman Vito Marzullo (25th), both Italian-Americans, to be their spokesmen at City Hall. Neither were likely to raise their voices on the behalf of these constituents.

In the 1940s, after Italians, Mexicans were the second most numerous among foreign born living on the Near West side.[9] However, drastic changes came to the Mexican community in the neighborhood of St. Francis with the triple threats of "urban renewal," expressway construction, and the takeover of the neighborhood by the University of Illinois at Chicago. Approximately 45 percent of the families and 33 percent of single residents displaced by the university were Mexican. As with Italians and blacks, many of the Mexican families and businesses were uprooted more than once.

Juan Velasquez, Cook County supervisor of elections, lived at Halsted and Maxwell, and remembers Latino residents scattered throughout the area, both north and south of Roosevelt Road, and many Latino businesses along Halsted Street and Blue Island Avenue. He stated that when Harrison-Halsted fell to the University it affected Mexican people all the way to Kedzie Avenue, because the area surrounding Taylor Street was like Pilsen is now, a center of Mexican shopping and other activities.[10]

In 1961 when the southern boundary of the site proposal for the university campus was moved north to Roosevelt Road, this meant that area clearance would not require the demolition of a second prominent Catholic church. St. Francis was temporarily saved. As we now know, the southern boundary was extended to the 15th Street viaduct as funds and public relations' damage control permitted.

In the immediate vicinity of St. Francis of Assisi Church was the Maxwell Street Market. Not only was it physically close to the church because it extended along Newberry to Roosevelt Road, but about one-third of the vendors and many of the shoppers were Mexican. They depended on the market

Photos by Carolyn Eastwood.

Above: Mexican vendors have a long tradition of selling a wide variety of produce and other goods at the Maxwell Street Market.

Left: Mexican vendors were among the most vocal in defending the Maxwell Street Market and participated in this demonstration march to City Hall to protest the closing of the market.

for their livelihood and to help stretch their household budget.

Alfonso Morales, who worked in the market as part of his dissertation research, concluded that not only was the market important economically to the Mexican population, but it reinforced other aspects of their culture.[11] It was a place where a whole family could work together in cooperation, sharing the work and the benefits of having a fledgling business, so that parents could pass on values and practices to their children. Families shopped together and could find ethnic food items and enjoy other facets of their culture.

Salvador Ceja, a former resident of the area, commented on the meaning of the market. "We've always gone to the market. When my father retired he used to stay with my sister and me in turns, and I would ask him where he wanted to go. The first thing he'd say, 'Son, I love Maxwell Street—take me to Maxwell Street.' He'd start talking there with different people about all the old times."[12]

Rev. Peter Rodriguez, former pastor of St. Francis, said he believed that the market benefited from St. Francis and St.

Photo by Carolyn Eastwood.

Sons learn from their fathers as they work together selling leather belts on Sunday morning at the Maxwell Street Market.

Photo by Carolyn Eastwood.

The close physical connection between the Maxwell Street
Market and St. Francis of Assisi Church could be seen from this
corner of Newberry Avenue and Maxwell Street—a mutually
beneficial relationship in many ways, according to some.

Francis benefited from the Maxwell Street Market. People
came to the area to go to church and also to do their shopping.
He said, "Now St. Francis is an island."

St. Francis of Assisi Church

THE SPIRE OF St. Francis of Assisi Church is a beautiful landmark
in the Halsted-Roosevelt neighborhood that can be seen from
a considerable distance. St. Francis originated as the first
German parish on the West Side of Chicago. When it was
founded, Germans were one of the three largest ethnic groups
in this neighborhood. The cornerstone of the present building
at Roosevelt and Newberry was laid in 1866, and by 1875 the
brick structure with its 190-foot tower was in place. Later a
convent, school, and rectory were built to complete the complex.

In the first quarter of the twentieth century the brick

building of St. Francis experienced two major traumas. First of all, the building caught fire on February 15, 1904. Although extensive damage was caused, the church was rebuilt as much like the old one as possible. Secondly, in keeping with Daniel Burnham's Plan, the city formulated plans to widen Roosevelt Road by 32 feet. It was a difficult decision for parishioners, but they opted to save the church and to move the 190-foot tower and entire front of the church 32 feet south.

Although there were thousands of Mexicans on the Near West Side by the mid-1920s, there was only a small chapel on Polk Street to meet their needs. At that time the only Spanish parish in the entire Chicago area was the one in South Chicago, and there was clearly a need for Spanish-speaking services in the inner city.

The first Sunday mass for Mexicans of the Near West Side was celebrated by the Claretian Missionary Fathers in St. Francis of Assisi on November 20, 1925, and there was a "wall-to-wall" crowd according to the records.[13] That started the ball rolling to make St. Francis of Assisi an entirely Spanish-speaking parish, with the Claretians in charge. The largest inner city Mexican settlement was on the Near West Side, and St. Francis was the first Catholic church within this area of Chicago to offer services in Spanish.

The count of baptisms is often used as a measure of participation in a parish, and it was noted that 195 out of 238 baptisms in the parish in 1926 were Mexican. The 1978 parish history of St. Francis shows that the number of baptisms kept increasing each year from the 1950s onward. The greatest number of baptisms was 1,799 in 1957.

As a student, Salvador Ceja learned English at St. Francis. His father and mother were both from Mexico, and his father worked 51 years for International Harvester. Yet his father never let them speak English at home and would say, "While you're here you speak your native tongue." Salvador said when he went to St. Francis most of the students were Latin Americans, " . . . in my room was one black, three whites, and the rest were Latin Americans." In 1965 the school of St. Francis was closed and the building was razed; the land was taken over by the University of Illinois at Chicago. The Sisters of St.

Francis from Joliet, Illinois, had staffed the St. Francis of Assisi school for nearly 100 years.

By 1980 many of the parishioners of St. Francis had left the neighborhood; some left voluntarily and others were forced out by urban renewal or the University of Illinois. Yet they continued to come to St. Francis for mass, Sunday school, weddings, funerals, and special fiestas. Also, the church continued to serve the parishioners through ESL and GED classes and legal aid.

Dark Years for St. Francis of Assisi Church

IN SPITE OF rumors and gloomy predictions, parishioners hoped for the best for St. Francis and prayed that talk of St. Francis being closed or merged with another church was just that— talk. At the end of 1993, the Archdiocese of Chicago was $4.5 million in the red, and the leadership had decided that many of the aging churches in the old immigrant neighborhoods would have to go. During the period from 1982 to 1996 the Archdiocese closed 81 churches.[14]

There was a difference in the case of St. Francis, however, because unlike many other churches, weekly attendance there remained high, averaging around 3,000. This was twice the average of other Catholic churches in the city. There were five masses every Sunday, all in Spanish, and annual donations were around $200,000. This loyalty was maintained in spite of the fact that the surrounding neighborhood had been largely demolished. Parishioners faithfully traveled significant distances from all over metropolitan Chicago to attend mass at St. Francis.

In the oral history that follows in the next chapter, Hilda Portillo relates the sequence of events leading to the closing of the church from her personal point of view. The stark fact of the closing came in the form of a *Chicago Sun-Times* article (January 12, 1994) rather than through any dialogue of church officials with parishioners of St. Francis.[15]

The article stated that it was recommended to Cardinal Bernardin that St. Francis be sold and the parish merged with

Holy Family Church. It continued, "Archdiocesan officials said there was little objection to the closing of St. Francis, but some parishioners Tuesday night said some people were upset." This statement was far from the truth because for a long time the Archdiocese had managed to ignore the parishioners' 4,000 signatures on petitions, their demonstrations, and their requests for hearings.

During that period I asked Rev. Andrew Greeley, priest, sociologist, and well-known author, if he had any inside information concerning plans for the closed church. He replied that he was not privy to any plans, adding, "The so called 'death squad' are those diocesan 'planning' officials who make decisions about closing parishes. They never consult anyone. And, of course, they have no professional qualifications, which is why I presume they have the job!"[16]

On November 20, 1994, mass was said for the last time at St. Francis and the doors were closed. Religious statues and other artifacts were removed from the church and eventually the pews, organ, and stained glass windows were also taken away. There were no utilities—the heat and the lights were shut off, pipes froze, and the condition of the building deteriorated. Some parishioners made the move to Holy Family, some went to other churches, and some stopped going to church altogether. But the St. Francis of Assisi Preservation Committee continued their fight to save the church. At one point a priest who was visiting from Mexico conducted a mass on the sidewalk in front of the church and many parishioners attended.

At the end of January, 1996, increasingly ominous signs foretelling the end of St. Francis could be seen. Wrecking equipment suddenly appeared outside the back of the church. On January 31st the parishioners marched in front of Cardinal Bernardin's mansion to "pray for a miracle," but none seemed forthcoming; they learned that on February 4, the Archdiocese had obtained a demolition permit from the city.

In the meantime, on January 24, 1996, it had been announced that a new bishop, Rev. John Manz, was being appointed to the vicariate of the Near West and Northwest Sides. His long history with the Spanish-speaking community

Photo by Carolyn Eastwood.

Parishioners occupied St. Francis on February 4, 1996, in order to protect
the church from demolition with their physical presence. Winter coats and
tents of paper gave them some protection from sub-zero temperatures.

presented the first small window of opportunity to St. Francis
parishioners pleading to be heard, and he did meet with them
on February 2 and listened to their side of the story.

On a freezing Sunday morning when the temperature
broke the 1895 record with a minus 14 degree reading, parishioners occupied the church. During the week following the
occupation Bishop Manz acted as liaison and indicated that
there was some hope that the church might be saved, at least
it would not be torn down for the time being. The following
Sunday, February 11, 1996, still under frigid conditions, the
church was packed for mass, the first held since its closing in
November of 1994.

By March 9, 1996, Cardinal Bernardin issued a statement
that " . . . perhaps we were not fully aware of the tremendous
commitment and attachment to the church." Taking into account the countless demonstrations and thousands of petition
signatures collected and delivered to the Archdiocese, at the
very least there appears to have been a disconnect somewhere
along the line if the cardinal believed that the number of

Photo by Carolyn Eastwood.

Parishioners of St. Francis of Assisi met with Cardinal Bernardin at his request to resolve some of the friction that had been caused by the issue of the dissolution of the church.

protesters was small. A press release confirming the reopening of the church was the prelude to an overflowing Easter mass.

Cardinal Bernardin had been diagnosed with terminal cancer, and shortly before his death in the fall of 1996 he met with a group of St. Francis parishioners outside his mansion in a reconciliation gesture. Approximately a week before his death he ensured that St. Francis would return to its status as a self-contained and separate parish.

State senator Jesus Garcia consistently supported the people of St. Francis and was there the cold day in February

Members of the St. Francis of Assisi Preservation Committee are shown here with Hilda Portillo at the meeting at Cardinal Bernardin's mansion that occurred a month before his death.

Photo by Carolyn Eastwood.

when they first occupied the church. Concerning the problems that poor people have in making their voices heard and their needs respected Sen. Garcia later told me, "It's clout versus poor people; that's why no one has been able to come up with a compromise, because clout doesn't feel that they've got to compromise with anyone who doesn't have any clout. That's why the victory of getting St. Francis to stay is a victory over overwhelming odds that wasn't supposed to happen. It couldn't happen. But it did!"[17]

As Juan Velasquez remarked, "There are only three ways of succeeding—through money, politics, or people. And if you don't have money or political power, you have to have people." Hilda Portillo's oral history in the next chapter is an example of the extraordinary effect that dedicated people power can have.

Notes to Chapter 10

1. Anita Jones, "Conditions Surrounding Mexicans in Chicago" (Ph.D. diss., University of Chicago, 1928), 42.

2. Louise Año Nuevo Kerr, "The Chicano Experience in Chicago, 1920-1970" (Ph.D. diss., University of Illinois at Chicago, 1976), 28.

3. Allen Davis and Mary Cree, *Eighty Years at Hull-House* (Chicago: Quadrangle Books, 1969), 143.

4. Jones, "Conditions," 44.

5. Ibid., 42.

6. Ibid., 53.

7. Robert Redfield, "Mexicans in Chicago," *Diary* (Chicago: Special Collections, University of Chicago, 1924-25), 99.

8. Interview, 1997.

9. Sibylle Allendorf, *Local Community Fact Book Chicago Metropolitan Area: Based on 1970 and 1980 Census* (Chicago: Chicago Review Press, 1984), 75.

10. Interview, 1997.

11. Alfonso Morales, "Making Money at the Market: The Social and Economic Logic of Informal Markets" (Ph.D. diss., Chicago: Northwestern University, 1993), 50.

12. Interview, 1997.

13. Rev. Msgr. Harry Koenig, ed., *A History of the Parishes of the Archdiocese of Chicago*, Vol. 1. (Chicago: New World Publishers, 1980), 282.

14. Steve Kloehn, "Beloved but not always obeyed," *Chicago Tribune*, 17 November 1996, 15.

15. Andrew Herrmann, "West Side Parish to Merge with Rehabbed Holy Family," *Chicago Sun-Times*, 12 January 1994, sec. 1, 15.

16. Correspondence, 1995.

17. Interview, 1997.

Courtesy of Norma Portillo.

Above, left: Hilda Portillo on her honeymoon in 1957.

Above, right: Hilda Portillo working at St. Francis of Assisi in 1977.

Below: Hilda Portillo (right) with her daughter Norma.

11

HILDA PORTILLO

FAMILY AND CHILDHOOD

I WAS BORN in Mexico in Chihuahua, Chihuahua, the biggest state of Mexico, on December 18, 1940. I was the fifth child of six. My father passed away when I was two years old so my mother was a widow very young. But we survived. My father had a lot of land and cows and horses; he was a farmer, but he also grew animals. My mother used to sew. When the monies were running out my mother left Chihuahua and came to Ciudad Juarez which is across the border from El Paso, Texas. She crossed the border and she went to El Paso with some of her samples and one of the most polished stores, La Popular, gave her a job. And that's how she supported us.

I was in a Catholic boarding school from the ages of 5 to 15 years old in Chihuahua. It was wonderful. I didn't know it was wonderful back then, but now I realize the nuns were very, very good. Still some of them are alive and they visit in Chicago so I have a chance to see them again. Every time I go to Mexico I go to visit them and I took my children along to know where I grew up.

My sisters weren't with me in the boarding school. The three oldest ones were girls, but when my father died they were around 10 or 11 years old. Then there was a brother, then me, and then the baby who was a boy. So the older ones were helping my mother, going to school themselves. She needed all the help she could get. So that's why they didn't go to the boarding school although they finished high school in Mexico. That was the highest grade they went, my sisters, the oldest ones, my mother made them go through high school.

When I was in the boarding school, I didn't feel like my mother left me because she was there once a month, or at the most, every six weeks, and she used to write to me because she used to suffer a lot because I was there. The reason I was in a boarding school was because I had an older and a younger brother and they used to baby-sit for me. I was always playing baseball and things like that. My brother owned gloves and the baseball bat and all that stuff. They were wonderful and they used to give me money to be nice. And then my mother said, "No, no, no, that's no good, something could happen to her."

So she sent me to the boarding school, but I never felt isolated. I had my bad days, but overall I would say I liked it; I learned a lot. When my mother used to visit me every month or two she would bring all these beautiful clothes for me.

When I was in boarding school I visited my family in the winter because back then in Mexico the vacations were in November, December, and January, and I used to go home for the vacations. My grandparents were very close to the capital of the state (Chihuahua), and I had relationships with grandparents on both sides. My uncle, my mother's brother, had a fruit farm and the truck used to come to the convent with free fruit. So that's why I was very well treated at the convent.

Also, I didn't come every year to my home because the nuns used to encourage us to travel to the interior of Mexico to get to know our country. So in two of those 10 years I went for the whole three months to visit different states in Mexico. Of course, my mother paid for it.

We went to Guanajuato, Jalisco, Morelia, Mexico City, Puebla, San Luis Potosí, and the other one we went to was on the coast of Mexico, Sonora. We used to sleep in religious provincial houses rather than hotels, and they used to take you to the cathedral where we were, and all the churches. And then sometimes we girls escaped in the night, you know. This was in 1953 and 1954 when I went there, but things have changed a lot. I enjoyed Oaxaca, especially the silver. I still have a lot of things that I bought there. When I took the trips my family gave me money to buy things for them and for myself.

I had an aunt who was three years older than me so when was home on vacation we'd go dancing. But we'd have a ball I remember. Of course, they bothered about chaperones; my aunt was one of the chaperones till my mother found out what was going on. Then my brother was very strict and he took like my father's place. They'd let me go to 12 noon mass every Sunday with my friends, and then we'd go to the show, or if we didn't want to go to the show we could go for ice cream or something, but be back by 3:30! And inside, no talking to strangers or anything like that.

In my mother's time the weddings there used to last as much as three days. All the village around would come to the wedding. And they danced day and night, and then they were tired and they'd sleep and then wake up. Lots of food—they used to hire many, many women to cook. The relatives used to cook but it wasn't enough. My mother had seven sisters but they couldn't cook enough for that many people, and it was beautiful. I never heard of any problems, only in one wedding in Sierra Madre where my mother was born. I was very, very little when that happened, but there was a big fight at the wedding and five men were killed. But that wasn't all the time. There were weddings and parties all the time. It was beautiful. I used to go there when I was 13 years old and I really enjoyed it.

I had one friend who was the son of a teacher, very, very handsome guy. He asked me to be his girlfriend when I was 14 and I said, sure, why not? And this was the only boyfriend I ever knew because then I married this other guy who never asked me to be his girlfriend, just to marry him and go to New York.

I came out of the boarding school when I was 15. By then my oldest brother was in the service here in the United States because the store where my mother used to be a seamstress fixed my mother's permanent residence in the United States. So all of us were legally here in the United States although we were living across the border. Because of that my brother went to register for the service at 18 years old for three or four years.

Marriage

So when I came out of school at 15 years old I met my brother's sergeant, Daniel Payan, and he liked me. He was 15 years older than myself. He said, "If you marry me I will take you to New York." I said, that's a deal. So I married him and went to New York. He was 30 and I was 15.

My family opposed it. I was very young, he was very old, he wasn't Hispanic either, but I said, I want to marry, I want to go with him. If you don't let me marry I'll probably just run away. Because New York in those days was like the capital of the world, so exciting for a child who was in a boarding school. And then here comes this gentleman, handsome, and with little things for me. My mother had to give permission in Mexico for me to be married at such a young age. But remember this, this was my oldest brother's friend, it wasn't anyone from the streets. And my mother also married when she was 15 years old.

In those days (in 1954) many people thought that you study just to be a good homemaker. At first my main motivation for getting married was that I wanted to go to New York, but my husband was a very good man, and with time I got to love him very dearly. But we only had five years.

I met my husband's mother and father on my wedding day. They were opposed to our marriage. They were Greek, I was Mexican, and I wasn't right for him. They were very unhappy. My mother-in-law just came to tell me how sorry I was going to be. My husband was an only child.

After my marriage my husband did take me to New York for a week. He offered to take me to New York to see Fifth Avenue, the UN. Then we went to Washington, D.C. He took me to the Capitol and the White House; it was my dream. Especially the designers in New York clothes. Not that we could afford anything, but I just wanted to see. New York is still big, but it seemed even bigger then, and I just wanted to see. It was so beautiful and I was so young. Can you imagine what it's like going to New York? It's like going to another world. We didn't have the Empire State Building in Mexico

City or anything like that. Different country; it's different, no matter what.

When we were married my husband still had one more year to go in the army. He had enlisted. Although his parents weren't poor, they were tight with the money and if he served he would have a scholarship, so that's why he did it. He was a sergeant in the army air force and used to work in helicopters and planes. That's a reason he and my brother got along so well because my oldest brother used to own a small plane, and until today he loves to fly.

We were in Philadelphia for that year after he got out of the army. He was studying at the same time, and he got his law degree. Back then I was so young; so ignorant with many things that I never got very interested in his credits. And most of the time I was pregnant and sick. I had a very, very hard time, especially alone and with no food to eat. I was very anemic and my first child, Dan, was born anemic. And the reason I was so anemic was that we were living with my mother-in-law in Philadelphia.

The connection is that she used to feed me, like two ounces of milk and one slice of toast every morning, and half a sandwich and half a glass of orange juice for lunch. And I was hungry, always hungry, because I was always used to eating whatever I wanted, you know. Just before my husband came from work she would give me a piece of fruit or something like that and tell me not to eat. She was so mean, you don't have any idea what I went through.

I told my husband and he said he would talk to her, but he used to give the money to her because she said I don't know how to manage money. Which was true, but at the same time, so I was anemic and so was my son. I went to a doctor and he got on to it, but by then it was kind of late. My son was born by C-section and he had to stay in the hospital three weeks. He wasn't full term; none of my children were full time.

So one time when I took my baby to the hospital for a check-up, I took some money from my husband and I went back to Mexico. I took the bus. My son was four months old. I thought it was my money too, but they called it "stole." So I left with no more than my son in my arms and what I was wearing.

I hadn't written to my family about what was going on. So when I got to El Paso, Texas, I called a neighbor because back then my family didn't have a telephone; only the very rich had telephones. I said, O.K. go to my house and tell my mother and my brother to come here to pick me up. Maybe three or four hours after that my brother got there. And when they arrived they saw me with the baby in my arms and crying, and I told them the reasons why I left.

They treated me very well. I got strong, my baby was well fed, and no signs of my husband. I didn't tell him where I was but he must have known. I wasn't there and the money wasn't there any more. So something happened. So I was living there with my family, and then I discovered I was pregnant. But I didn't hear from my husband asking if I was alive or anything. But then one day he just appeared after two months and he said he was there to take me back.

He was afraid of my brothers too. They told him, we didn't want her to marry you, but she wanted to marry you and you better treat her well. My brother spoke to my husband before he let him see me, and then my brother said, "If you want to go with him, that's fine with us." They didn't tell me I'm going to lose my family or anything like that if I went back with him. But I had a baby and I was pregnant with him, and I loved him because he was good to me, you know, but not his mother.

He said I hadn't told him what was really going on, but I said I told him. To her I never did anything right, so he said, "We're going to go away from her. We're going to live in a different state. I love you, that's it, so come back with me." What took him so long? He was afraid of my brothers and he was mad and his mother told him it was the best thing that I disappeared. And he used to have a Greek girlfriend that his mother really wanted for him and she thought it was an opportunity. Looking back on all of that some is funny, some is painful.

COMING TO CHICAGO

SO THAT'S WHEN we came to Chicago in May of 1957. We moved

to Oak Park and we had a nice house, but I knew nobody there. I had been a Catholic all of my life so my husband found a church for me because it was the most important thing for me, you know, to find a church and in Spanish. St. Francis of Assisi at Roosevelt Road and Newberry was the only church we found for mass in Spanish, and so he brought me one day during the week and we spoke to the pastor. My husband explained that he was Greek Orthodox and that I was Catholic and that he wanted to bring me and my son every Sunday to mass, and the priest was very nice.

The priest back then was Manuel Jimenez, the pastor of St. Francis. So he gave me a very warm welcome, and every Sunday my husband used to go to the Greek Orthodox church at Polk and Ashland, but I was in St. Francis for a good two or three hours every Sunday. I made a lot of friends at that time because they knew I was lonely, I was new in the city. It was not like now you see Mexicans all over, stores all over, back then there were two Mexican stores in the area, you know, very, very limited. When Pilsen became more Mexican was when they built the university, when they moved the businesses. They had business, but it wasn't what it is now.

Little Village didn't exist then as it does now. Mostly the Mexican people started to moving to Pilsen in the '60s when the University and the city started buying their houses to build the university and the expressway. It was Mexican there in Pilsen but not like we know Pilsen now. The main shopping center for Mexicans was Halsted between Roosevelt and Taylor. There were two or three restaurants and there was a dance ballroom there, Spanish theaters, one Mexican and one Puerto Rican.

When my husband and I went for that first visit, the pastor said he would take care of me and so he told my husband all these beautiful things, and he told me what time to be there and he was going to have somebody to help me with my son. So when I came back to mass it was beautiful. There was an association that was composed mostly of young women, and they gave me a list of names and telephone numbers, and said these are families where you can go to their houses and visit there. It was like I had something of my own; finally I had a wonderful, wonderful place, and nobody could ask for anything better than I saw there.

They showed me a place where I could get my tortillas; it was a tiny, tiny room then. It's [El] Milagro and now it's a big corporation. This was on Halsted between Roosevelt and Taylor. So they took me there and I bought my tortillas and I bought other things, Mexican things, so when my husband came to pick me up he was so happy because I was so happy, and I said, look what I found, tortillas and cheese, and you know, many things. So to me Sunday was like going to a big event because I was talking to my people who buy the kind of food I was used to having. And especially to be perceived with my son! Everybody used to love my boy; they took pictures and pictures of him. They had photo classes there. I just cannot tell you how it was with words; you have to go through it. These were wonderful, wonderful, wonderful!

So we were living in Oak Park and I had Dan and then I was expecting the twins, but I lost them. My mother-in-law came to my house one time for a visit. She wasn't staying with us, but every single day she was visiting me to inspect the house, to see clothes, to see if everything was right. So one day my husband told me to make some Mexican stew with potatoes and a lot of vegetables. I didn't know very well how to cook, but he was very patient and nice. And so this was what I was doing, a stew, boiling. And she came there and she started telling me about how do I expect my husband to eat this food for pigs?

So I took the stew and threw the water on her, the boiling water. I was just so upset, you know. She was badly hurt, I burned her. She didn't bring a suit against me because she attacked me in my house and my husband stood by me, by my side. She didn't come around after that, never, never more. When my husband died she took me to court to take the children away from me. I know I did something wrong, but I was so fed up with her telling how bad a wife I was, how bad a mother, bad everything. And you know I begged her many times to stop coming to my house, to leave us live our lives.

I lost the twins. I was so upset I started having cramps. I was $6\frac{1}{2}$ months. So she went to the hospital and I went to the hospital. They tried, but they couldn't save the children because they said I waited too long. And we didn't know a thing. Now they know all of these things, but back then, you know, they didn't know as much about premature babies. After that I had my son, David, and then my daughter, Norma. My daughter was 11 weeks early and she weighed 2 lb. 11 oz.

Some of the medical practices we have are from Mexico. For example, I try to have herbal teas and things like that, natural medicines. I learned that from my mother because she is from the Sierra of Chihuahua and she knows a lot of remedies. Sometimes they work, sometimes they don't work, you know. Now these remedies are coming to the United States, a good many things. Before we used to be criticized so much. Now you go to a house and they serve you all kinds of tea.

In some ways I think the midwives are better than the doctors. In Mexico it's normal; it's still the traditional way. In the big cities you can see doctors; in small towns maybe they have one doctor or two, but generally, people don't have money to pay hospitals and doctors. You know, the most amazing thing is, in Mexico when I was very young, I used to hear these things; for example, if the baby was breech the midwife used to turn it around. And she would do this on the outside, not going inside. I don't know how. But I never really believed it.

So now, not too long ago, my oldest godchild was going to have her second baby and the baby was the wrong position and there was a lot of pressure on her. The doctor kept telling her that she would have to have C-section because the baby was in that position and the baby could die. Her mother found a Mexican lady here in Chicago who said, "That's nothing, I can turn the baby around." My godchild called me and asked, "What do you think?" I said, well, I don't know, and she said, "She is going to do it from the outside." Her doctors didn't want her to do it, but eventually she did it anyway. She went to her doctor another time and they took an ultrasound again. They were watching her very closely.

Then we took her to the lady and the lady worked and worked with her, maybe an hour and a half (massaging her stomach). So right after that we took her back to the doctor's office, and they did an ultrasound again, and that time the baby was in a normal position. These ladies know so much! The lady we took her to was a midwife in Mexico. She's living now with her children here. So this young woman didn't have to have a C-section. And the lady charged $15. They gave her $50, but she only charged $15. My godchild told her doctor after it was all over.

My mother was, and still is, an excellent human being. Now she's in a wheelchair, she's paralyzed, and she lives on the second floor of this house with me. She was the best friend of my husband and he said because she's my mother she's not going to work any more. That she was to come and live with us. She was living six or seven months a year with us and then she'd go back to Mexico because my brothers and sisters were single. Remember, I married very, very young so my brothers and sisters weren't yet married. But my husband and my mother used to get along pretty good.

I was living in Oak Park when I lost the twins and I was living there when I lost my husband. In the meantime I had my other son, David, and was expecting my daughter, Norma. My son Dan was four years old when he was killed with my husband.

My husband used to work for the government. He was a lawyer, he was an undercover agent, but a regular lawyer. Sometimes it was nine to five, but other times he had to get up at like one in the morning and run for three days, things like that. I didn't ask what he was doing. I worried about him. I didn't know much in the beginning. He told me before we married because he already was with them. He told me that there were secrets, but I don't like secrets. That's one of the reasons I became a citizen six months after I came to this country because he could not be married to an alien.

I married him in 1956 and he passed in 1961, September 25, 1961. It was in the afternoon; my husband and Dan were on their way to a ball game. David didn't want to go and I didn't feel good because I was pregnant with Norma. I had very hard pregnancies. This was in the afternoon, I don't remember the time, I have everything written down for the records, but I don't know. Then that evening about nine somebody from his office came to my house and talked to me that my husband

and son were killed. Someone shot them and then they crashed the car with a truck. They thought he was by himself. It was something to do with a case he was working on.

That's when my daughter was born at five and a half months. God gives us the strength. My mother was with me then and then my whole family came. None of them were married yet except for my sister, Nicholas's mother. She died when she was 24-25 years old. There's something that never compensates for the loss of a husband. My son, I don't think I ever until now let myself really feel the pain because I thought I was going to go out of my mind.

I remember they tied me because I was just crazy. I didn't want to believe, I wanted to walk out of the hospital, I wanted to see my husband, I wanted to see my son. I didn't see them in the funeral home, I didn't go to the cemetery. I missed everything. I had a C-section, so there was no way they could let me go. And I was in such a mental state that it was dangerous to let me go. I understand that now. And then somehow I learned to block that from my mind to survive. Then after that I learned my son, David, had leukemia. I really went wild then. Oh, he survived; he was four when they diagnosed it, but he died when he was 11 years old. They didn't know as much then as they know now.

From the hospital I came to the city. I never went back to my house in Oak Park. Never, never. I don't have a thing from the house. I've never been to the front of the house. I don't even know if the house still exists. It was too hard, and now it's no sense doing that. The lawyer sold the house. The priest helped me a lot. The parishioners were by my side all the time.

After three months when my baby daughter came home from the hospital it was the happiest day of my life after so many things had happened, and after losing my husband and my son. My mother was living with me all that time. And my mother is a very religious person, and my brothers watched for me too. When I had all those problems a number of men told me I wasn't going to make it. I had never in my life worked before, but then I started working a year after that happened.

GOING TO WORK

I GOT INTO that work because my husband left me some money, and his life insurance, and I sold the house. Then I hired a person to investigate who had killed my husband and my son. Then people from the government came to my house and they said, "Don't waste the money; they're not going to find who killed them." They investigated, they did everything, but my husband wasn't the first or the last one to get killed in the city. It was a very dangerous job. I found out things here and there, yes, but I realized at a certain point of my life that it wasn't worth it. My husband was gone and my son was gone and nothing could bring them back. What I was doing was taking away from my other two children and myself.

So nine or ten months after he was killed they came and asked me if I wanted to work for them. I felt good about that because I wanted to get out of the house. Although I had a pension, they gave a pension to the children and to me, I gave up my pension and I started working. And I think it was very good that I did. Everybody told me I was crazy going to work, but I said, no, I need to go. I thought if I was inside I would find more about what business my husband was to get killed for. It didn't happen that way, but that's what I thought. I did get some information, but not everything I wanted, and now I thank God for that.

I was never in the office; I was in the field traveling around and meeting people. I was bringing documents to this country or taking them out, all over. My mother looked after my children. When I learned about my son's disease, I stopped traveling and I just did things locally or in the States. But I always was working with Spanish-speaking people.

They sent me to college. They paid for it. I received a RN degree; then I went for a political science degree. Then I wanted to learn some more to be able to help in church; then I became a social worker not many years after that. I ended up with degrees as a registered nurse, a social worker, and in political science.

I was able to use all of this. I was even a very good nurse. I was there doing something else such as collecting information, but at the same time, I was doing my job. It was Passavant Hospital then, now Northwestern. I was in cardiology, although I worked in the delivery room for a while. And I used to work in schools because there's a lot of fraud in the schools, especially with the programs to learn English. It's awful how they exploit the country, people are just collecting the checks; sometimes they go, sometimes they don't go.

There was never any sign of life from my mother-in-law (my father-in-law had died), but remember, after my husband died she took me to court to get the children. But she lost. When my daughter was going to be 15 years old, my mother-in-law wrote a letter to her. She said she wanted to see my daughter, she wanted to talk to her, and she wrote, "If this letter ever reaches your hands, please answer me," like if I was going to read the letter. I didn't open the letter or anything. After dinner I sat with my daughter and said, I wanted you to know your grandmother wrote to you.

I also raised two nephews. They were like my own children, and they call me "Ma." Nicholas was older than my daughter, Norma, and Alfredo was 10 days younger than Norma. One is the son of my sister who died, and my brother-in-law brought the baby to me when he was three months and a week. The other nephew is my other sister's son. She was divorced right after she was married, and they annulled the marriage, and so he came to me when he was five months old. I raised both of them and sent them to school.

When I traveled for my work my mother was with the children and I was always back home by Saturday. When I used to come home my children were my life. I didn't have a husband, nobody else but them. If I go to the store, they go with me, to the movies, I never go any place without them. When you're married it's more difficult because the husband needs attention, but also there's two people to give attention to the children.

When I was growing up my mother used to keep us busy, and we were always too tired for gangs or any activities like that. It was my main reason that when my children reached 13 or 14 I sent them to work in the summer because I was working. I didn't want them watching television all day and fighting with each other or going out. Many businesses are willing to take young people to teach them. I think that's great if you can find a place like that, even if they don't pay you. They take your children and the children learn and they're not out on the streets with a gang. But people have this mentality that the businesses are going to exploit the young people because they're not going to pay them. I'm sorry, but I cannot see the point. The point I see is that it's going to keep the young people busy which is more important than any money they can bring.

I used to volunteer help with Catholic Charities with the Cuban refugees in 1981. For three years I was helping them, and I learned a lot. At that time I was still working for the federal government and I told my boss, I'm fed up with this; I want to have my pension because at that time I had the hours to retire. I said I'm going to retire and I'm going to work for my church. He was kind of sarcastic (he was Catholic, too), and he said, "You're in for a surprise." I said, maybe, maybe, but I want to learn for myself.

So I went to Catholic Charities to help them with the refugees, but I learned so many things. Catholic Charities and the Archdiocese are separated up to a certain point, but they are very supportive of each other. Catholic Charities makes millions and millions because all the industries and businesses give money. And they have collections each year at church and all churches in the world give money for Catholic Charities, so they have the money. The cardinal decides what percent goes to Catholic Charities. The portion for Catholic Charities is big, but then out of that portion money goes for administrative expenses. I don't say what happened in the whole world, but I know what happened in Chicago. If it happened in the best country in the world, you can imagine what happens in the other ones.

What happened was they used to have meetings where they ordered the best caviar, or you name it. Next day I asked, how much are they paying for this? He answered, "Oh, you enjoy it?" They could have had hamburgers or anything. But when someone is paying $700 for a pound of caviar for the staff, O.K., that wasn't right.

Father Holbrook was administrator there, and now it's Father Conway, and Conway and I used to talk about that. He's Irish but he speaks very good Spanish. I said, Father, how they can do this? He said, "Well, you know, people before him used to do the same thing." I said, but we, the ones who give in church to support the poor, we don't give the money to buy these things.

I was the representative for many years, and also I was in the cabinet of Placido Rodriguez, the bishop, to help him distribute $6 million every year to not-for-profit organizations. So we used to have a meeting with the cardinal every month, from nine in the morning till four in the afternoon, and they used to give us lunch there, too. They didn't want us to carry brown bags. And they ordered these, a little box with a sandwich, an apple, and coffee and soda.

So one day Father Conway was there. I don't know the reason, but he was there, the Director of Catholic Charities, and I was behind him and Bishop Rodriguez was behind me, and the cardinal (Bernardin) was standing right by the side. And when Father Conway grabbed his little lunch box I said, "Well, I don't think you're going to like that Father Conway, that's not caviar." And he was red, and the cardinal said, "Who has caviar for lunch?" And I said, they do, at their meetings. He said, "You're kidding?" I said, no, I'm not kidding, isn't that right, Father Conway? And Bishop Rodriguez was laughing. I don't want to make trouble for nobody, but I don't think it's fair. That's when I started opening my eyes really more about what was going on.

Photo by Carolyn Eastwood.

In early 1996 the Archdiocese of Chicago had obtained their
demolition permit, and Midwest Wrecking was poised
to demolish the historic St. Francis of Assisi Church.

12

HILDA PORTILLO

(CONTINUED)

St. Francis, a Community

When I came to Chicago in 1957 St. Francis was already full of Mexicans. St. Francis was the first church that opened its door to Hispanics, the railroad track workers. So we feel gratitude to the Franciscans. The Franciscans didn't speak Spanish, so the cardinal wrote to the Provincial Father in Spain about sending priests (the Claretians) here to work with the Hispanics. In those days, in the '20s, it was hard to get priests from Mexico. They were hiding, etc. So they got the priests from Spain. They were excellent persons. They worked with us very, very good and I believe they gave us the best they could.

The church of Our Lady of Guadalupe in South Chicago also had Spanish services, but South Chicago was farther out and St. Francis was an inner city parish. Our Lady of Guadalupe has never been 100 percent Hispanic; they still have some white people in the church.

St. Francis was unique and different to all other churches in the Chicago area because it was the first step for the new immigrants, just like for me. The port-of-entry relationship was really different. We always gave them a welcome and helped them look for a job or a house. There was not a week went by that we weren't looking for refrigerators, stoves, etc. for the newcomers because they don't have anything. It was really a special relationship. And most of the churches you go for a mass, you have bake sales, you have maybe a banquet a year, but that's it; that's not a family thing.

When the immigration started arresting the people in the '60s and '70s, in the '60s especially, we closed the gym for sports. We had a big, big gym, and we closed the gym because we had a lot of people staying there. We asked for mattresses and refrigerators. The gym is one, big room, so we put the beds and mattresses for 100–150 on the floor for them to sleep. The second floor was for the married couples because we have rooms, and the third floor was for the women only or women with children. But men, single or married, working by themselves, they were on the first floor.

If they had relatives here the relatives start the papers for them or they start working and the employer requests them to be here. They were there only for a short time because they didn't have a house to go to. They didn't have anything, they just came to the church like in California or Mexico. If someone wanted to come to Chicago they just called St. Francis. It was the same thing in the '40s when the cardinal at that time was Cardinal Meyer. It was the same thing then so it was nothing unusual. We had to move fast and we had to ask for food and everything to feed all these people. The church helped, but also many companies, e.g., Campbell's Soup, Nabisco, many companies gave us a lot.

There was a big Mexican population by the '60s, but most of the churches refused to give us a mass, including St. Pius. They would have mass one day in the basement but not in the church. We don't go for that because we believe we've got children and they deserve mass in the church, so we went to St. Francis because we can use the main doors, the main church. It was different. And anybody who is anybody these days, like businessmen, bankers, they still feel that gratitude, and they are willing to help if we get St. Francis back.

When they'd appear in Mexico, people would say to them, "When you go to Chicago, go to St. Francis and they will help you." They'd come from Mexico with only the name of St. Francis. They were told that when they got to St. Francis someone's going to do something for them, you know. They'd put a mattress for them on the floor of the gym and feed them.

Sometimes we had 10 a day, 20 a day. Some families they don't have documents. And we know how these people suffer, and we know all the things they went through, and we went with them in a way because we have to contact many people in order to buy them a stove, refrigerator, some clothes, everything. We used to have a place where we used to store all year round, everything, where people could call us with stoves or refrigerators. We had them in a storage place. So sometimes people came and we didn't have anything to give them. And if we didn't have what they needed then we would collect the money between us and buy for the children. That's the most important thing. The clothes never were a problem because everybody can give you clothes. I would go here to my neighbors, you know, knocking on doors.

There wasn't room there for everyone who came to St. Francis for help so we used to have them in houses. I had a big house so I used to accommodate them in my house, only women and children, sometimes couples, but never men alone. But also the Holy Name Society did a very good job in taking the men with them. They would find them a place to eat, and to sleep, and an apartment to settle down.

At St. Francis they would look for jobs for the newcomers, but in those days it wasn't difficult because the industry here was big. It was very easy because they would come and in two or three days they were working. That's why all of us, and the people who make it, never forgot St. Francis because they spend the money to help others who were in the same situation they were when they came here.

We had money for the poor parishioners and we had a pantry because I used to go one day a week to collect from Campbell's Soup and other companies such as Dominick's, places that were giving food, juice, canned food for the poor. They would give things every week and like hundreds and hundreds of loaves of bread on a Saturday, and then on Sunday we would say to the parishioners, go in and help yourselves, and they could just go in to the storage room and take what they needed. People used to get vegetables for the week, beans, rice, whatever. Campbell's Soup was just wonderful. They even said to me, "Just be there, we will send a truck." La Preferida, all of them helped until Father Jesus Carrero came to

St. Francis.

He wanted to have everything clean, and I asked him, what do you mean by clean? He said, "Well you know, I don't like to have this many people here because they come every day to pick up food, and I'm sure they have food. This is not a public organization. There are pantries at 17th and Halsted and at Racine and 18th." I said, Father, we've done this for years and years. The people feel more comfortable with a church organization than with the government. Everybody used to take. God knows, I don't have a necessity, but I used to take something sometimes. It was like a family, you know, and nobody felt embarrassed because we were equal. We used to make a joke, you're so fat because you're taking so much. Because we were like in a family. But when Father Carrero came, he didn't want it.

We cried and cried because of all the people who came to the pantry, especially the people who don't have documents. They can't go to public pantries, they aren't going to go to any place because they won't give them anything. He even had the hard heart to send the trucks back; he didn't let the trucks deliver the goods. I went to the Claretian priest, my friend; I went to the Provincial, the head of the Claretians. He said, "I agree with you, I'm going to call him, and he has to do that. He said he used to be a pastor and we used to do the same thing for the poor. The priest before and the pastor after him, they were all alike. We used to do that for our people." But when Father Carrero came he just stopped everything.

St. Francis was made up of families, single women and single men, widows and widowers, but mostly family. The difference is how we help, how we get organized. I never felt that they discriminated because I wasn't a man. We worked together. We used to have Holy Name Society, only men. Holy Name Society was an organization for them to grow spiritually and to grow any way they can.

For example, we used to have painters, carpenters, electricians, and they used to do everything for St. Francis. We never paid for anything. The only thing we paid was to the Art Institute every time the church needed to be painted. They charged a lot of money; we can find somebody else for a little over half of what they charged. We had them because we wanted to have the best that we can for the church. In my lifetime St. Francis was painted six or seven times. The ones we hired the time before the last one, they did a sloppy job. It looked fine after they finished, but then the gold leaf was peeling four or five months after that. We paid $48,000. Then three years after that we painted again because it was so awful.

So that's when we talked with these Art Institute people and we hired them. We told the people (the congregation), we're going to do this and this, and it's going to cost us a lot of money, but it's going to be more beautiful and it's going to last more. We want you to come to the rectory and tell us how much you're going to give because we have to ask the man for the money. So we asked to borrow the money for three years; we're going to pay them in three years with an open contract if we can pay it before. So nine months and we paid the whole thing. With the paint and varnishing the pews and everything it was close to $80,000.

Then we asked the people to pay for the gym too, because we have a new gym, and the gym cost then, back in the '40s, over $100,000. So it was a lot of money, and most of the people were making about $1 an hour, and we said we have to pay it so you have to sign that you will give $150 a year because we have so many years to pay for the gym. In four months all the money was paid! Because people cared. This is something they don't understand; if I say I'm going to buy an extra dessert or some extra thing I don't buy it, and we talked to the parishioners and said, do this, and then you're going to save the extra dollar. And we're a family, we have to come out with the money. And that's why all of them felt like it really was their house.

I was talking with the priest the other day where my children went to school, Nativity of our Lord, and the priest said, "Too bad they closed your church." I said, yes, very bad. He said, "That's because the Mexican people don't give any money." Oh, I was very, very upset. I said, who told you that? He said, "Well, that's what I hear." I said, where did you hear that? He said, "Well, I hear they had financial problems." I said, tell whoever told you that to tell you the truth and not to lie. I said, we were in excellent shape; we were doing very well. We used to help two churches, one school and one church, every year. We are poor people, working-class people, but we give the most we can to our church.

So the next time I stopped by I showed him some financial papers and said, these are for your information. He said, "O.K.," so he told me the next week, "You know those financial papers were very interesting. I was talking to some priests about that because all of them, including me, we were told that they closed St. Francis because of financial problems."

Another organization we had at St. Francis was Immaculate Heart of Mary. That was our ladies' organization, mostly to grow spiritually and visiting the sick in homes and hospitals, and helping the church in any way we could with mass and communion. Very big, about 160 members. This is a lot because in most other churches they don't even have an organization, much less like this. Back in the '60s and early '70s when they started the organization there were over 200 people, a lot because there wasn't the Mexican community around in the neighborhood anymore.

There was also an organization for young people and they had a lot of dances and classes and trips. Mostly they were our children and grandchildren. These activities are really needed for the young people because of the gang problems. Just this weekend there were three killed in Little Village. The Mexican families that keep their customs are different.

Generally, what we found in talking to the young people was that many Mexican women are Americanized or they work. Women send their children out to play and they want to rest. They send the children to school and then when they come from school they stay by themselves. There's nobody home, you know, waiting for them or to feed them or something. Parents send the children in summertime out to play because they want to rest, especially the fathers—set down, you know, watch television. The mother cooks and so the children don't find love, they don't have attention, they don't find anything in their homes. So they find someone to play with them, give attention to them. That's what the young people tell us over and over.

In a village in Mexico everyone would be looking out for the children, but here in the neighborhoods, in Little Village, where there's most Mexicans, 99 percent, most of them come from little villages. What has broken down is in the family, the extended family. In Mexico there are a lot of people who move from one town to another, from one state to another, and they survive pretty good. I don't think there's a problem, the moving. I think the problem is the parents. Some of them make so little money, and they work so hard, and they don't have any time for the children. Some of them have no education and they can't help the children.

In Chihuahua where I lived there's no gangs, killer gangs, or at least when I was there. They don't have YMCAs like we have over here where everyone can get together. I don't know, but here in Chicago it's mostly because they don't have attention from their parents. We heard it from gang members. We had very good communication with them.

It's not just a matter of the guns gang members have. I remember my relatives, they used to have real guns, and never, never did my cousins or my brother do anything wrong with the guns. My oldest brother used to supervise the carrying of the milk from the village to the city and he had a big gun, hard to carry. And they never did anything. They carried guns because there's no police there. There are good people there but when they cross deserts or empty places somebody can attack them. But my brother was seven years old and never, never misused the gun. He learned to use the gun from my mother. After my father died my mother took over.

At St. Francis we promoted a banquet every year and raised money. I remember in 1957 when we were planning the first Our Lady of Guadalupe banquet. It was going to be the first banquet the Hispanic community ever had in the Midwest. We had a hard time finding places, O.K., because nobody would accept us. Remember, you know how Mexicans comb their hair (braids) and their dress, that's the impression many hotel owners had of what they would have coming to the banquet. So finally Father Jimenez, who was from Spain too, made a deal with the owner of the LaSalle Hotel. The hotel exists no more, but it was very nice, very pretty.

So Father used to tell us from the pulpit every day. I want you to wear the best thing you can wear because we are going to represent the Hispanics, the Mexicans, so wear the best you can. And it was beautiful, that first banquet, because many people wear the same *rebozo* (shawl), but nicer. And the mariachi band was beautiful. People who had never been to Mexico thought we didn't know how to behave or dress for a special occasion. And many of the people from St. Francis were very, very poor. They didn't have the means to dress up elegantly, but they wear their best. But what a family at our parish banquet, once a year celebrating Our Lady of Guadalupe! In later years we went from there to the Palmer House. Another year we went to the Chateau Royale on Chicago Avenue; it's not there any longer.

And we had the biggest banquet in the Midwest in 1978 at McCormick Place, 6,000 people. They have had bigger, but not in a catered dinner. It was the 125th anniversary, so we were going to go big, so we went bigger than we thought. And many people wanted to get in. We brought Vicki Carr from Las Vegas, and we were happy. But overall, it was a fiasco because when we went to see the hall, they had red carpeting and they had all these beautiful lights. So when we arrived (the banquet was on a Saturday) there was nothing, just plain cement and no heat. The service was so bad so we didn't pay them. We were in all the newspapers.

They gave us the V.I.P. room; you know, where the cardinals and the bishops come. I never wanted to have the V.I.P. room, but others wanted it. They told us what they were going to serve, but they didn't serve what they promised and it was cold. We were paying a fortune and they promised us the waiters for the tables. What saved us was Vicki Carr, really. She was only supposed to be there for one hour and she was there for three hours. She put on a very good show. She was aware of what was happening to us. She was talking about that and she said, "We'll show these gringos, we'll have a good time, no matter what." And so people were happy, you know.

Mayor Daley was there every year when we had our annual banquet from 1957 until 1964 or 5 when he started sending somebody to represent him. And that wasn't every year, but in the beginning he was there. He was very charming, telling us, you know, how wonderful that we're together and how the community was growing. And if any of us needed anything, all we had to do was call, you know, the politicians. Vito Marzullo was good too and also D'Arco. He was nice because any time we wanted anything for the church, trees, sidewalks, anything. The next day they would go and do it. But that was the only thing we used to ask them.

We used to take organized groups on tours to Europe, to the Holy Land, etc. The first time we had good luck, but the second time they just kept putting us back. So then after that we told them we weren't going to pay them till we leave, remember there were no credit cards then. So we had very good service. We went with 150 people on the trips. But it's hard to organize anything; it's a lot of work.

Another thing we did was that we went from St. Francis to California to march with Cesar Chávez. A bunch of us used to go there to be with him and he used to take us to the fields. And the overseers used to throw us out because they thought we were inspectors or something.

The connection we had was that Father Pat, a Claretian, had been a priest at St. Francis and then he was transferred to California. There he became friends with Cesar Chávez and became involved in the union. So he used to call us for two reasons; one because they had a picnic there every year, a sort of reunion that we used to go to, and at the same time we'd march with Cesar Chávez and talk to people. We'd let them know that they weren't alone, that even here in Chicago there were people who understood the cause.

In those days there used to be children five years old working. The farm owners would say, "We don't know why these people complain because we give them a house and job." But you should have seen these houses—oh! And then they would pay them nothing. No schools, no nothing for the children. That's so sad, but nobody would believe that. If you go see and work with them, you cry. That's what I did. I just cannot take it. Cesar Chávez was here in Chicago several times, and he came to St. Francis too. He and the union made a big difference for those workers.

We had some contact with migrant workers here in the

Chicago area because they used to come to church on Sunday. Especially Father Rodriguez took an interest in them. He used to go and talk to the owners and try to make them realize that they were exploiting these people, and to better their conditions.

Father Rodriguez is a Claretian, and he's at Holy Cross now. He was with us for some 11 years. He was a very young priest in his late 20s, and it was his first church here in Chicago. The Immigration used to come to the vestibule of the church and ask for papers. We stopped them from doing that, but they used to be right in the door, right by the door waiting. We complained so much that they disappeared from there, but one time they were waiting there again. A parishioner told Father Rodriguez something while he was at the altar celebrating mass. So he took the microphone off and rushed out of the door and he fought with the immigration officers. He told them to leave and they refused to leave. They were getting very smart with him so he just rolled up his sleeve. All the priests at St. Francis were like that. Only Jesús Carrero was an exception.

So they went to court with the case. They sued him; it was so bad, he was four years in a court. He lost the first time he appeared. Then he won, and it was like that for a long time until finally an appeal court found in his favor. They never, never came back to St. Francis. He's from Spain and he's great; he's one of us. He gives us a lot of moral support, a lot of love. He started the English classes in the church and different things to learn. They tried to shut St. Francis before, but then the pastor came to us and said, "Well, we have to defend St. Francis again. It's going on, so get ready."

Every year we used to have a festival to raise funds. We used to have rides for the children on Newberry Avenue, and we had food in the gym. And people from all different regions of Mexico used to cook food. It was very good, very colorful, Michoachán food, Chihuahua food, things like that. This was in the summertime in the '60s, '70s, '80s. Sometimes it was in May, sometimes in September because June, July, and August are very difficult because everybody is on vacation.

It slowed after the university was built. Then we only used

to have the food and dance floor. And they can go there all afternoon and not pay anything if they don't want to buy anything. They can dance and be with their families; it was something very good. And then we have games like bingo and prizes; it was nice. Indoors we had something like a fair. After the University came in there wasn't room for the rides.

When the University announced their plans to build, the Mexican parishioners who lived in the area were devastated. They were in a shock! They fought because they tried to keep their houses, but to no avail because the University is the state, you know. But they were in shock. They were displaced from what they knew as their second home because that was the only Mexican neighborhood that had products, Mexican products, and everybody lived just around. So it was a very, very sad day, notifying them about what was going to happen. They went to court. There were no Hispanic aldermen then, nobody. We didn't have anyone in City Hall or state. Just Richard J. Daley.

We used to have a lawyer at St. Francis who worked free of charge and we also had social workers. And then in those days we had six or seven priests. There were a lot of masses and a lot of work with the community. People didn't go to Hull-House. They were scared to go any place. They were just secure in St. Francis or with St. Francis families.

The Closing

In the *Chicago Sun-Times*, January 12, 1994, was the announcement of the closing of St. Francis. It was just included with other church news. Without the picture of St. Francis I never would have found out. In the article they were saying the building would be sold. The article said, "The official said there was little objection to the closing of St. Francis, but some parishioners said some people were upset." They just spoke to the secretary and she said she didn't want to give her name; she was scared, too.

If only they had come to us as we wanted them to do in the beginning. When we learned in the newspapers that they were going to close St. Francis, we called for a meeting and we asked, "What's going on? Let us know!" Even the pastor refused to have a meeting. And that's why it hurt because people were hoping. They felt betrayed, they felt that the church officials don't have any respect for them. They felt they treated us like dirt, which is true, and they don't care. I heard one of the officials calling us "a bunch of wetbacks," but what could we do about it?

Our Lady of Pompeii was going to be closed and then it was left open, and that's when they closed St. Francis all of a sudden.

We formed an organization of 22 people in a core group, people who worked together to make the decisions about how to fight for St. Francis. We never met in church because we never were allowed. They saw us as the troublemakers. One time Father Carrero even called the police on us because we were collecting signatures on petitions. We met in houses. Some members have big houses, big basements. Sometimes we met in restaurants. We would go with our families and stay the whole day, the afternoon. They're very nice, the restaurant owners, they put aside a room, especially for us. We're all from church and we've known each other for years. We used to just call ourselves St. Francis of Assisi Committee, but we found that if we have money in the bank under that name the Archdiocese could take it away, so we began to call ourselves the St. Francis of Assisi Church Preservation Committee because we have been fighting to preserve St. Francis.

Alderman Ocasio introduced a bill in the City Council to make St. Francis of Assisi a historical monument. At that time he was chairman of the Preservation Committee. Who was really helping was Luis Gutierrez, the U.S. Congressman from Chicago. He was moving all the aldermen. He was baptized in St. Francis and Alderman Ocasio, all of them, they used to come to St. Francis. Billy's (Ocasio) father-in-law was a deacon in St. Francis.

We wrote a letter to Mayor Daley about the landmark situation reminding him we're still here and we're still fighting for our church, and we want him to do something naming St. Francis a landmark. There are papers many, many times in the past for St. Francis to become a historic landmark because it's Hispanic, but to no avail. But we have to convince the City Council, but the power is with Daley. That's what Luis Gutierrez told us.

We talked to Cardinal Bernardin on two occasions. When we went for the first time in April of 1994 to the cardinal's house, we saw him then. He said he would reconsider his decision, or study the decision that the planning committee gave him. We didn't hear from him in May. Then in June we went back to the mansion in four chartered buses. He wasn't there when we arrived, but he was just getting in. I was walking in the back of everybody because we were ready to leave. People who were on the sidewalk and those who were already in the bus saw him arriving and they ran out and started telling him why we had come.

But then some people started yelling to let Hilda talk. Then he saw me in the back of everybody. He said, "You're leading them; these people don't know what they want." When he said that some people got really upset. Although my English is relatively poor, some of them speak English very good. They were born here, they have college degrees; none of us is stupid. Some people were saying, "It's not Hilda—we're here to talk to you." They said, "They [his advisors] are lying to you. We never agreed; nobody ever told us anything about this." He said, "I will reconsider the decision."

This was in early June; then the 19th of June was the final decision to close St. Francis. It was in the *The New World*, the Catholic paper. The *Sun-Times* called on Saturday morning to ask my reaction. When I read the paper (*The New World*), I cried all night. He made the decision to close St. Francis of Assisi the 12th of June, and he didn't tell anybody. He publicized it on the 19th, that was Saturday and Sunday. You have the news of his decision seven days after the decision and can't do anything until Monday, 10 days after the decision. But he didn't give us the opportunity to appeal. He promised us he would reconsider what he did to us.

We spoke to a lawyer about what our rights were because they didn't give us the opportunity to appeal. The lawyer told us, "We're going to do something because they did so much wrong in so many ways; for example, not publicizing the notice for the 10 days. They don't have the decrees, they don't have anything." And he said, "We certainly can do something and start seeing how you can raise money because we're going to Rome."

So what we decided to do was to send everything we can to the Vatican or to people who are going to Rome because we cannot write the Vatican directly from here. Everything you send the Vatican from here goes to the East Coast. It doesn't go directly to the Vatican, but they screen it here in this country. When I first heard that I said, this cannot be. But we have a member in our group who is a supervisor in the post office. She said, "Oh, yes, it is." So the only way we can send letters directly to the Vatican is to send them by friends who are going to Europe. Only one time we had a response saying that they received our documents and can we fill them out a little more about the situation. This was encouraging to us.

We spoke to a former priest in Evanston, this was a church with high middle-class parishioners, but they closed it. They took the case to Rome, and Rome said the church could be reopened. When they took it to the Cardinal Bernardin to reopen the church, he said, "No, because I'm the boss." So they tried for another year. Finally he opened the church in June, I believe, but it's not the church the parishioners used to know. What he did was sell the church to some place, India or Africa, and they have missions there. They don't have masses like they used to, so the parishioners lost. Because when he said no, they took the case back to Rome, but in Rome they said, "He's the boss."

So I spoke to the priest back then and he said he couldn't do much for us because he was the priest there, but he referred us to the lawyer who was a parishioner in the same church who took their case to Rome. But after this case, the lawyer even said the Archdiocese tried to hire him to be on their side because he learned so much about everything that was going on and they were afraid of him. So I got in touch with him and we met with him a few times, and he said he would help us.

We asked for the closing decree, which the Archdiocese

didn't have. They didn't bother to make one, because who would have thought the ignorant Mexicans would ask for it. They just did it with no papers, no nothing. So we were fighting with them because we wanted the decree. About three months after this they finally sent us three. One dated in June 12th of last year (1994), another on November 20, and another in December. The closing of the church was November 20th.

So he said he could do something. He (the lawyer) was very optimistic and he called the president of the committee and he called me. He said he was very optimistic and he wanted to meet with us. This was Friday so I said, O.K., let's meet on Monday, because that's easy for all of us to meet during the week. This was Friday morning, and I don't know what hit him between Friday morning and four Monday afternoon, because when he got there he had really changed his mind. He said, "There's nothing to do. There's nothing to do; they covered themselves, and they own the land and no matter what you do, it won't do any good."

But we said, "How come you've changed?" And he said, "Well, I've studied the decree very carefully." We said, "But we talked about this decree over the phone; that's when you were so optimistic." He said, "Well, I made calls here and there and I spoke to somebody." But he said, "You know, you guys still have a chance; you can get like a quarter million signatures to name St. Francis of Assisi the Hispanic cathedral."

He said if we could collect a quarter of a million or more signatures to present these to Cardinal Bernardin it might help. But we had petitions before. We had petitions for all the parishioners and for all the friends, you know. But he said this was our only chance. He was trying to give us some busy, big work. So I said, "Consider it done. You just make up heading for the petition and we will collect the signatures in one month. No problem." And he was in a trap. He said, "You think you can do it?" Yes, we will do it.

This was Monday, so he said, "By Thursday you are going to have it in the mail. O.K.?" No! We didn't have the wording of the petition in the mail. We called him and asked, "What's going on?" He said, "Well, I've been so busy." Then when other members of the group called him he said, "Well, before I do this you've got to have a contact." I said, "We already have 250 businesses ready for us to collect signatures. We called about 1,600 people to go and collect signatures in the Hispanic community." And he said, "Really!" Like he never expected us to do anything like that.

So then he told us he was going to take a week's vacation. It was a Wednesday. He said, "Friday's going to be my last day, but before I leave I'm going to put these papers in the mail and you can make the copies. On Friday you will have it." I said, O.K. Nothing! He came back from vacation and nothing happened.

He seemed very brave as if he wasn't afraid of anybody, so I decided to call him and ask him to be honest. Then he said, "You're not going to find a lawyer because there's nobody in the city with experience in canonical law." As far as he knows, they (the Archdiocese) have nine lawyers and they can bring as many as they need from all over the United States or from other countries because they have the money. So there's the problem.

When we collected the first signatures the Archdiocese said it wasn't fair because we said we opposed the closing St. Francis. They said they weren't *closing* St. Francis, they were just *transferring* St. Francis. We said, "O.K., we'll go back and get the signatures again saying we oppose the closing and merging." And we never had a response from the cardinal or anybody.

Later we went up in fumes when we read in the newspapers that the city wanted to build a stadium where is St. Francis now. We wrote a letter to Mayor Daley and he didn't answer us. We went to see every alderman in the city. When I went to see my alderman, the mayor's brother, John Daley, was there. And I said, well, we need help, you know. They closed our church and the land is on the border and many, many people live in the neighborhood, and we want you to support a bill in the City Council.

John Daley said yes, he would support the bill and that it wasn't true that his brother (the mayor) wanted the stadium there. He said he was just thinking about the idea, he hadn't made a final decision. But I said, "How can he say let's build the stadium on some land that he doesn't own?" So anyway, we went back to City Hall and searched the title and it was still the Archdiocese that was the owner.

We have a letter from the University telling us that they are not interested in the land. That they never before or after this had spoken of buying the land. They don't need it and they don't have the money. And they don't want to have the Hispanic community against them. That's the plain truth.

After the closing was announced they destroyed the inside of the church; the lights, the heaters, the murals, they didn't remove then, they just pulled them out. The images, you know, the statues of the saints, were gone. They were in the basement and lying on the floor of Holy Family Church.

When we met with Bishop John Gorman, that was when we were making a lot of noise, he said the decision was made and asked us to be nice and quiet. He said, "If you help move the parishioners from St. Francis to Holy Family, I will help make you our leaders in Holy Family." We got so upset, so upset, I just don't believe what my ears were hearing. That's an insult, that's an insult because you cannot make a leader. It's awful. So we walked out of his office very upset. He's not going to buy us with a bone. We said to each other, we're not going to do this. We're going to keep fighting.

The parishioners who went along and went to Holy Family were just waiting for St. Francis to be open. Those people are not allowed to use some of the facilities of the church. For example, they are forced to use portable toilets in the back of the church. The church leaders brought two toilets and they put them in the backyard because they wouldn't let the Hispanic members use the ones in the basement. How do you like that?

This kind of thing happened in most of the churches in Chicago in the '50s and '60s. They locked the doors in the Hispanics' face. I don't see any other motive for them stopping them from using the toilets in the church other than that they are Hispanics, O.K.? The children, I have seen children and old people in the snow walking to use those toilets.

Twice the Jesuits used the church for something at the

time of the Hispanic mass at 11:30. They know that's a permanent mass with a lot of people there and they sent them, the Hispanic congregation, to the basement. Why don't they do their arrangements for another time?

They are abusing our community, of course, all of those guys who call themselves followers of God. God wasn't white. He didn't come for one but for all of us. And you know, the Hispanics who wanted to study for the priesthood weren't allowed to go into the Chicago seminaries until the middle or late '70s because they were Hispanic. The seminaries sent them to Florida, California, or to Texas, but not in Chicago. Other states, but not in Chicago. Many people don't know this. This is plain discrimination. They were so mad with me because I opened my mouth to talk about this, but this is the truth. It is all these little things; they don't let our people use the toilets and they don't let our seminarians use the seminaries either. Because the plain truth is, we're Hispanic.

There have been many, many effects from closing St. Francis. We had a man that started getting sick after they closed St. Francis, and he was getting sicker and sicker and he started having heart problems. And we have many, many sick people, emotionally, especially the old. Mainly I'm very upset because of the people who have small children. They stop going to church because they don't believe any more, and they're disillusioned.

Now the family is going different ways. Especially if there are teenagers. They say, well, we don't have anything to go to church for any more. We have so many families with these problems; many are having bad grades in school. They don't go to church anymore. Among some of them the wife is trying very hard to take the children to church but the children say, "If our father doesn't go to church then we don't want to go." We have already two divorces because one wants to go to church and the other doesn't. They (the Archdiocese) doesn't have any idea. If they call us fanatics, we are not.

In September of 1995 we had a mass outside St. Francis because the inside was closed to us. We were all excited; people were happy, although being on the outside was not the same as being at church. We enjoyed mass. People came that

Photo by Carolyn Eastwood.

A Mexican priest visiting relatives in Chicago agreed to say
a mass for St. Francis of Assisi parishioners outside the locked
church on the corner of Newberry Avenue and Roosevelt Road.
Guadalupe Portillo, Hilda Portillo's mother, is in the front row (left).

I haven't seen for a long time. At the beginning, the president
of our Preservation Committee made the announcement. He
thanked the people for being there and he said that we were
offering that mass for God to give us strength and to move the
cardinal's heart to reopen our church.

There was nothing in the newspapers, but on Channel 9
and Channel 32 they had news at 9 PM and again on Monday.
They talked to the priest and to many of the parishioners. They
took a lot of film, but they just showed small portions. They
said that we flew this priest from Mexico in order to have this
mass, but that's not true. They asked me and asked me, both
of the reporters, and I said, no, the priest was here visiting his
relatives, and so we asked him to celebrate the mass. We
didn't want to give the name of the priest because there could
be consequences. He said he will be back. He said he was
offering the mass hoping that God would help us and our
church. And he spoke very, very nice you know.

And there were spies there because they sent them from

Photo by Carolyn Eastwood.

Parishioners of St. Francis of Assisi demonstrated in front of the cardinal's mansion, hoping to talk to Cardinal Bernardin and present reasons why their church should not be closed.

Holy Family and there was a lady from the Archdiocese. She got there early and I know her. And I said, what are you doing here? She said, "Well I came just to observe." She had a notebook and started taking notes. She works very close with the bishops.

I had two phone calls; they told me to stop, one from the Archdiocese and one from the Claretians. They said, "The church is closed, it's not going to open. What are you doing there?" I said, well, there's a lot of people. You refuse to meet with us, the cardinal refused to meet with us. And so we're not going to listen to them. We're going to do whatever we can. One who called from the Archdiocese said, "Well, it's not going to be a long time till we tear down the church." I said, well, we'll see that day because we never did anything wrong, and he hung up.

What I don't understand is why they wanted to stop us. If they were very sure they were going to knock the church down, why were they bothering us? The man who spoke at the beginning of the mass, he had a call too, but the only thing was, the person didn't identify himself. And, if like they say, we are nothing, we are fighting for a lost cause, why bother? I said, well, if you're telling me how you feel, why are you bothering calling me?

They say we have done a lot damage to the church, especially me. I have done a lot of damage to the church because I have told the people many things that people aren't supposed to know; for example, that they didn't accept Mexicans in the seminaries. I said, well, I'm just telling the truth. You tell me if I'm lying. They said, "Well, not exactly, but these people aren't supposed to know things like that."

OCCUPATION OF ST. FRANCIS

EVEN THOUGH WE knew our church had suffered a lot inside, and we had demonstrated many times, when we found the demolition machinery outside the rear of the church at the end of January (1996), it was a terrible shock. When we discovered that machinery, we had prayers in front of the church and we sent faxes to the cardinal to stop the demolition. We went to the cardinal's mansion, a few of us, because it was very, very cold then, to ask him to stop the demolition, but he didn't come out because he was very ill. That's what we were told. But Robert Quackenbush came out and said, "We're going to stop the demolition for now."

That was Wednesday night. Thursday I went by St. Francis and was surprised to see Father Rowe from St. Ignatius with two trucks in back and two trucks in front carrying away our most precious things. They were demolishing our altars and in the balcony they took the pipe organ, a beautiful pipe organ, and now that's in the basement of St. Ignatius. I followed them and I know they put it there. They had already taken away all our stained glass windows and our statues. They made holes in the ceiling and took the suspended panels in the front of the church. They took the confessional doors, all beautiful wood. I said, Father Rowe, why are you doing this? They promised us last night. He said, "I have permission of higher authorities." Then he said, "Get out of here, you're in the way."

Then I called the media (Channel 66) when I saw that. They arrived and took pictures of what was going on. Channel 66 called the cardinal's office and they weren't able to answer why, when in front of the TV Wednesday night they said they were going to stop everything, then why Father Rowe was

Photo by Carolyn Eastwood.

Many times during the long struggle to save St. Francis of Assisi Church there was media coverage, but without some dramatic turn of events the coverage tended to die away and the destruction seemed to be inevitable.

there. They had no answer and they said Quackenbush would get back to them later on, which he never did.

So then Friday, February 2nd, somebody noticed that there were little cords around the church, like where you're going to dynamite something. You just connect it and everything blows up. I didn't notice it but about 3 PM one of our committee members, Gerardo, called me crying. He asked me to call Rome, to call Mexico. I didn't call, but when he called, they told him there's nothing they can do for us, that everything was in the cardinal's hands. So then when I was talking to him, a call came in from another committee member, Jorge. I was crying and upset. Such a long, long time we've been fighting, and I said, they lied to us again, and I said, what can we do? Then he said, "Take the church over."

I said, how are we going to do it? He said, "I don't know." But he told me that he was going to pray and he'd call me back. So then I was reading the paper early in the morning that Friday and I saw that Father Manz was going to be made a bishop, so St. Francis would be part of his area. I had called him earlier in the week and he had never, never returned my call. So that Friday about one or two o'clock I called his office. He wasn't there, of course, but I told the secretary that I wanted to leave a message for him. I said we were going to be there at his church at six with the media. If he's there, fine, but we're going to be there. So Bishop Manz called me back at 4:30, before five, and he wanted to know more. Why we want to meet with him, why we're going to take the media with us, what we want to achieve with this.

At that time only two of us knew that we were thinking of taking over the church, nobody else. So we met with Bishop Manz. He was pretty nice about it. He had kept me on the phone from 4:30 till fiveto six, and I said Father, you have to let me go because I have to meet with you in five minutes. So I was just at the door ready to leave my house when Jorge called, and he said, "I know now how we're going to do it, but we have to ask the others if they are willing to do this. Once we are in the church we have to keep doing it."

In the middle of the meeting Father Manz had to go and celebrate mass and I didn't go to mass because I wanted to talk to Gerardo of our committee. I said, we are thinking about occupying the church. Are you willing to do it? He said, "Yes, I'm willing to do it. I'm willing to do anything, but how are we going to do it? Who else knows about it?" I said, nobody else knows about it. So after the meeting we go for a cup of coffee. I only told four persons because I was afraid of it getting out, but I said we're planning this and we wanted to know if you are willing to do it. They said, "Yes." Then we started arranging to get generators, water, blankets. At that time the church wasn't locked. It was open for anybody day and night. So we asked Jorge to bring nails and wood so we could lock the doors from the inside.

Earlier Saturday I called Father Carrero and said, Father, we need your help, you know we're fighting for St. Francis. He said, "So what?" I said, we need your help. Are you willing to help? He said, "What can I do?" I said, listen, I know how badly you've been treated and how our people have been treated. Help us. Don't come out before eight for the eight o'clock mass tomorrow at Holy Family. Don't come out early because we need two minutes of the mic to tell the people that we're going to walk to St. Francis. We need your help after mass, but not before mass. He said the deacon is going to be there and he is very close to the cardinal, but finally he said O.K.

Saturday we called all the people we know to meet at St. Francis or to go to Holy Family and then walk to St. Francis. The church was open, remember, but much to our surprise, about 10 PM Saturday a priest called me to say they had locked the church and now they had a guard. When we talked to the bishop on Friday we talked about how they left the church open and people could come and steal things. So we believe up to this day that it was he who alerted them to the danger of vandalism. We'll never know.

So anyway, when they told me the church was locked and somebody was inside, there was no way I could reach everybody. Father Carrero was in bed by then but I called him. I said, they locked the doors. He said, "I know." I said, if you knew, why didn't you tell me? He said, "I thought you'd have a person watching there." I said, no we didn't know. I said, you have to give us a key. He said, "I'm not able to just walk in and out." But he said, "Well, I have a master key and I will leave it at the priest's house." So he did.

He said I should pick it up, but at that time my car wasn't running because of the cold. And I said, I'll have to send somebody, but he didn't want nobody else to get it. He said, "Who are you going to send?" And I said, I'm going to ask Jorge, and he said, "O.K." So Jorge and his wife went there at two in the morning and got the key. Father Carrero said, "O.K., I'll give you the key and I'm going to be standing at the corner of Roosevelt and May at six in the morning for you to give me back the key."

So we thought, if we have to return the key at 6 AM, then we have to be at the church by at least 4:30 to let everybody in. When Jorge went for the key Father was waiting for him in the door. He said, "Give it to Hilda and tell her she can keep it."

So Margarita, of the committee, and I were the first ones to walk inside. But in the front of the church were two police cars and one a little farther away. And we said, that's the only thing we need! But it was too late, we're going to go in. So then we figured out a way to distract the police from the church for a minute or two. This was about 6:30 AM.

So then the police car in front of St. Francis moved, and I jumped out of the car and went to open the door. But it didn't open! Margarita's husband, Carlos, was in the car and I said, what are we going to do? And he tried it and he couldn't open the door. Oh, I was so mad! So Jorge went to Father Carrero and said, "Father, you didn't give me the right key." He said, "Well, I thought I did," but then he gave him another key—the right one. By the time he returned with the right key we had two police cars again there and I was very, very nervous. But by the time the police got out of their cars and came to the door, we were inside. We closed the door and then we used another door that was there to prevent anyone else from opening it with a key.

And then we have to deal with the watchman that was on the second floor. We were afraid he was going to shoot us. We knew he was on the second floor because somebody had seen his light. As soon as we were inside we went running to the back of the church and opened the door because the others were there. The police wanted to know what was going on and we said we were taking over. They didn't say anything.

About the watchman, even though there were police there, he was afraid. He didn't know there were just two women downstairs. We didn't give him a chance to come down because we were running to the back, not as fast as we thought we were going to because there was a lot of garbage on the floor, and dark. And by the time he found out what was going on, he left.

By that time the people from Holy Family were walking to St. Francis and Channel 66 was there. I had had trouble getting them to come because they didn't have news on Sunday then and they didn't have cameras. And I said to this lady who is director of Channel 66, we need it, please, please.

I did the same thing with the newspaper, *La Raza*, and I said, please be there. So they were there and took pictures and told everything. They talked to the community at Holy Family and were on the walk to St. Francis. And we sent faxes to the media that we were going to take St. Francis over at a quarter to eight. So all the TV channels in the city were there and did interviews and took pictures of us walking in a large circle and carrying signs in the church.

We didn't know how it was going to turn out, but the Archdiocese had been lying over and over again and they treated our community so badly, and what a big injustice. That's what we were fighting, and we were willing to give our lives for that. We prayed. When we got together to discuss our plans we knew we didn't have the money to rent what we needed to rent such as the generators, and we knew we didn't have a lot of the answers. But we prayed, and God used us as instruments.

All of us stayed there after we got in because we didn't have a master plan. We just said, "Get in and that's it." And so, most of us were there for two weeks. Some took off from work or took vacation or whatever, but we knew we could not keep that up so then we started taking turns. One person has been sleeping there since we took over until today.

At first we were sleeping on cots out in the open part of the church before they made the "bedroom" blocked off with plastic in the corner of the church. We fixed the little room when we decided that four or five people would spend the night. At the beginning we didn't want to lock ourselves in a little room. We wanted to be where we could see everything because we were afraid that something was going to happen. But God helped us.

We had no toilets, no running water, no electricity, no gas, and no heat, but the day after the occupation we got a portable toilet. And it was below zero, and you could see your breath in the church. Most of those who stayed there have arthritis now, and I lost part of my little toe from frostbite. The restaurant people were very nice—they used to send coffee and food.

We never negotiated with the Archdiocese. We just occupied the church, and they never negotiated with us. They sent somebody like a priest and a deacon and the police to say we should leave because we're going to die there in the cold weather.

Some of the things that belonged to us, we just went to Holy Family and took them back. Nobody gave them to us. The same parishioners who had been forced to go to Holy Family, they went there and they claimed things. We were surprised because the first one to walk in Ash Wednesday was the Jesus of Nazareth statue, the statue with the many wounds. They never, never agreed; they gave nothing. So some of our things came back mysteriously. But our pews were gone and we had to buy folding chairs, and they sold our stained glass windows to another church so we will never have those back.

Salvador Ojeda was a member of St. Francis. He was sick for a long time and he heard about us taking over the church and knew what was going on through the television and the newspaper. Right after we were in he decided to have his funeral mass at St. Francis. That was the only way he could help us, being in bed and sick. We didn't find any priest here that would do it, so friends called Father Pat in Los Angeles, he's a Claretian. He used to be in St. Francis when Ojeda was young; they grew up together and Ojeda was his driver.

So Father Pat came to St. Francis from Los Angeles to celebrate the mass. We told him when we called him, "Well, we don't know how they are going to react or if they will close the church." But he wanted to call the media and talk to them and tell them what was going on. To us it was like a stream of light because the conditions we were living under were very, very bad. All these big shots came from all over the United States and especially television from Chicago. None of them brought their cameras in with them because they were scared. But it was really special that day, many people came, many people saw how it was. And something beautiful happened. The week before that a florist started donating hundreds of roses every week. And for us it was very nice.

We never believed that they were going to throw us out. Never! Never! A few had some doubts. In fact, when they sent somebody to tell us they were going to dynamite the building after removing us, we prayed. What's going to happen? And we read in the Bible where if you fight for justice, God is with you.

The first day they didn't talk to us. They called the cardinal's office and called the high organization, and nobody commented on us being there. But the police was there very often, every hour or so. They said you have to leave, but they

Photos by Anthony Eastwood.

Above: Bishop Manz, who was first to really listen to the parishioners of St. Francis of Assisi concerning their threatened church, returned to the reopened church to celebrate mass on Easter Sunday in 1996.

Left: Some of the interior destruction of St. Francis of Assisi Church can be seen where the murals and stained glass windows had been removed.

weren't aggressive because we had created a good relationship with the 12th District within the last two years before we took over. We had to get their permission before we had a demonstration or when we walked to the cardinal's mansion, and in the beginning, like in early '94, they didn't want us to do different things, but then they began to know us and they were very nice to us.

In fact, they told us that the Archdiocese wanted them (the policemen) to arrest us, to take us out. They said that they were radioing them everything that was happening in St. Francis because they don't want anybody to die there. And that's why the Archdiocese didn't respond so quickly. They took a long time because the police were informing them that we had hot food, that we had generators, but it was very cold. So the policemen asked us just to send the old people and children home, but many children stayed anyway. They didn't want anyone to die, but also they didn't want the scandal of putting us out.

The week after we took over St. Francis, Bishop Manz went to talk to the cardinal. Then Cardinal Bernardin ordered an investigation and that's when Father Nevins stepped in to lead the investigation to see what was going on. By February 14th we had the first mass there since it was closed and Father Carrero preached.

Finally the investigation was over and they found that the

Bishop Manz presiding, a reading by Hilda Portillo, and a mariachi band were all parts of the celebration of Easter and the reopening of St. Francis of Assisi in 1996.

Photo by Anthony Eastwood.

reasons they used for closing St. Francis were false, and they sent the report to the cardinal and the Archdiocese said that St. Francis would be open. Bishop Manz came to celebrate Mass Easter Sunday to let the parishioners know that St. Francis will remain open. Now we have five masses celebrated every Sunday.

At first, officially, St. Francis and Holy Family were made one parish. It meant that when they originally closed St. Francis, St. Francis as an entity didn't exist any more, but they just called it Holy Family/St.Francis of Assisi parish to quiet the people. Holy Family was the administrator of St. Francis. Because of this decision a lot of strange things were happening. After the church reopened there were five masses at St. Francis, but they were taking our weddings and our quinceañeros (celebrations for 15-year-old girls). And they are forcing people. They say, if you want to be baptized, you have to go to Holy Family. They baptized children in St. Francis on Sunday, but Saturdays when more children are normally baptized, they had to do it in Holy Family. And to baptize they had to go over there for a conference. They said we had no room, which was false. And they were charging $200 for the wedding and $200 for the quinceañeros.

We have two or three weddings every Saturday and we have two or three quinceañeros every week. What happened was, the parishioners said to Father Nevins, "We want to have the quinceañeros at St. Francis. If you don't want to open the doors, we're going to have it on the sidewalk." So he said they could be held inside.

There was a wedding and they planned to have it in St. Francis, and Father Nevins said it had to be in Holy Family. People cried, and the bride said, "Father, we don't want to go there, don't force us to go there. My grandmother married here, my mother married here, and I want to marry him here." But he (Father Nevins) just kept denying it. And people said, "We want to baptize our children here in St. Francis." Then when these people refused to have the baptism in Holy Family and wanted St. Francis, they were given a certificate that said "Holy Family." And some people tore the certificate up and said, "No, we want it from St. Francis."

We met with the dean of the area. He doesn't understand why we don't have our own bulletin, and he doesn't understand why we shouldn't have our own weddings and quinceañeros at St. Francis. If a person wants to celebrate there, there's nothing wrong with that. We talked about money. We gave him the letter Cardinal Bernardin sent us saying we're going to be two parishes with one pastor and separate our money. Two parishes with one pastor, and every parish would have to survive with their own people. The pastor spent two days a week at Holy Family and he calls on our sick and elderly, but there was no pastor at St. Francis during the week. He never came to St. Francis except Saturday and Sunday. We were supposed to have control of our money, but that's not how it was; that's why we went to the dean.

And he said the thing that the cardinal said was that he doesn't know if we will ever become independent from Holy Family and only the future will say. The day we met with the dean he said he doesn't know why they are complicating it so much; he figures it's simple. The dean said he would talk to the cardinal and he would ask him to free St. Francis from Holy Family. The dean is good; when they had the area meetings he was the only person who never said, "St. Francis must be closed." In the '70s and '80s the other priests were fighting for St. Francis to be closed.

We needed a parish council, but we did not have one, and now there are disputes within the Preservation Committee over who will be in control. This trying to take control is stupid. They are good people and all of us want the same thing, O.K.? But there's no trust anymore.

The Sunday school is beautiful. There were problems getting it started and they didn't want us to refurbish the rectory because there is talk that they may pull it down, but we wanted the Sunday school for our children. When we had registration it was a madhouse; altogether there are about 270 children. And we can't accept any more because there's no room. They start at 9:30 and they end with the mass at 11:30, and it's going well because we have a lot of experienced teachers.

We fought to preserve St. Francis, and now that it's pre-served we have to move ahead.

Photo by Carolyn Eastwood.

The new market still has several produce vendors, plus an upsurge in the number of food stalls with tents and tables where Mexican food is served.

EPILOGUE

Photos by Carolyn Eastwood.

Above: Foreign visitors to Chicago often visit the new market, including these two Japanese students who are students at Roosevelt University.

Below: Many vendors, such as this shoelace salesman, made the transfer from Maxwell Street to Canal Street when the historic market was closed.

EPILOGUE

THE EVENTS AND issues that have affected the lives of residents of this Halsted-Roosevelt neighborhood, as related in these four oral histories, continue to produce constant change, but the power equation has not changed. Ordinary people still struggle to elicit information about future plans for their neighborhood in order to wage an informed fight for their own interests. Some changes that have occurred after the interviews were completed are individual and others involve the whole neighborhood.

Harold Fox died at the age of 86 on July 28, 1996. In one conversation he had speculated that contracting skin cancer was probably a result of all the years of pursuing his favorite sport of fishing. Previously, when I visited him for the two-day interview in Florida, his usual exuberance overflowed when he described the pleasures of fishing and of giving away some of his catch. Typical of Hal's nature, a family member told me that near the end he still wanted to answer some more of my questions and was very frustrated because he did not feel up to it. He would be fascinated to know that today his zoot suit design has gone full circle and is influencing fashion again.

Fox Brothers Tailors is still in business on Roosevelt Road just east of Jefferson. Three mainstay employees of the business that worked for Harold Fox continue at Fox Brothers, for a combined total of over 100 years of service.

A few Jewish owners retained businesses on Halsted, but most are gone. Some members of the Jewish community, blues musicians, and preservationists have been involved in an effort to save some remnant of the old Maxwell-Halsted complex to commemorate the community that was, but most of the buildings are disappearing.

In this century of Near West Side history, no single reason can be isolated for the sequence of events that has occurred in the neighborhood. Leadership and economic, social, and political factors have constantly interacted and produced new conflicts and coalitions. Recent interlocking developments involve four major areas of the neighborhood: the new market that has been developed on Canal Street after the Maxwell Street Market was closed; gentrification in the Little Italy area; expansion of the University of Illinois throughout the area they call their "South Campus"; and the futures of the two churches that stand in the path of University expansion.

After the closing of the Maxwell Street Market, a smaller, gentrified version of the market was reconstituted on Canal Street, about a half mile away from the former site. It was called the "New Maxwell Street Market." Few who knew the Maxwell Street Market see Canal Street as an actual reincarnation of the old market. There is a completely different "ambiance," to use an upscale description. Ironically, Maxwell Street itself has actually been eliminated at the point where it intersected with Canal Street, due to a new Dominick's mall.

Most people who enjoy markets believe the new market is certainly better than nothing, which is what the city would have provided without the protests. Thousands of shoppers are there every Sunday, and it is a lively place with an ethnic mix that you are unlikely to see elsewhere on a weekly basis. Everyone has welcomed the greater sanitation and security efforts; these had been regularly requested for the old market by vendors and shoppers, but they were consistently refused by the city.

What is most important is that there has been a subtle change in the character of the market. You still see crowds of people and you see many of the same vendors, but some of the eccentric, free-wheeling spirit of the market is gone. There are some practical reasons for this. Now, control of sites is from the top down rather than by self-governing arrangements of the vendors themselves, so some of the independence and also abuse of the system has disappeared.

Also, the city has instituted vendor fees of $30 a day for a space; this is compared to no fee in the old market. These fees are prohibitive for the really impoverished vendors who are not likely to earn as much as $30 in a day. For them, a day's vending in the market would be a losing proposition, and with this, the market has lost an important component of its 120-year history—a means of making a start when you have almost nothing.

Given the history of the closing of the Maxwell Street Market, there is an insecurity that hovers over the new market. If the city could shut down the old market after 120 years, in spite of the protests and arguments from high and low circles, how can anyone believe that the new market may not also be under threat?

An intangible yet real result of the closing of the market has been a certain erosion of faith in the democratic process. Supporters of the market found that lack of information hurt their cause and that public meetings were public relations shows conducted in the spirit of appeasement rather than being held for the purposes of informing and decision-making.

Since the takeover of a large part of Little Italy by the University of Illinois at Chicago, an abiding skepticism has remained concerning investors who buy property under the guise of urban renewal. Many changes have come about in the area, apart from the loss of neighborhood property, during the more than 30 years since the campus was built. Property values, property taxes, and rents have escalated out of the reach of many residents as increasing numbers of upscale townhouses are built, and much of the gentrification has been brought about through informal agreements between developers and city government.

Recently, such an agreement came unstuck when former Alderman Ted Mazola and Oscar D'Angelo, who chairs the local urban renewal advisory board, both friends of Mayor Daley, attempted to shortcut the urban renewal process and were informally offered tax increment financing (TIF) by the Daley administration.[1] Homeowners in the targeted area raised an outcry that gained media attention. They did not want their homes condemned and bulldozed, and the accompanying publicity brought the administration up short. A developer may still build townhouses in the area, but now the bidding must be open, and there is a possibility that the new townhouses may not be as concentrated as previously planned. The homeowners have been promised that their homes will remain.

A look at the gentrification process that has occurred in this neighborhood is instructive because it is so typical of many areas of Chicago. Because of escalating rents and property taxes, working-class residents are forced out and, as upscale residents move in, the character of the neighborhood that the new residents sought is changed or no longer exists. In Little Italy new townhouses are selling from $300,000 to $500,000, and older two- and three-story homes are going for $250,000 to $400,000. Apartment rentals range from $500 to $1,500 per month. Long-time resident homeowners have found that if they want to continue living in the area, they must rent out part of their buildings in order to pay the higher taxes.

Florence Scala worked with others on a committee to establish a branch of the Chicago Public Library on Taylor Street. Negotiation and cooperation among Chicago Public Library officials, UIC, and local interests helped to bring about the opening of this library for the public.

After closing the Maxwell Street Market the University of Illinois surrounded the area with chain link fences and installed parking lots and athletic fields; but with the announcement in 1996 of plans for a partnership with big-time developers, the University entered a new phase in land acquisition and demolition.[2] The University has proposed private projects for the 45-acre "South Campus" site bounded on the north by Roosevelt Road, by 16th Street on the south, Morgan Street on the west, and Union Avenue on the east. The area includes the line of shops on both sides of Halsted from Roosevelt to Maxwell and the few buildings still left on Maxwell. The plan proposes new housing, a hotel, and a performing arts complex. Four competing teams of developers submitted their plans. At the time then-UIC Chancellor David Broski said, "Most private developers want to work with a partner that can get things done without having to jump through bureaucratic hoops."[3]

One of these "bureaucratic hoops" is acquiring eminent domain rights. In order to bypass public questioning of this arrangement in usual eminent domain proceedings, Illinois's Republican-led General Assembly added a special provision to an otherwise non-controversial bill just before adjourning in the summer of 1996. This tactic practically precluded public discussion of the University takeover of land in this area. The provision would allow the University to develop the site without the approval of any state board or agency, including the Illinois Board of Higher Education, so carte blanche for the University's plans is well in place.

Two forms of protest have surfaced since the announcement of the University's latest expansion plans. One of these is an Internet and letter writing campaign by people who are interested in immigrant history, blues, markets, and in retaining a vestige of the old Maxwell-Halsted area through saving some buildings and instituting a museum. The city has put a certain amount of pressure on the university to make some token concessions, such as saving some facades and a few buildings.

The most vocal protest against the proposal is precipitated by economic concerns. Black and Hispanic leaders from the neighborhoods surrounding the expansion area have no real hope of stopping the University expansion, but they object to being left out of the planning process because this new phase will affect their communities. They are concerned that the gentrification that is likely to take place will price them out of their own neighborhoods. When these community leaders met with Broski, he explained to them, "We're trying to make the place look a little more hospitable, warmer, a little friendlier."[4] He mentioned a Starbucks coffee shop as part of that vision.

This was not what the community leaders had in mind as an example of hospitality and warmth. These non-profit groups maintain that they have been trying to revitalize their neighborhoods without driving out poor and working-class residents, which is exactly what Little Italy residents were working at over 30 years ago when the University moved in. On April 10, 1997, some 200 leaders and residents of Pilsen and Little Village met with the University spokesman, James Foerster. The meeting was billed as a "public informational meeting" with the usual poster-sized map showing the expansions projected by the University. All speeches by leaders or members of the audience were in both English and Spanish making it a long evening.

The Pilsen/Little Village residents had many questions relating to the effects of the expansion on housing prices, jobs, and on local business participation and development. There was a high level of skepticism and anger because of the history of the University regarding local residents, many of whom were displaced in the initial takeover of the Harrison-Halsted neighborhood. The fact that most of the difficult questions were answered by the familiar refrain, "We plan to do an impact study on that," was not reassuring because impact studies, like "forming a committee," are a facile way of avoiding controversy, delaying decisions, and burying real issues.

The congregation of the Gethsemane Missionary Baptist Church has had to come to terms with their isolated situation and has decided to leave their church and go to another location, according to Gethsemane's pastor, Eric Roberts.[5] Although the University has not overtly forced them out, the city used a familiar form of pressure by sending inspectors who easily found code violations in the 138-year-old building. According to Rev. Roberts, a 1978 court decision excluded Gethsemane from the Halsted-Roosevelt urban renewal area. In order to obtain the site, the University would have to go back to court, and not only would they have to prove that they

Children carrying roses prepare to line the aisle to welcome Cardinal George to St. Francis of Assisi on July 6, 1997, soon after his appointment to Chicago as Cardinal Bernardin's successor.

Photo by Carolyn Eastwood.

Photo by Carolyn
Eastwood.

Carlos Villaseñor
of the St. Francis
of Assisi
Preservation
Committee
greets Cardinal
George outside
the church
and expresses
concern about
the return of
the church's
original stained
glass windows.

need the property, but they would be required to give reasons why it would be essential to the University's plans. Rev. Roberts stated that meeting repair bills to bring the building up to code would cost the congregation $250,000 and that is beyond their means. So it appears inevitable that a historic building full of meaning for the Jewish community and the African-American community will go down to make way for condos.

St. Francis of Assisi has fared better. The Archdiocese agreed not to demolish the church and has since made substantial investments in what appears to be a good faith effort, by renovating the steeple, redecorating the interior, replacing the pews, and rebuilding the rectory. The stained glass windows, sold to another church by the Archdiocese, were replaced rather than restored. Perhaps to indicate his commitment to Cardinal Bernardin's decision to reopen St. Francis, Cardinal George, who replaced Cardinal Bernardin after his death, chose St. Francis for one of his first parish masses.

Given the kind of publicity engendered when they bulldozed the Holy Guardian Angel Church in the 1960s, the University is probably not prepared to risk removing St. Francis of Assisi Church. But the University/City of Chicago combination continues to make life more difficult for the parishioners by tearing up Newberry Avenue next to the church and narrowing the sidewalk where vendors have always sold food and religious relics before and after the services.

On December 3, 1993, the University of Illinois at Chicago launched their Great Cities Program with a formal luncheon and guest speakers. One of their goals was " . . . establishing partnerships with organizations in the neighborhoods immediately adjacent to UIC to help improve quality of life in these areas for current residents and businesses."[6] They have been selective in their choice of organizations to support, and they are rarely the "ordinary people" of the neighborhood.

At this luncheon Mayor Richard M. Daley was the keynote speaker, and he began by thanking the University for naming the newly renovated campus library after his father, Richard J. Daley. Then, although he had a prepared speech, he could not resist some ad lib comments, and he began to talk about his father's decision to place the University campus in its present location. These remarks were omitted from the University's published text of his speech, but it was recorded on video by a cameraman.

Mayor Daley became more and more vehement as he described opposition to his father's decision, the people who said he was wrong. But, Mayor Daley concluded, "His dream was *right* then, many, many years ago, and it's *right* today." This scene, and the passionate defense of his father's point of view, is symbolic of the relationship between the Daley dynasty and this Halsted-Roosevelt neighborhood. It is emotional and it is personal, even in this most bureaucratic of worlds.

This simplistic point of view takes little account of the complexity of needs and views of ordinary people. When ordinary people are heard, it is usually because extraordinary people lead the struggle and inspire innovative, fervent action that is sustained over a period of time. There is absolutely no guarantee of success and almost certain substantial costs in terms of time, money, comfort, and even safety, but these oral histories show that such people do exist and can fight, and fight hard, in the effort to retain the identity of their embattled communities.

Notes to Epilogue

1. "No shortcuts to urban renewal" (Editorial), *Chicago Tribune*, 13 November 1996.

2. Steven Strahler, "UIC private-sector pitch," *Crain's Chicago Business*, 27 May 1996, 4.

3. Michael Hawthorne, "General Assembly grants UIC carte blanche on campus plan," *Crain's Chicago Business*, 17 June 1996.

4. Gary Marx, "Neighbors fear UIC expansion," *Chicago Tribune*, 12 March 1997, sec. 2, 4.

5. Interview with Rev. Eric Roberts, May 20, 1997.

6. "Great Cities," (Chicago: University of Illinois at Chicago, December 3, 1993).

Photo by Carolyn Eastwood.

The final weeks before the closing of Nate's Deli were busy,
with customers crowding up to the counter to place their
orders, and staff hustling to keep up with them.

BIBLIOGRAPHY

Books

Abbot, Edith. *The Tenements of Chicago 1908-1935.* New York: Arno Press, 1970, orig. University of Chicago Press, 1936.

Addams, Jane. *Twenty Years at Hull-House.* New York: Macmillan, 1910.

Adelman, William. *Pilsen and the West Side.* Chicago: Illinois Labor History Society, 1983.

Balkin, Steven. *Self-Employment for Low-Income People.* New York: Praeger, 1989.

Berkow, Ira. *Maxwell Street: Survival in a Bazaar.* New York: Doubleday, 1977.

Bisno, Abraham. "Chicago." In *The Russian Jew in the United States*, ed. Charles Bernheimer. Philadelphia: Winston, 1905.

Branham, Charles. "Black Chicago: Accommodation Politics Before the Great Migration." In *Ethnic Chicago*, ed. Melvin Holli and Peter d'A. Jones. Grand Rapids, Michigan: Eerdmans Publishing Company, 1984.

Burgess, Ernest and Charles Newcomb. *Census Data of the City of Chicago, 1930.* Chicago: University of Chicago Press, 1933.

Castells, Manuel. *The City and the Grassroots: A Cross-Cultural Theory of Urban Social Movements.* Los Angeles: University of California Press, 1983.

Chicago Fact Book Consortium. *Local Community Fact Book, Chicago Metropolitan Area.* Chicago: Chicago Review Press, 1984.

Cipriani, L. *Italians in Chicago and Selected Directory of the Italians in Chicago.* Chicago, 1927 and 1933-34.

Cutler, Irving. *The Jews of Chicago.* Chicago: University of Illinois Press, 1996.

———. *Chicago: Metropolis of the Mid-Continent*, 3rd edition. Dubuque: Geographic Society of Chicago and Kindall/Hunt Publishing Company, 1982.

Davis, Allen and Mary McCree. *Eighty Years at Hull-House*. Chicago: Quadrangle Books, 1969.

Drake, St. Clair and Horace Cayton. *Black Metropolis: A Study of Negro Life in a Northern City*. New York: Harcourt Brace and Company, 1945.

Duis, Perry. *Chicago: Creating New Traditions*. Chicago: Chicago Historical Society, 1976.

———. *Challenging Chicago: Coping With Everyday Life, 1837-1920*. Urbana and Chicago: University of Illinois Press, 1998.

Eastwood, Carolyn. *Chicago's Jewish Street Peddlers*. Chicago: Chicago Jewish Historical Society, 1991.

Ewen, David. *American Popular Songs*. New York: Random House, 1966.

Frazier, E. Franklin. *The Negro Family in Chicago*. Chicago: The University of Chicago Press, 1932.

Gerth, Hans and C. Wright Mills. *From Max Weber: Essays in Sociology*. New York: Oxford University Press, 1965.

Glazer, Nathan. "Social Characteristics of American Jews." In *The Characteristics of American Jews*, ed. Marshall Sklar. New York: Jewish Education Committee Press, 1965.

Grossman, James. *Land of Hope: Chicago, Black Southerners, and the Great Migration*. Chicago: University of Chicago Press, 1989.

Hayner, Don and Tom McNamee. *Streetwise Chicago*. Chicago: Loyola University Press, 1988.

Horwich, Bernard. *My First Eighty Years*. Chicago: Argus Books, 1939.

Ianni, Francis. "The Mafia and the Web of Kinship." In *The Italians: Social Backgrounds of a Social Group*, ed. Francesco Cordasco and Eugene Bucchoni. Clifton, New Jersey: Augustus M. Kelley, 1974.

Iorizzo, Luciano and Salvatore Mondello. *The Italian Americans*. Boston: Twayne Publishers, 1980.

Kenney, William. *Chicago Jazz: A Cultural History 1904-1930*. New York: Oxford University Press, 1993.

Kerr, Louise Año Nuevo. "Mexican Chicago: Chicago Assimilation Aborted, 1939-1954." In *Ethnic Chicago*, ed. Melvin G. Holli and Peter d'A. Jones. Grand Rapids, Michigan: Eerdmans Publishing Company, 1984.

Koenig, Rev. Msgr. Harry C., ed. *A History of Parishes of the Archdiocese of Chicago*, Vol. I. Chicago: New World Publishers, 1980.

Learski, Rufus. *The Jews in America: A History*. New York: World Publishing Company, 1954.

Lemann, Nicholas. *The Promised Land: The Great Black Migration and How It Changed America*. New York: Knopf, 1991.

Levitats, Isaac. *The Story of the Chicago Jewish Community*. Chicago: Board of Jewish Education, 1954.

Mayer, Harold and Richard Wade. *Chicago: Growth of a Metropolis*. Chicago: University of Chicago Press, 1969.

Meites, Hyman. *History of Jews in Chicago*. Chicago: Chicago Historical Society, 1990 (orig. 1924).

Miller, Ross. *Here's the Deal: Buying and Selling a Great American City*. New York: Knopf, 1996.

Nelli, Humbert. *Italians in Chicago, 1880-1930: A Study in Ethnic Mobility*. New York: Oxford University Press, 1970.

Pacgya, Dominic and Ellen Skerrett. *Chicago: City of Neighborhoods*. Chicago: Loyola University Press, 1986.

Philpott, Thomas. *The Slum and the Ghetto: Neighborhood Deterioration and Middle-Class Reform, Chicago 1880-1930*. New York: Oxford University Press, 1978.

Redfield, Robert. *Mexicans in Chicago 1924-25* (diary). Chicago: Special Collections, University of Chicago: 1924-25.

Rolle, Andrew. *The Italian Americans: Troubled Roots*. New York: Free Press, 1980.

Rosen, George. *Decision Making Chicago-Style*. Urbana, Illinois: University of Illinois Press, 1980.

Sawyers, June. *Chicago Sketches*. Chicago: Wild Onion Books, 1991.

Schiavo, Giovanni. *The Italians in Chicago*. New York: Arno Press, 1975.

Segal, Ronald. *The Black Diaspora*. New York: Farrar, Straus and Giroux, 1995.

Sorkin, Sidney. *Bridges to an American City: A Guide to Chicago's Landsmanshaften, 1870-1990*. New York: Peter Lang Publishing, 1993.

Sorrentino, Anthony. *Organizing Against Crime*. New York: Human Sciences Press, 1977.

Spear, Allan. *Black Chicago: The Making of a Negro Ghetto 1890-1920*. Chicago: University of Chicago Press, 1967.

Thrasher, Frederick. *The Gang*. Chicago: University of Chicago Press, 1960 (orig. 1927).

Townley, Eric. *Tell Your Story*. Chigwell, England: Storyville Publications, 1976.

U.S. Commissioner of Labor. Seventh Annual Report. *The Slums of Baltimore, Chicago, New York, and Philadelphia*. Washington, D.C.: U.S. Government Printing Office, 1894.

Vulliamy, Graham. *Jazz and Blues*. London: Routledge & Kegan Paul, 1982.

Wirth, Louis. *The Ghetto*. Chicago: University of Chicago Press, 1928.

Unpublished Material

Eastwood, Carolyn. "A Study of the Regulation of Chicago's Street Vendors." Ph.D. Diss., University of Illinois at Chicago, 1988.

Jones, Anita Edgar. "Conditions Surrounding Mexicans in Chicago." Ph.D. Diss., University of Chicago, 1928.

Kerr, Louise Año Nuevo. "The Chicano Experience in Chicago: 1920-1970." Ph.D. Diss., University of Illinois at Chicago, 1976.

Morales, Alphonse. "Making Money at the Market: The Social and Economic Logic of Informal Markets." Ph.D. Diss., Northwestern University, 1993.

Vecoli, Rudolph. "Chicago's Italians Prior to World War I: A Study of Their Social and Economic Adjustment." Ph.D. Diss., University of Michigan, 1963.

INDEX

Italicized page numbers indicate photos.

1st Ward, 159, 180, 249, 251
12th District, 325
12th Street, 21, 22, 38, 85
"12th Street Rags", 85
12th Street Store, 48, 225
13th Street, 224
14th Place, 29, 207, 208, 222
14th Street, 27, 139, 224, 239, 244, 251
15th Street, 21, 218
16th Street, 3, 37, 115, 202, 224
18th Street, 108, 266, 300
19th Ward, 112
22nd Street, 57
26th Street, 223
47th Street, 96, 99, 232
64th Street, 95, 232
79th Street, 231

Aberdeen Street, 124
Adams Street, 226
Addams, Jane, 21, 108, 110, 112, 146,
    153, 168, 172, 184
    housing, 186, 207
African-American
    neighborhood (*see* Black Bottom)
    neighbors, 139–140, 210
Alinsky, Saul, 29, 153–154, 157, 176–
    177
Ammons, Gene, *87*, 88, 89, 95, 97
Andrew Jackson School, 122
Apollo Theater (New York), *87*, 98
Aragon Ballroom, 141
Archdiocese of Chicago, 10, 11, 274–
    276, 294, 308, 310–311, 312–313,
    314, 306, 322, 325–326
Armando family, 127–129
Armstrong, Louis, 71, 87, 101
Art Institute of Chicago, 300
Ashland Avenue, 33, 134, 186, 190,
    287
Aykroyd, Dan, *242*–243

Back of the Yards (neighborhood),
    153, 176, 266
Balaban and Katz theaters, 63
Balaban, Barney, 29
Ballard, Russell, *160*, 162–163, 179

Barber Street, 207, 208, 222, 224
Basie, Count, 70, 87, 96
Battle of the Bands, 95–96
Beach, Agene, 212
Belushi, John, 242
Benson, Al, 233
Berkow, Ira, 203, 241
Bernardin, Cardinal Joseph, 274–*277*,
    294–295, 309, 310, 311, 317, 323,
    325–326, 327, 336, 337
    Cardinal's mansion, *316*, 317
Bieri, Father, *158*
Bikel, Theodore, 85
Binford, Jessie, *115*, 168–169, 179, *183*
Black Belt area, 202
Black Bottom (Detroit), 204
Black Bottom neighborhood, 13, 200–
    213, 218
    black merchants, 205
"Black Bottom Stomp", 205
Blackstone Hotel, 179
Blackstone Theater, 148
Blue Island Avenue, 107, 111, 123,
    129, 139, 193, 224, 269
Blue Note, 232
Blue, Steve, 233–234
"blues" bus (Maxwell St. Market), *243*,
    244
"blues culture", 203
Board of Education, 252
Bohemian immigrants, 4, 20, 106
Bolby, Pat, *91*
Borman, Whitey, *77*
Boys Club, 235, 251
Brabec, Irv, 70
Brockman, Gail, 88
Broski, David (UIC Chancellor), 334,
    335
Brown, Roslyn, 10–11
Bureau of Labor, 106
Burley, Dan, 79
Burnham, Daniel (Plan of Chicago of
    1909), 21, 273

Cabrini Street, 111
California Avenue, 150
Cambridge University, *9*

Campbell's Soup, 298
Canal Street, 13, 29
  new market, 330, 332
Capone, Al, 42, 143, 147
Carmi's hat shop, 127
Carpenter Street, 133
Carr, Vicki, 304
Carrero, Father Jesus, 299–300, 306,
  308, 319–321, 325
Caruso, James, 109
Catholic Charities, 294–295
  director, 295
Catholic Church, The, 93, 140, 176.
  See also Archdiocese of Chicago
Catholic Youth Organization, 115
Ceja, Salvador, 271, 273
Central National Bank, 162
Central Park, 223
Central Park Theater, 51
Century of Progress World's Fair
  (1933), 62, 108
Channel 66, 321
Charleston (dance contests), 62
Chateau Royale, 304
Chávez, Cesar, 305
Chernin, Dorothy, 207
Chicago, City of, 164, 251–252
  Great Cities Program, 338
Chicago Avenue, 215, 304
Chicago Daily News, 174
Chicago Defender, 203
Chicago Fire of 1871, 19
Chicago Garment Workers Strike of
  1910, 108
Chicago Hebrew Institute, 28
Chicago Housing Authority's Jane
  Addams project, 153
Chicago Land Clearance
  Commission, 113
Chicago Park District, 209
Chicago Public Library, 194, 267, 334
Chicago River, 202
Chicago Sun-Times, 114, 115, 274,
  307, 309
Chicago Taxpayers Foundation, 182
Chicago Temple, 235
Childers, Buddy, 72
Citizens' Housing Committee, 170,
  181–183, 188
Chicago Park District, 222, 223, 227
Citizens Poverty Committee, 181

City Colleges, 149
City Council, 113, 157, 163–164, 170,
  181, 185, 212, 308, 309, 312
City Hall (Chicago), 3, 6, 8–12, 167,
  169, 170, 172, 176, 254, 269, 270,
  313
civil rights movement, 186–188, 196
Claretian Missionary Fathers, 273,
  297, 305, 316
Clark Street, 129
Clinton Street, 150, 223, 224
clout, 5, 202, 278
Club Riviera (St. Louis), 90, 91
Cole, Nat "King", 30, 69, 97–98, 232
Colosseum (on Wabash), 129
"Concerto to End All Concertos", 96
Congregation Paole Zedeck Anshe
  Sfard, 27
Congress Parkway, 150, 166
Conservation Area Program, 166
Conway, Father, 295
Cook County, 164, 269
corruption, 143, 147, 173
Cottage Grove Avenue, 95
crime, 112–113, 142–145, 194
Curtiss Candy Company, 42
Cyrus the Great (cigar shop), 39

Daley, John, 312–313
Daley, Richard J., 12, 111, 114, 164–
  167, 171–175, 174, 181–183, 304,
  307, 308, 309, 312, 338
Daley, Richard M., 11, 252, 333, 338
Dan Ryan Expressway, 8, 9, 23, 24,
  111, 115, 201, 206, 208, 210, 222,
  226, 251, 258
D'Angelo, Oscar, 252, 333
D'Arco, John, 144, 156, 159, 163, 165,
  172, 249, 251, 305
Davis, Sammy, Jr., 85
De Laurentis, Gloria, 183
de Nancrede, Edith, 137–139, 138
De Salvo, Antoinette, 178
Decision-Making Chicago-Style, 113
Dempsey, Mary, 194
Department of Streets and
  Sanitation, 155
Depression, the, 126, 153, 268
Diamond Horseshoe, 86
Diggles, Joe, 183
Diggles, Mary, 183

Dirkson, Senator, 241
Dolnick, June, 170, 181
Dominick's, 299, 332
Dorsey, Tommy, 70
Douglas Park, 222
Dover, Bill, 73–74
"Downbeat", 80
du Sable, Jean Baptiste Point, 202
Duncan family, *199*
Duncan, James (Nate's brother), 218
Duncan, Kenny (Nate's brother), 240
Duncan, Milton (Nate's father), *199*,
    215–219
Duncan, Nate, 6, 13, 24, 25, 199, 201–
    202, 204, 207, 212–213, *214*, 215–
    263, *248*, *260*
    in the army, 228–232
Duncan, Roberta (Nate's Mother),
    215–219, *217*, 240, *242*
Duncan (Webster), Patsy, (Nate's
    sister), 218, *239*, 240
Dunne, George, 144

Eckstine, Billy, 70, 232
Edelweiss Beer factory, 57
Edible Nuts, 109
Egan, Monsignor, 175
Eisen, Maxie, 54
Eisenhower Expressway, 111, 166
El Grotto, 73–74
El, the, 231
Ellington, Duke, 70
Ellis Island, 33
Encyclopedia Britannica, 189
Eng, Jonathon, *91*
entrepreneurship, 109
Evanston, IL, 223, 310
Exodus, 168
expressway, 7, 269, 287

Federal Theater Project, 148
Federal Writers' Project, 148
Ferguson, Maynard, *72*
Ferrone, Phil, 126–127
Filibert, Sr. Mary, *183*
Fire of 1874, 20
First Congregational Church, 235
First Roumanian Congregation, *27*,
    200
Fitzgerald, Ella, 232
Flash magazine, 78

Fligelman Watches, *24*
Flugg, Michael, 204
Foran, Tom, 179–180
Ford Park, 223
Foster (public grade school), 29, 39,
    207, 219, 220
Fox, Aaron (Hal's brother), 68, 78, 84
Fox Box, 71
Fox Brothers Tailors, 25, 29–30, 37,
    48–50, 60, 67–86, 91, 94, 97, 98, 99–
    101, 206, 331
Fox Brothers Woolen Company and
    Tailor's Trimmings, 25, 37, 48–50
Fox, Conrad (Hal's grandfather), 33
Fox Family, 33–43, 63, 67–68, 99–101
    Victor (Hal's brother-in-law), 78,
    84
Fox, Harold "Hal", 6, 7, 13–14, 17, 18,
    19, 25, 27, 29–30, 32–101, *60*, *90*,
    92, *100*, 206, 227, 331
Fox, Healy (Hal's uncle), 34, 67
Fox, Helen (Hal's 2nd wife), 63–64,
    68
Fox Lake, 53–54
Fox, Leo (Hal's father), 34, 67
Fox, Marie (Hal's 3rd wife), 99, *100*
Fox, Sam (Hal's uncle), 42
Fox, Sarah (Hal's mother), *69*–70, 78,
    101
Fox, Vivian (Hal's 1st wife), 63
Foxx, Redd, 232
Franciscans, 297
French
    immigrants, 4, 110
    neighbors, 127
Friends of the Market, 252
Friends of the Roosevelt Library, 193
Fuchs, Bill, 83

gangs, 139–148, 222, 293–294, 303–
    304
gangsters, 159, 172, 181
Garcia, Jesus (State Senator), 277–278
Garfield (school), 251
Garfield Park, 113, 165
Garment Workers Union (Amalga-
    mated Clothing Worker strike), 172
Garroway, Dave, *82*, 84
Geertz, Charlie, 39
"generation gap", 106
George, Cardinal Francis, *336*, *337*

German
immigrants, 4, 21, 110
neighborhood, 272
school, 27
German Evangelical United Church, 27
Gethsemane Missionary Baptist Church, 27, 28, *200*, 210–*211*, 218, 336–337
Giancana, Sam, 146, 180
Gilbert, Ray, 78
Gillespie, Dizzy, 81, 98, 232
Giovangelo, Alessandro (Florence Scala's father), 118
Giovangelo, Ernie (Florence Scala's brother), 120, *159*, 161–165, 189
Giovangelo, Mario (Florence Scala's brother), 120, 189–191
Giovangelo, Teressa (Florence Scala's mother), *118*
Glessner House, 173
Glickman, Maxie, 44
Glickman, Red, 44
Glickman Theater, 41
Goldberg, Arthur, 29
Goldblatt's Department Store, 62
Goldman, Max, 40
Gold's Restaurant, *37*, 48, 93
Goodman, Benny, 30, 87, 90
Goose Island, 165
Gordon, Irv, 234, 248–249
Gorman, Bishop John, 313
Gottlieb, J., 19
Granata, John, 144–145
Grand Avenue, 94
Grant Park, 129, 218, 220
Gray, William, 74
Great Migration, 202–205
Great Northern Theater, 148
Greek neighborhood, 123
food, 206
neighbors, 139, 210
Greeley, Rev. Andrew, 275
Green, Paul, 6
Guardian Angel Social Center, 111
Gutierrez, Luis (congressman), 308–309
Gutstein, Rabbi Morris, *17*

Gypsy
immigrants, 4

neighbors, 207, 220–221

Halsted-Maxwell area, 12, 201, *246*, 332, 335
Halsted-Roosevelt neighborhood, 3–4, 6–8, 9, 11–12, 15, 19, 263, 265–278, 331, 334, 338
Halsted Street, *2*, 3, 9, 19, 21, 24, 29, *37*, 47, *104*, 106, 108, 110, 115, 123, 139, 142, 144, 169, 201, 202, 205, 212, 222, 225, 239, 251, 255, 264, 266, 267–278, 279, 287, 300
merchants organization, 254, 256–257
Halsted-Taylor area, 139
Hampton brothers, 75
Hampton, Lionel, 72, 88, 90
Handbook of Jive, 79
Haring, Tibor, 168
Harlem Globe Trotters, 223
Harrison-Halsted area, 9, 103, 114, 157, *171*, 182, 269, 336
Harrison-Halsted Community Group, 114, 166
Harrison Halsted Renewal Project R-10, 166
Harrison-Halsted-Roosevelt area, 105
Harrison Street, 115, 123, 266
Harriss Pies, 61
Hart Schaffner and Marx, 108, 121
Harvey Company, 53
Hebrew Literary Society, 29
Henry Booth Settlement House, 209
Herman, Woody, 70
Hill Street Blues, 234
Hines, Earl, 73–74, 98
Hispanic neighbors, 207, 220, 223
Holbrook, Father, 295
Holiday, Billie, 68, 96–97, 99, 232
Holy Family Church, *2*, 111, 124, 169, 175, 275, 306, 313, 316, 321, 322, 236–327
Holy Guardian Angel Church, 111, 114, 115, 124, 164, 166, 173, *183*, 337
Holy Guardian Angel School, 114, 115
Holy Name Society, 299
Housing Act, 116
Housing and Finance Agency, 181
Howlin' Wolf, 203
Hughes, "Mother", *210*–211

Hulbert, Eri, 152, 153–155, 157, 159, 161–162, 165
Hull-House, 13, 21, 28, 30, 91, 106, 108, *110*, 114, 124, 125, 136–141, 149, 153–154, 156, 160, 161–164, 168, 173, *174*, 178–179, *180*, 183, 184, 190, 195, 197, 210, 263, 266–*267*, 307
  Board of Directors, 268
  Bowen Hall, 91
  Mary Crane Nursery, 125, 268
  Theater Group, 148
  Visiting Nurses Association, 125
Huston, John, 148
Huston, Walter, 148
Hyde Park, 170, 188
Hymie's (original hot corned beef place), 47

"icicle look", 79, 99
Illinois Board of Higher Education, 335
Illinois Central Train, 231
immigrants, 4, 8, 139. *See also under* specific ethnic group entries
Independent Voters of Illinois (IVI), 181, 185
Indiana Avenue, 173
INS (Immigration and Naturalization Service), 268, 306
Institute of Juvenile Research, 176–177
International Harvester, 94–95, 155, 162, 206, 273
"Irish" (criminal), 145
Irish
  immigrants, 4, 21, 110, 122
  neighbors, 123, 127
  parish, 111
Italian
  culture, 134, 206
  immigrants, 4, *103*, 210, 105–116
    anti-immigrant sentiment, 107
    assimilation, 107–112
  neighborhood, 9, 105–116, 123, 204, 252, 266, 269
Italian Socialist Women, 108

Jackson, Chubby, 80, 81
Jay's Potato Chip factory, 206
Jefferson Street, 3, 8, 21, 24, *26*, 33, 36, 139, 202, 207, 208, 218, 220, 222, 223–224, 225, 226, 331
Jeffrey Avenue, 231
Jesuits, 175
Jewish
  bathhouse, 209
  immigrants, 4, 19–30
  merchants, 205
  neighborhood, 13, 19–30, 147, 203–204
  neighbors, 139, 220, 236–239
Jewish Training School, 29
"Jewtown", 203
Jimenez, Father Manuel, 287, 303
Jimmy Dale band, 30, 87–99, *90, 92*
Jim's Hot Dogs, 48, 85. *See also* Stefanovic, Jim
jitterbug, 55, 63, 98–99
Johnson, Walter, 195
Juvenile Protective Association, 168

Katz, Howard "Hotsie", 101
Kayser, Kay, 78
Kechum, Leon, 90
Kedzie Avenue, 269
Kennedy, John F., 185
Kenney, Fran, 84
Kenton, Stan, 30, 70, 81, 95–*96*
Kerner, Otto (Illinois governor), 169
King, Martin Luther, Jr., 181, 186–188, 213, 236
Konitz, Lee, 30, *91*
Korean immigrants, 238–239
Korean War, 228
Krupa, Gene, 70
Ku Klux Klan, 91

L. Klein's, 225
La Preferida, 299
La Raza, 321
"La Societa" groups, 130–31, 143
Land Clearance Commission, 173
landsmanschaften, 28
LaSalle Hotel, 303
Latoria family, 108
Latoria, Phillip, *108*
Lawndale (neighborhood), 19, 22, 34, 37, 182
Leavitt Bros. (corned beef), 47–48, 206
Leo Fox Tailors, 78–79
Leonard, Sheldon, 241
Lester, Buddy, 94

Lester, Jerry, 94
Levinsky, Kingfish, 47, 80
Levinsky, Leapin' Lena, 47, 80
Lewis, Jerry, 241
Lewis, John L., 215
Lexington Street, 151, 189
Liberace, 84
Liberty magazine, 66
Liberty (street), 218
Libonati, Roland, 149
Lincoln Park, 129, 218
  neighborhood, 182
Lithuanian immigrants, 20
"Little Italy". *See* Taylor Street
Little Richard, 89
Little Village (neighborhood), 287, 302, 335–336
Little Walter, 203
London House, 232
Loop, the, 4, 144, 165
Louis Prima band, 94
Low, Minnie, 28
Lyon, Ben, 24, 25, 212, 225, 226, 236–237, 238, 259
  wife, 249, 259
Lyon's Deli, 47, 48, 226, 231, 236–237

Mackevich (store), 225
Mafia, 86, 112, 172
Mance, Junior, 30, 88, 96
Manhattan Pickle Factory, 244
Manz, Bishop John, 275–276, 318–319, *324*, *325*–326
Mario's Italian Lemonade, *192*
Market Master. 44, 234, 248–249. *See also* Gordon, Irv; Glickman, Red
Market Street, 142
Marks Nathan Home, 39
Marquette Park, 188, 236
Marshall Field's, 35, 51
Mary Worth funnies, 91
Marzullo, Vito (alderman), 172, 269, 305
Mascione, Mrs., *178*
Mason, Hog, *91*
Maxwell Fur Company, *24*
Maxwell Street, *1*, 8, 9, 19, 21–25, 29, 33–42, 44, 101, 108, 185, 196–197, 200, *212*–213, 218, 220, 222–226, 233, 236, 243–249, 250, 251, 261, *272*, 330, 334

Maxwell Street area, 18, 43–50, 203, 255
  police station, 216, 233, *234*
Maxwell Street (book), 241
Maxwell Street Market, 3, *4*, 8–9, 11–13, 46, 101, 109, 142, 196, 200, 201, 205, 211, *234*, 261, 269–*272*, *271*, 332–334
  the "Chicken-man", 245
  new market, *329*, *330*, 332
  the "Strong Man", 244–245
Maxwell Street Market Coalition, 253–254
Maxworks, 252
May Street, 320
Mazola, Ted (alderman), 11, 193–194, 333
Mazzoni, Bessie, 146
McCormick Place, 304
McKinley High School, 141
Medinah Athletic Club, 141
Meigs Field, 113, 165
Mexican
  immigrants, 4, 139
  immigration, 265–272
  discrimination, 314
  neighborhood, 124, 147, 264, 265–278, 287
Meyer, Cardinal, 175, 298
Meyers, Mary, 146
Midwest Wrecking, *296*
migrants, 8
  African-American, 4, 202–205, 215–216
Milagro, El (tortilla factory), 288
Mill, Melody, 90
Miller Meadows, 113
Miller Street, *119*, 145, 150, 250
Miller Street Playlot, 158
Milton, Morris, 83
Minsky's Burlesque, 64
Minton, Skeets, *71*
Monk, Thelonious, 98
Monroe, Vaughan, 87
Montgomery Ward, 203, 216
Morales, Alfonso, 271
Moreland Bros. Beverage, 155
Morgan Street, 23, 106, 127, 130, 166, 251
Morten, Jelly Roll, 205
Moses Montefiore Hebrew Free

School, 29
Municipal Reference Library, 11
Musso, Vito, 95

Nabisco, 298
Nadler (dry cleaner), 83
Nate's Deli, 47, 212–213, *212*, 237–243, *240*, *241*, *257*, 258–261, *260*, *340*
  "Soul Food Cafe", 241
Nativity of the Lord School, 301
Near West Side (neighborhood), 4, 15, 18, 24, 26, 105–116, 204, 264, 266
Near West Side Community Committee, 176–177
Near West Side Planning Board, 113, *159*, 168, 171, 195, 197
Nevins, Father, 326
New World, The, 111, 309
New York Harlem Fronts, 74
Newberry Avenue, 10, 111, 222, 244, 250, 251, 269, *272*, 287, 306, *315*, 337
Newberry Center, 235, 250
Nicholson, Nick, 80
Northerly Island (Meigs Field), 113, 165
Norwood Park, 54
Notre Dame parish, 127

Oak Park, IL, 287–291
Oasis, The, 62
O'Brien, Bob, 78
O'Brien Street, 219, 224
Ocasio, Billy (alderman), 308
O'Connor, Len, 186
Ojeda, Salvador, 323
Organizing Against Crime, 113
Oriental Theater, 70, 94, 232
Our Lady of Guadalupe, 297, 304
Our Lady of Pompeii parish, 111, 124, *169*, 308
Owens, Jesse, *71*

Paley, Walter, 29
Palmer, Earl "Quack", 60, 78, 84
Palmer House, 85, 304
Parker, Charlie, 232
Passavant Hospital, 293
Patner, Andrew, 197
Paul's Bakery, 227

Payan, Daniel (Hilda's husband), 284–291
Pearson, Sarah, 39
Perez, Al *239*, 240
Perfection Pop Company, 42
Pershing Ballroom, 68, 73, 95, *96*, 232
Piano C. Red, *200*
Pilsen (neighborhood), 269, 287, 335–336
Pittsburgh Courier, 84
Player, Sam, *91*
Polish neighbors, 223
Polk Street, 29, 106, *110*, 129, 273, 287
Portillo, Guadalupe (Hilda's mother), 281–284, 290, 291, 293, *315*
Portillo, Hilda, 6, 14, 263, 265, 274, 278, *280*, 281–328
  children, *280*, 281, 285, 288–291, 292, 293
Portnoy Carpets, *258*
Portnoy, Jerry, *257*, 258
Powers, John, 112
Prohibition, 147
Protective Union, The, 73
Puerto Rican neighborhood, 287
Pulaski Road, 226
Pullman Company, 189

Quackenbush, Robert, 317, 318

Raby, Al, 188
Racine Avenue, 4, 111, 128, 151, 166, 235, 300
Rail Terminal site, 113
Ramos, Mrs., 264
"Red Rocket" streetcar, *37*
Redfield, Robert, 268
Regal Theater, 63, 85, 96–98, 99, 232
Rickover, Admiral Hyman, 29
Riley Printing Company, 170
Riverside Golf/Country Club, 113, 164
Riverview Park, 113, 129
Robert Brooks Homes, 151, 186
Roberts, Rev. Eric, 336
Robinson, Bill "Bojangles", 70
Robinson's Department Store, *23*, 226
Rodriguez, Rev. Peter, 268, 271, 305–306, 323
Rodriguez, Bishop Placido, 295
Rogers, Jimmy, 203
Ronan, Al, 189

Roosevelt Cafeteria, 48
Roosevelt Road, *2*, 3, 10, 21, 30, *37*, 38, 45, 46, 48, 93, 107, 109, 111, 115, 147, 151, 166–167, 185, 186, 187, 193, 202, 218, 222, 244, 249–251, 255, 264, 267, 269, 273, 287, *315*, 320, 331
Roosevelt, Theodore, 168
Roosevelt Torch, 30
Roosevelt University, 30
Rosen, George, 113
Rosenberg, Moe (alderman), 28
Rosenthal, Bernard, *77*
Ross, Barney, 39, 225
R.O.T.C., 56
Roti, Fred (alderman), 269
Rowe, Father, 317
Rugolo, Pete, 85, 95
Rush Street, 151

Savoy Ballroom (New York), 98, 232
Scala, Antoinette (Florence's sister-in-law), 109
Scala, Charles "Chick"(Florence's husband), 150–152, 177, 179, 185, 186, 191, 195
Scala, Ernie (Florence's brother), 120, 151, 159, 161, 162–165, 189
Scala, Florence, 6, 12–13, 103, 105, 107, 109, 112, 113, 114, 116, 118, 119–197, *126*, *159*, *160*, *183*, *184*, *190*, 252, 334
bombings of home, 177–179
family, 118–129, 177
Florence Restaurant, *190*–191, 193
holidays, 131–133
Scala, Mario (Florence's brother), 120, 151, 189–191
Schuh, Bernice, *108*
Schwartz, Bernard, *158*
Scola, Father Etalo, 164, 167
Scotch Woolen Mills, 121
Scout Council of Chicago, 235
Sears Roebuck, 203
Sedgwick Street, 129
Segal, Joe, 30
Shaare Tikvah Schul, 17
Shaw, Robert (alderman), 259
Shaw, Artie, 90
Shearing, George, 232
Sheridan Park, 140

Shiloh Baptist Church, 187
Skelton, Red, 241
Slum Clearance and Urban Redevelopment, 113
Smokey Joe, 78–79
Smythe (public grade school), 29
Soldier Field, 224
Sorrentino, Anthony, 113
"Sorrento", 95–96
South Chicago, IL, 297
South Parkway (King Drive), 96, 232
South Water Street Market, 109, 205
St. Agatha's parish, 188
St. Charles Correctional Institution, 162
St. Francis of Assisi Church, *2*, 10, 13, 14, 48, 91, 93, 111, 166–167, 257, *263*, 268, 269, 271–278, *272*, *276*, *280*, 287, *296*, 297–328, *315*, *324*, *336*, *337*
closing, 307–317
Holy Name Society (men's organization), 299, 300
Immaculate Heart of Mary (ladies' organization), 302
occupation of, *276*, 278, 317–325
parish community, 297–307
reopening, 325–328
St. Francis of Assisi Preservation Committee, 275, *277*, 308, 327
members,
Gerardo, 318–319
Jorge, 318, 320–321
Margarita, 320
Villaseñor, Carlos, *337*
St. Francis of Assisi School, 111, 273, 274
St. Francis of Assisi, Sisters of, 273–274
St. Ignatius, 158, 169, 175, 317
St. Jude Society, 94
St. Louis World's Fair, 266
St. Pius Church, 298
Stan Kenton band, 72
Stanford Park, 29, 30, 91, 93, 147, 207–209, *208*, *214*, 222, 227
Youth Council, 209
Starbucks, 335
Stardust Hotel, 86
Starr, Ellen Gates, 110
State of Illinois, 113, 307, 335

"State Street of the Ghetto", 23
Stefanovic, Jim, 47, 48, 85. *See also*
    Jim's Hot Dogs
Stella, Bob, 86
Stella d'Oro Cookies, 86
Stewart Avenue, 21
Stitt, Sonny, 88
Storm, The, 151–152
Stovepipe (Maxwell St. musician), 243
streetcars, 37, 129, 224
Strong, Larry, 205, 207, 210

Talmud Torah, 29
Taxpayers Federation, 170
Taylor Street, 28, *104*, 105, 107, 111,
    112, 119, *120*, *126*, 127, 129, 133,
    139, 186, *192*, 194, 222, 235, 261,
    269, 287, 334
Taylor Street neighborhood ("Little
    Italy"), 6, 8, 12, 42, 252, 332
Taylor, Hound Dog, 203
Temporary Organizing Committee,
    113
Terkel, Studs, 148, 176
Toffenetti's, 142
Tormé, Mel, 84
Touff, Cy, 88
tumbolo (game), 130
Tuscany restaurant, 127

U.S. Supreme Court, 114, 115
Union Avenue, 8, 23, 27, 29, 39, 44,
    202, 206–207, 208, 210, 218, 219,
    220, 222, 226, 244
Union Park Temple, 94
United Methodists, 235
United Nations Relief Association,
    153
University of Illinois, 113, 162, 164–
    166, 181–184, 211–212. 254–255,
    313, 336–337
    at Champaign, 149
    at Chicago, 9, 10, 12, 111, 112–116,
        157, 171, 239, 269, 273–274, 287,
        306–307, 338
        "South Campus", 332, 334
    Navy Pier program, 113
urban renewal, 6–8, 12–13, 23, 113,
    115, 156–157, 163, 165, 166, 181–
    183, 249–263, 269, 201, 274, 333,
    336

Valentino, Lee, 166–167
Van Buren Street, 121, 166
Varelas, Constance, *183*
Vatican, the, 310
Vaughan, Sarah, 84, 232
Velasquez, Juan, 269, 278

Wabash Avenue, 129
Walker, John, 205–207, 210–211, *214*
Washburne (public grade school), 29
Washburne High School, 223
Washington, Harold, 10
Waters, Muddy, 203
Watkins, "Billy the Tailor", 83, 206
    shop, *206*
Watkins Kyler, Yvonne, 206–207, 209
Weber, Max, 11
Weiboldt Foundation, 163
Welk, Lawrence, 87
West Central Association, 165
West Side Bloc, 145
West Side Christian Parish, 187–189
West Side Community Committee,
    113
West Side Organization, 187–188
Western Avenue, 94
Wirth, Louis, 204
Withers, Jane, 94
Wittenburg Mallin, Mildred, 24–25,
    28
Wittenberg Matzoh Company, 24, *26*,
    35
Women's Loan Association, 28
Woodlawn (neighborhood), 176, 177
World War I, 202
World War II, 8, 149, 155, 217
World's Fair of 1893, 21
WPA, 148
Wright, Frank Lloyd, 49

Yiddish culture, 29, 41–42
YMCA, 250–251, 254, 303

Zahed, Leo, 84
zoot suit, 66, 74–75, *76*, *77*, 78, 79–80,
    331
    era, 98–99
"Zoot Suit (For My Sunday Gal), A",
    78

ACKNOWLEDGMENTS

THIS HAS BEEN a long term project, and as I begin to contemplate the people to whom I owe thanks I am overwhelmed by the number of those who have helped in many different ways from encouragement and inspiration to providing information.

First of all, I'd like to thank Professors Perry Duis and Charles Hoch at the University of Illinois at Chicago, who not only taught me about neighborhoods and city ways but encouraged me in my writing efforts. For her advice on publishing matters and her unfailing support and optimism I am grateful to Professor Carol Sherman at College of DuPage.

I am most appreciative of the efforts of Lori Grove who came through for me in finding specialized bits of information and for making my map presentable. I am also grateful to Joseph Lorenz for his video recording, which captured information that would have been otherwise unavailable. I would like to express appreciation for the generosity of the following people who loaned photographs from their personal collections: Harold Fox, Florence Scala, Nate Duncan, Leo Zayed, Philip Albert, Norman Schwartz, Bishop John Walker, and Jeff Fletcher. I am also pleased to acknowledge Greg Stepanek in the Publications Department of the Chicago Transit Authority for his help in tracking down the streetcar photograph.

A special thanks goes to Larry Zimmerman, Tom Hryhorsak, and my son Chris Eastwood and his wife, Susan, for saving my sanity when computer problems threatened destruction.

For valuable and much needed advice concerning the form and content of the manuscript, I owe a great debt of gratitude to Dr. Irwin Suloway and to Patrick Reardon, both of whom were extremely generous with their time and expertise in providing helpful suggestions.

It goes without saying that I have been dependent on various libraries through my years of research, but I would particularly like to acknowledge the help of reference librarians at the Spertus Library, in the Special Collections library of the University of Illinois at Chicago, the Chicago Historical Society, and the Wheaton Public Library. Credit lines for photographs from the Special Collections of the library of the University of Illinois at Chicago are designated as JMAC if they are from the Jane Addams Memorial Collection or the Wallace Kirkland Papers; those from the Italian American Collection are cited as IAC photographs.

I have continually gained knowledge about the Halsted-Roosevelt neighborhood and its history from conversations over a long period with Irving Cutler, Norman Schwartz, and Steven and Barbara Balkin, and I am grateful for all the help they have given me. I would also like to acknowledge the continuing friendly help I have received from Marine Curtis of

Gethsemane Missionary Baptist Church. I cannot begin to name all the people who I interviewed for this project, but each added information and flavor to the book and they are identified throughout the text.

I am especially grateful for the warm-hearted acceptance I have received through the years from Maxwell Street Market vendors with whom I became friendly, and for the welcome that I receive as I return to visit St. Francis of Assisi Church and Gethsemane Missionary Baptist Church.

I am thankful for a supportive family. In addition to Chris's valuable computer help, our daughters, Wendy Collier and Victoria Sumner, and son Peter and his wife, Julia, have all given assistance and encouragement in their own ways, and the open-minded outlook of our grandchildren, Holly Collier and Ian Eastwood, always renews hopes for the future. My husband, Tony, has given the most enduring support because he too enjoyed the market, Nate's deli, the two churches, and, most of all, the people we met. Throughout all the ups and downs he has never failed to discuss problems encountered, read the manuscript, and encourage and help in any way that was needed.

I cannot adequately express my admiration for Sharon Woodhouse, Lake Claremont Press publisher, who combines courage and sensitivity in accepting this project, and I am also thankful for the editing and technical assistance of Bruce Clorfene and Karen Formanski.

It hardly needs to be said because it is so obvious, but my greatest gratitude and admiration belongs to the four people, Harold Fox, Florence Scala, Nate Duncan, and Hilda Portillo, who gave their time and honest narratives to make this project a reality. Their stories are unique and personal and yet they reveal so much about life in this corner of Chicago during this past century. I am saddened that Hal Fox is no longer here to greet this publication with his usual boundless enthusiasm and commentary.

LAKE CLAREMONT PRESS IS . . .

Regional History

NEW!
Chicago's Midway Airport: The First Seventy-Five Years
Christopher Lynch

Midway was Chicago's first official airport, and for decades it was the busiest airport in the nation, and then the world. Its story is a reflection of America, encompassing heroes and villains, generosity and greed, boom and bust, progress and decline, and in the final analysis, rebirth. A celebration of the rich history of an airport and a window to an earlier era.

1-893121-18-6, Spring 2002, softcover, 200 pp., 140 historic photos, $19.95

Great Chicago Fires: Historic Blazes That Shaped a City
David Cowan

As Chicago changed from agrarian outpost to industrial giant, it would be visited time and again by some of the worst infernos in American history—fires that sparked not only banner headlines but, more importantly, critical upgrades in fire safety laws across the globe. Acclaimed author and veteran firefighter David Cowan tells the story of the other "great" Chicago fires, noting the causes, consequences, and historical context of each. In transporting readers beyond the fireline and into the ruins, Cowan brings readers up close to the heroism, awe, and devastation generated by the fires that shaped Chicago.

1-893121-07-0, August 2001, softcover, 167 pp., 80 historic photos, $19.95

The Chicago River: A Natural and Unnatural History
Libby Hill

When French explorers Jolliet and Marquette used the Chicago portage on their return trip from the Mississippi River, the Chicago River was but a humble, even sluggish, stream in the right place at the right time. That's the story of the making of Chicago. This is the *other* story—the story of the making and perpetual re-making of a river by everything from geological forces to the interventions of an emerging and mighty city. Author Libby Hill brings together years of original research and the contributions of dozens of experts to tell the Chicago River's epic tale—and intimate biography—from its conception in prehistoric glaciers to the glorious rejuvenation it's undergoing today, and every exciting episode in between. Winner of the 2001 American Regional History Publishing Award (1st Place, Midwest) and the 2000 Midwest Independent Publishers Association Award (2nd Place, History).

1-893121-02-X, August 2000, softcover, 302 pp., 78 maps and photos, $16.95

Literary Chicago: A Book Lover's Tour of the Windy City
Greg Holden, with foreword by Harry Mark Petrakis

Chicago has attracted and nurtured writers, editors, publishers, and book lovers for more than a century and continues to be one of the nation's liveliest literary cities. Join Holden as he journeys through the places, people, ideas, events, and culture of Chicagoland's historic and contemporary literary world.

Includes 11 detailed walking/driving tours.
1-893121-01-1, March 2001, softcover, 332 pp., 83 photos, 11 maps, $15.95

"The Movies Are":
Carl Sandburg's Film Reviews and Essays, 1920-1928

Ed. and with historical commentary by Arnie Bernstein, intro. by Roger Ebert
During the 1920s, a time when movies were still considered light entertainment
by most newspapers, the *Chicago Daily News* gave Sandburg a unique forum to
express his views on the burgeoning film arts. *"The Movies Are"* compiles
hundreds of Sandburg's writings on film, including reviews, interviews, and his
earliest published essays of Abraham Lincoln—which he wrote for his film
column. Take a new look at one of Hollywood's most exciting periods through
the critical perspective of one of America's great writers. A passionate film
advocate, Sandburg early on grasped and delighted in the many possibilities for
the new motion picture medium, be they creative, humanitarian, or technologi-
cal; intellectual, low-brow, or merely novel. In doing so, he began defining the
scope and sophistication of future film criticism.
1-893121-05-4, October 2000, softcover, 397 pp., 72 historic photos, $17.95

Hollywood on Lake Michigan: 100 Years of Chicago and the Movies

Arnie Bernstein, with foreword by *Soul Food* writer/director George Tillman, Jr.
This engaging history and street guide finally gives Chicago and Chicagoans
due credit for their prominent role in moviemaking history, from the silent era to
the present. With trivia, special articles, historic and contemporary photos, film
profiles, anecdotes, and exclusive interviews with dozens of personalities,
including Studs Terkel, Roger Ebert, Gene Siskel, Dennis Franz, Harold Ramis,
Joe Mantegna, Bill Kurtis, Irma Hall, and Tim Kazurinsky. Winner of the 2000
American Regional History Publishing Award (1st Place, Midwest).
0-9642426-2-1, December 1998, softcover, 364 pp., 80 photos, $15

Ghosts and Graveyards

Chicago Haunts: Ghostlore of the Windy City

Ursula Bielski
From ruthless gangsters to restless mail order kings, from the Fort Dearborn
Massacre to the St. Valentine's Day Massacre, the phantom remains of the
passionate people and volatile events of Chicago history have made the Second
City second to none in the annals of American ghostlore. Bielski captures over
160 years of this haunted history with her unique blend of lively storytelling,
in-depth historical research, exclusive interviews, and insights from parapsy-
chology. Called "a masterpiece of the genre," "a must-read," and "an absolutely
first-rate-book" by reviewers, *Chicago Haunts* continues to earn the praise of
critics and readers alike. Our best-seller!
0-9642426-7-2, October 1998, softcover, 277 pp., 29 photos, $15

More Chicago Haunts: Scenes from Myth and Memory

Ursula Bielski
Chicago. A town with a past. A people haunted by its history in more ways than
one. A "windy city" with tales to tell . . . Bielski is back with more history, more
legends, and more hauntings, including the personal scary stories of *Chicago*

Haunts readers. Read about the Ovaltine factory haunts, the Monster of 63rd Street's castle of terror, phantom blueberry muffins, Wrigley Field ghosts, Al Capone's yacht, and 45 other glimpses into the haunted myths and memories of Chicagoland.
1-893121-04-6, October 2000, softcover, 312 pp., 50 photos, $15

Graveyards of Chicago:
The People, History, Art, and Lore of Cook County Cemeteries
Matt Hucke and Ursula Bielski
Like the livelier neighborhoods that surround them, Chicago's cemeteries are often crowded, sometimes weary, ever-sophisticated, and full of secrets. They are home not only to thousands of individuals who fashioned the city's singular culture and character, but also to impressive displays of art and architecture, landscaping and limestone, egoism and ethnic pride, and the constant re-minder that although physical life must end for us all, personal note—and notoriety—last forever.
0-9642426-4-8, November 1999, softcover, 228 pp., 168 photos, $15

Guidebooks by Locals

New!
A Cook's Guide to Chicago: Where to Find Everything
You Need and Lots of Things You Didn't Know You Did
Marilyn Pocius
Pocius shares the culinary expertise she acquired in chef school and through years of footwork around the city searching for the perfect ingredients and supplies. Each section includes store listings, cooking tips, and "Top 10 ingredi-ents" lists to give readers a jump start on turning their kitchens into dens of worldly cuisine.
1-893121-16-X, Spring 2002, softcover, 275 pp., $15

Ticket to Everywhere: The Best of *Detours* Travel Column
Dave Hoekstra, with foreword by Studs Terkel
Chicago Sun-Times columnist Dave Hoekstra has compiled 66 of his best road trip explorations into the offbeat people, places, events, and history of the greater Midwest and Route 66 areas. Whether covering the hair museum in Independence, Missouri; Wisconsin's "Magical Mustard Tour"; the Ohio Tiki bar on the National Register of Historic Places; Detroit's polka-dot house; or Bloomington, Illinois—home to beer nuts, Hoekstra's writings will delight readers and instruct tourists.
1-893121-11-9, November 2000, softcover, 227 pp., 70 photos, 9 maps, $15.95

A Native's Guide to Chicago, 4th Edition
Lake Claremont Press, edited by Sharon Woodhouse
Venture into the nooks and crannies of everyday Chicago with this unique, comprehensive budget guide. Over 400 pages of free, inexpensive, and un-usual things to do in the Windy City make this the perfect resource for tourists, business travelers, visiting suburbanites, and resident Chicagoans. Called the "best guidebook for locals" in *New City*'s "Best of Chicago" issue!
1-893121-23-2, Summer 2002, softcover, photos and maps, $15

ORDER FORM

Near West Side Stories	_____	@ $17.95 =	_____
Chicago's Midway Airport	_____	@ $19.95 =	_____
Great Chicago Fires	_____	@ $19.95 =	_____
The Chicago River	_____	@ $16.95 =	_____
Literary Chicago	_____	@ $15.95 =	_____
"The Movies Are"	_____	@ $17.95 =	_____
Hollywood on Lake Michigan	_____	@ $15.00 =	_____
Chicago Haunts	_____	@ $15.00 =	_____
More Chicago Haunts	_____	@ $15.00 =	_____
Graveyards of Chicago	_____	@ $15.00 =	_____
A Cook's Guide to Chicago	_____	@ $15.00 =	_____
Ticket to Everywhere	_____	@ $15.95 =	_____
A Native's Guide to Chicago	_____	@ $15.00 =	_____

Subtotal: _____
Less Discount: _____
New Subtotal: _____
8.75% Sales Tax for Illinois Residents: _____
Shipping: _____
TOTAL: _____

Name_____

Address_____

City_____State_____Zip_____

Please enclose check, money order, or credit card information.

Visa/Mastercard#_____Exp. _____

Signature_____

Discounts when you order multiple copies!
2 books—10% off total, 3–4 books—20% off,
5–9 books—25% off, 10+ books—40% off

—Low shipping fees—
$2.50 for the first book and $.50 for each additional book, with a maximum charge of $8.

Order by mail, phone, fax, or e-mail.
All of our books have a no-hassle, 100% money back guarantee.

4650 N. Rockwell St.
Chicago, IL 60625
773/583-7800
773/583-7877 (fax)
lcp@lakeclaremont.com
www.lakeclaremont.com

About the Author

CAROLYN EASTWOOD was born in Canton, Ohio, and grew up in Detroit, Michigan. She relocated to the Chicago area in 1943, but has lived and worked in many locations across the United States and throughout the world, including Washington D.C., England, Israel, and Italy. Her extensive travels have concentrated on markets, vendors, and ethnic occupations in low-income communities.

Carolyn received a B.A. in Sociology from the University of Wisconsin, an M.A. in Anthropology from Northern Illi-

Photo by Anthony Eastwood.

nois University, and a Ph.D. in Public Policy Analysis from the University of Illinois at Chicago with the dissertation, "A Study of the Regulation of Chicago's Street Vendors." She published *Chicago's Jewish Street Peddlers* with the Chicago Jewish Historical Society in 1991.

Carolyn is an adjunct professor of Anthropology at the College of DuPage and at Roosevelt University. She resides in Glen Ellyn, Illinois, with her husband, Tony.